The Nature of the Japanese State

The Nissan Institute/Routledge Japanese Studies Series

Other titles in the series:

The Japanese Numbers Game: the Use and Understanding of Numbers in Modern Japan, *Thomas Crump*

Ideology and Practice in Modern Japan, *Roger Goodman and Kirsten Refsing*

Technology and Industrial Development in pre-War Japan, *Yukiko Fukasaku*

Japan's Early Parliaments 1890–1905, *Andrew Fraser, R.H.P. Mason and Philip Mitchell*

Japan's Foreign Aid Challenge, *Alan Rix*

Emperor Hirohito and Shōwa Japan, *Stephen S. Large*

Japan: Beyond the End of History, *David Williams*

Ceremony and Ritual in Japan: Religious Practices in an Industrialized Society, *Jan van Bremen and D.P. Martinez*

Understanding Japanese Society: Second Edition, *Joy Hendry*

The Fantastic in Modern Japanese Literature: the Subversion of Modernity, *Susan J. Napier*

Militarization and Demilitarization in Contemporary Japan, *Glenn D. Hook*

Growing a Japanese Science City: Communication in Scientific Research, *James W. Dearing*

Architecture and Authority in Japan, *William H. Coaldrake*

Women's *Gidayū* and the Japanese Theatre Tradition, *A. Kimi Coaldrake*

Democracy in Post-war Japan, *Rikki Kersten*

Treacherous Women of Imperial Japan, *Hélène Bowen Raddeker*

Japanese–German Business Relations, *Kudō Akira*

Japan, Race and Equality, *Naoko Shimazu*

Interpreting History in Sino-Japanese Relations, *Caroline Rose*

Japan, Internationalism and the UN, *Ronald Dore*

Life in a Japanese Women's College, *Brian J. McVeigh*

On the Margins of Japanese Society, *Carolyn S. Stevens*

The Dynamics of Japan's Relations with Africa, *Kweku Ampiah*

The Right to Life in Japan, *Noel Williams*

The Nature of the Japanese State: Rationality and Rituality, *Brian J. McVeigh*

Society and the State in Inter-War Japan, *Elise K. Tipton*

London and New York

The Nature of the Japanese State
Rationality and rituality

Brian J. McVeigh

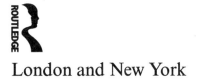

London and New York

First published 1998
by Routledge
11 New Fetter Lane, London EC4P 4EE

Simultaneously published in the USA and Canada
29 West 35th Street, New York, NY 10001

© 1998 Brian J. McVeigh

Typeset in Times by RefineCatch Limited, Bungay, Suffolk
Printed and bound in Great Britain by
Mackays of Chatham PLC, Chatham, Kent

British Library Cataloguing in Publication Data
A catalogue record for this book is available from the British Library

Library of Congress Cataloging in Publication Data
A catalog record for this book has been requested

ISBN 0–415–17106–7

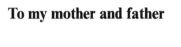To my mother and father

Contents

List of figures and tables

FIGURES

TABLES

Series editor's preface

Japan as the new century approaches is going through a turbulent period, in which some of its most entrenched political and economic institutions and practices are being increasingly questioned. The financial crisis which occurred in the latter half of 1997 affected most of the so-called "tiger economies" of East and South-East Asia, and did not spare Japan. The collapse of several important Japanese financial institutions signalled not only that the system was in crisis but also that the government was no longer willing, or able, to rescue ailing institutions. The sense of crisis quickly dulled the luster of the "Asian model" in the eyes of the world's media, but also concentrated minds within Japan on the task of reforming the system. The extent to which the system needed reforming remained a matter of sharp dispute, but a consensus was emerging that many entrenched practices which derived from the immediate post-war period of the "economic miracle" needed to be radically rethought. At the beginning of 1998, the extent and timescale of the desired revolution remained in doubt. Elements of the old regime seemed to be falling apart, but the shape of the new was still but dimly discernible.

Reading the world's press in the aftermath of the financial crisis one could well derive the impression that East Asia (including Japan) was heading for collapse and that the world could safely direct its attention elsewhere, notably to the dynamic and successful market economies of North America and Europe. Such an impression, however, was manifestly erroneous. Japan and its surrounding region remained a zone of intense economic production and interaction, resourceful and dynamic. Though there was a financial crisis, it was far less clear that there was an economic crisis. To use a hackneyed phrase, the fundamentals of the Japanese economy remained sound. Radical reform was no doubt needed, but the occurrence of crisis made the road to that rather easier. If the world thought that the

East Asian region could safely be ignored, it was likely to be in for a rude shock in a short span of years.

The Nissan Institute/Routledge Japanese Studies Series seeks to foster an informed and balanced, but not uncritical, understanding of Japan. One aim of the series is to show the depth and variety of Japanese institutions, practices and ideas. Another is, by using comparisons, to see what lessons, positive or negative, can be drawn for other countries. The tendency in commentary on Japan to resort to outdated, ill-informed or sensational stereotypes still remains, and needs to be combated.

In this book Brian McVeigh applies the tools of the social anthropologist to some of the most fundamental issues in our understanding of contemporary Japan. For instance, what in Japanese society is the relationship between rationality and ritual? Who runs Japan: is it the government bureaucrats that run Japan, or the politicians? To the first question he responds that rationality and ritual, far from being polar opposites, are in the Japanese social context interlinked and mutually reinforcing. "For many Japanese," he argues, "rituals are regarded as a very rational way to organize social life." The implications of this view are wide-ranging, since if rationality is not just a hard, cold calculation of individual interest, but also embraces the kind of ritualistic behavior designed to promote societal harmony and curb the naked expression of selfish personal interest, then many of the assumptions underlying contemporary theories of rationality need to be looked at with a critical eye.

In responding to his second question, McVeigh argues for the irrelevance of much of the debate about who runs Japan, because, in his view, not only the government bureaucracy *strictu senso*, but also politics, the economy and other spheres of life are essentially bureaucratized. Now this is obviously an argument in the Weberian tradition, and may be applied to a greater or lesser extent to many advanced societies. But McVeigh takes it further in applying it to Japan, and argues that there is so much bureaucracy around that it largely negates the existence of an effective civil society. This, like the first, is a highly controversial point, but if it stimulates the cut and thrust of debate, the book – quite apart from its other merits – will have performed a signal service.

J.A.A. Stockwin

Preface

The seed of this book was an article in which I attempted to demonstrate how Japanese state policies and economic interests encourage, via rationalization, a style of thinking that ritualizes (e.g. hierarchizes, centralizes, compartmentalizes, standardizes) social existence. As I wrote this article, I became convinced that there were linkages between different topics that deserved clarification in order to bolster my argument. But as I tried to squeeze sections on bureaucracy, rationality, civil society, education, and legitimacy into thirty pages, it became apparent that one article could not possibly contain all my arguments. This book is the outcome of my efforts to show how state and subjectivity meet in Japan, and in many ways it is informed by my mundane experiences of living and working in Japan.

This work is about political science, though I suspect certain political scientists, more accustomed to approaches hinging on case studies, the processes of policy making, or the history of an institution, will question a work that does not fit into the conventional academic genres. Moreover, this work will appear particularly enigmatic for those who have adopted assumptions and methodologies shaped by the expectations of Anglo-American-style politics: parties, elections, legislatures, executive branches, free markets, etc. These are certainly not absent, but their role in Japan's political scheme of things is remarkably different from what some researchers (though it needs to be emphasized, not all) seem to realize. Though it may be comforting to some, the view that Japan is a carbon copy of the United States or the "West," with some differences perhaps attributable to "cultural(ist)" traits, is not useful. Unless the real differences are recognized, researchers, policy makers, and the public on both sides of the Pacific (or anywhere else for that matter) will not be well served. But besides merely recognizing these differences, I feel it is imperative that we come to terms with the *implications* (both academic and practical) of these differences: for better or for worse, there are many modernities, and Anglo-American-style democratic liberal capitalism, with its particular view of state/society, government/individual relations, and public/private, is only one. Anthropologists, however, used to radically different and multiple pasts and presents, will not be surprised to hear that Japan's modernity diverges from what many might expect.

As a rule, anthropologists are more used to highly focused studies primarily based on interviews and long-term, on-the-ground observations, and may wonder why I have cast my net so wide rather than ethnographically exploring one topic. I have done so because this work is about the *linkages* – the ideological and institutional chains – that bind the disparate parts of Japan's sociopolity together. Stated simply, this work is about the anthropology of the state, or more specifically, the ideology of the Japanese state. The ideological chains I investigate, however, are for the most part not explicit but implicit; not coherent but unsystematized; not neatly arranged once and for all but assembled and reassembled on a daily basis. These connecting ideologies have neither scriptures nor spokespersons to which one can readily point. Instead, they exist beneath the surface of everyday practices, behind words glibly spoken, and under institutions taken for granted. The hidden nature of these connecting notions makes them less attractive as research targets, but not any less important, since their obscure nature only enhances their binding power. Not being obvious, these linkages are usually not looked for by many researchers.

I also suspect some colleagues may be disappointed that certain issues I raise in this work have been dealt with in too cursory a fashion. Space precludes their extended treatment, and in any case, the reader should note that the goal of this work is to highlight linkages between areas that are usually not considered related. There are many other topics that could have been included, and, as in all works, my choice is selective. If readers note other subjects and linkages that appear to confirm this work's argument, I will be satisfied that this book has achieved its purpose.

Acknowledgments

Many friends and colleagues have given me their time, support, and suggestions in the course of writing this book. For this I owe many thanks to Hildred Geertz, Takie Sugiyama Lebra, Ellis Krauss, Ted Bestor, Thomas M. Huber, Ueno Makiko, and Gregory Starrett. I owe special thanks to Chalmers Johnson, whose support and advice were invaluable. I would also like to express my gratitude to Keith Knapp, Tom Arrison, Donna Storey, and Guven P. Witteveen. They have furnished me with directions, comments, and general support.

In Japan, the people who offered advice and various types of support are too many to enumerate, but I owe special thanks to Chuck Weathers, who greatly assisted me by reviewing and commenting on the entire first draft. Also, the many discussions I have had with Katalin Ferber furnished me with ideas, inspiration, and confirmation of some of my own lines of reasoning. For this I am most grateful. I also owe thanks to Adam Schneider, Beth Coleman, Chuck Muller, James Roberson, John Brine, Kawahashi Noriko, Marcia Johnson, Ōuchi Hirokazu, Owen Griffiths, Satō Izumi, and Steven Murphy-Shigematsu. I would also like to express my thanks to Professors Miyanaga Kuniko, Ogawa Kōichi, Kogane Yoshihiro, Morita Akira, Ikeya Akira, David Lehney, Kathy Tegtmeyer Pak, Steven Reed, and Ken Ruoff. I am also grateful to the students I have taught in Japan, particularly those in the Faculty of Policy Studies at Chūō University, who taught me much about sociopolitical life in Japan. I am also grateful to Chairman Uda Masanaga, President Shishido Toshio, and Dean Namekata Akio at Tōyō Gakuen University, who have all made my teaching and researching there both enjoyable and productive. Also, I would like to thank Kawatō Akio (Deputy Director-General of the Cultural Affairs Department, Ministry of Foreign Affairs), Honma Masao (Director of the International Affairs Planning Division of the Science and International Affairs Bureau, Ministry of Education),

Watanabe Akihiko (Director of the Foreigners' Education Office of the Science and International Affairs Bureau, Ministry of Education), and Professor Mitsuta Akimasa, a former official of the Ministry of Education who shared with me his years of experience. Their assistance has been most helpful.

I would like to express my thanks to the staff at Routledge, especially Victoria Smith, whose encouragement is greatly appreciated. Also, I owe a debt of gratitude to three reviewers, whose comments and suggestions strengthened my arguments.

Special thanks go to Lana Yuen, whose companionship and commitment has kept my sights on matters non-academic in proper focus. Her keen discernment of human relations in Japan has also enriched this work. Finally, I am grateful to my family, who as always, have supported my work in ways that are solid, constant, and invaluable.

I would like to thank the Educational Foundation of Tōyō Gakuen for granting me permission to use my previously published material from *Tōyō Gakuen Daigaku Kiyō* ("Rationality, Bureaucracy, and Belief in the Japanese State," 4: 125–40, 1996) and *Kenkyūshitsu Dayori* ("Shaking State and Society in Japan: Problems of an Over-Rationalized Society," 27: 75–84, 1996).

Note to the reader

James Fallows writes that for decades the United States and the United Kingdom have dominated world politics, granting them the dubious honor of being able to ignore what others have said about political economy in languages other than English. The consequence is a sort of smugness among those who accept as "common sense" certain political and economic principles grounded in the Anglo-American experience (1994: 179–80). In this book I occasionally employ the term "Anglo-American" (and for a somewhat different stress, "Euro-American"); my intention is not to dichotomize the societies of Japan with the United States and the United Kingdom, as if everyone in the world looked toward these two societies as the only competing models. Rather, I use "Anglo-American" because, being an adjective that has encapsulated a set of hegemonic ideas for so long, it acts as a sort of convenient intellectual foil that highlights what Japan is all about. My apologies to those who feel that "Anglo-American" neglects or subsumes more specific societies.

Abbreviations

AEN   *Asahi Evening News*

CGD   *Chū gakkō: dōtoku kyōiku jūjitsu no tame no kōnai kenshū no tebiki* (A Primer on School Training For Realizing Moral Education in Junior High School)

CG   *Chū gakkō: dōtoku kyōiku shidō jō no shomondai* (Various Problems Concerning Guidance for Moral Education in Junior High School)

CGO   *Chū gakkō: omoiyari no kokoro o sodateru shidō* (Guidance for Cultivating a Heart of Empathy in Junior High School)

DK 1   *Dōtoku kyōiku suishin shidō shiryō – shō gakkō: yomimono shiryō to sono riyō 1* (Materials to Promote Guidance in Moral Education – Reading Materials and Their Use for Primary School 1)

DK 2   *Dōtoku kyōiku suishin shidō shiryō – shō gakkō: yomimono shiryō to sono riyō 2* (Materials to Promote Guidance in Moral Education – Reading Materials and Their Use for Primary School 2)

DK 3   *Dōtoku kyōiku suishin shidō shiryō – shō gakkō: yomimono shiryō to sono riyō 3* (Materials to Promote Guidance in Moral Education – Reading Materials and Their Use for Primary School 3)

DK 4   *Dōtoku kyōiku suishin shidō shiryō – shō gakkō: yomimono shiryō to sono riyō 4* (Materials to Promote Guidance in Moral Education – Reading Materials and Their Use for Primary School 4)

DKS 1   *Dōtoku kyōiku suishin shidō shiryō – chū gakkō: yomimono shiryō to sono riyō 1* (Materials to Promote Guidance in Moral Education – Reading Materials and Their Use for Junior High School 1)

DKS 2   *Dōtoku kyōiku suishin shidō shiryō – chū gakkō: yomimono*

	shiryō to sono riyō 2 (Materials to Promote Guidance in Moral Education – Reading Materials and Their Use for Junior High School 2)
DKS 3	*Dōtoku kyōiku suishin shidō shiryō – chū gakkō: yomimono shiryō to sono riyō 3* (Materials to Promote Guidance in Moral Education – Reading Materials and Their Use for Junior High School 3)
DY	*Daily Yomiuri*
JT	*Japan Times*
MTY	*Monbu tōkei yōran* (Summary of Statistics on Education)
SGD	*Shō gakkō: dōtoku kyōiku jūjitsu no tame no kōnai kenshū no tebiki* (A Primer on School Training For Realizing Moral Education in Primary School)
SGDK	*Shō gakkō: dōtoku kyōiku shidō jō no shomondai* (Various Problems Concerning Guidance for Moral Education in Primary School)
SGO	*Shō gakkō: omoiyari no kokoro o sodateru shidō* (Guidance for Cultivating a Heart of Empathy in Primary School)
SGSH	*Shō gakkō shidō sho: shakai hen* (Primary School Guidance Manual: Social Studies)
SGTH	*Shō gakkō shidō sho: Tokubetsu katsudō hen* (Primary School Guidance Manual: A Compilation of Special Activities)
WBBG	*Waga kuni no bunka to bunka gyōsei* (Our Country's Culture and Culture Administration)
WBS	*Waga kuni no bunkyō shisaku* (Our Country's Education Policy)

1 Introduction
Where rationality and rituality meet

JAPAN: A RITUALIZED OR RATIONALIZED SOCIETY?

For many, Japan presents a paradox. On the one hand, popular images portray it as a land where ancient arts and colorful festivals flourish. Steeped in a venerable past, Japan is instinctively associated with tradition. Buddhist temples are heirs to a spiritual wisdom that defies logic, and Shinto shrines, wrapped in misty legend, pay homage to nature. It is a society where complex codes of etiquette are scrupulously observed and rich ceremonialism and quaint customs move solemnly to a rhythm of ritualism. Exchanging gifts, seasonal events, the popularity of etiquette manuals, self-effacing meetings, and the endless entry/exit formalities of school and workplace permeate Japanese society. Indeed, as a Japanese saying phrases it, "there are formalities even between close friends."[1] But other images suggests that Japanese society moves to a much more modern rhythm; it is where proficient workers march lock-step to the tune of powerful corporations and government bureaucracies; school and employee uniforms are ubiquitous; public transportation is invariably punctual; and a general sense of practical efficiency and public orderliness reigns.

These views – the ceremonially permeated, enigmatic oriental Other versus the efficient, economically miraculous "Japan, Inc." – speak as much about Western perceptions as they do about Japanese society.[2] Nevertheless, they at least hint at some salient characteristics of Japanese society, such as a predilection for order, predetermined patterns, and set procedures. Many have observed that life in Japan is highly ritualized, organized, and regimented. One might answer that this ritual orderliness is a matter of tradition, frozen patterns of behavior from the feudal past. But this does not answer why such behavior patterns have (apparently) persisted for so long and what present roles they fulfill. Another, more banal answer might be that ritualization is merely a preference, governed by an aesthetic sense of order, for doing things in a set manner. But such a response is at best unsatisfactory, and at worst a form of circular reasoning, since it leads to another question: why do so many Japanese have this preference? Japanese do not devote consider-able amounts of time to purchasing and exchanging gifts just because "they like to"; they do not spend vast sums of money on weddings just because "they like formality"; and they are not sensitive to status dis-tinctions embedded in language use just because of their "national character." To respond that the Japanese behave the way they do because of "tradition," "customs," or "national character," or any other ghostly non-explanation, is not merely tautological; it also mis-leads by divesting Japanese, as social actors, of any agency or intention. Furthermore, it depoliticizes social life in Japan.

PURPOSES AND PREMISES

At this point, I pose two questions that this book addresses: why is life so regulated, ordered, and patterned in Japan? And, how can two seem-ingly contradictory images of Japan, the rituality of an ancient culture versus the rationality (in the classical Weberian sense) of an economic-ally super-efficient nation-state, be reconciled? My answer to these two questions is that life in Japan is characterized by what may be termed a bureaucratic ethos,[3] a distinctive sensibility that reveals a certain syn-onymy between two prevailing images of Japan: an "expressive" cultural rituality (e.g. consensus, cooperation, harmony, loyalty, and ritualized behavior) and an "instrumental" economic rationality (e.g. control, coordination, management, compulsion, and regulated behavior). Another way to state this is that Japanese sociopolitical pat-terns reveal the rituality in rationalism and the rationality in ritualism.

A set of conceptual markers has provided intellectual direction for average Japanese and Japanologists alike. Taken together, these markers form a discourse that constructs national identity and expresses: (1) "vertical society" (*tate shakai*) and "senior/junior relations" (*sempai/ kōhai*); (2) "groupism," *uchi/soto* (inner/outer), *ura/omote* (back, hidden/front, exposed), and *honne/tatemae* (true opinion/stated policy); and (3) "cultural homogeneity," "consensus," and "harmony."[4] Many Japanese and not a few researchers have regarded these notions as com-prising an essentialized Japanese identity that is part of a vague but immutable "tradition," or rooted them in the past: Tokugawa feudal-ism, Confucianism, an agricultural past, or Japan's history as an "island country." These culturalist mythologies and the aforementioned terms pervade accounts of Japanese society and are often employed by elites (as well as non-elites) to legitimate power arrangements, thereby ignoring *existing* political and socio-economic structures that produce them. But the aforementioned Japanese terms point to a bureaucratizing tendency and may just as well be described as: (1) hierarchization (and a related process, centralization); (2) sociopolitical categorization; and (3) sociopolitical standardization and regimentation. The Japanese expressions are merely dressed in the softer language of "tradition" and the "uniqueness" of Japanese culture. In any case, they define and reproduce class, age, gender, and nationality divisions, operate in families, schools, workplaces, and political institutions. The rituality of the Japanese concepts in fact resonates with rationality, which in turn leads to bureaucracy. After all, ritualization, rationalization, and bureaucratization actually share fundamental defining features, at least if viewed abstractly: verticality, classifying, centralizing, and routinizing.[5]

If stated in the barest terms, then, this book is premised on the notion that self, society, and state are linked by rationalizing and ritualizing practices that constitute a bureaucratic ethos. The argument that a bureaucratic ethos shapes sociopolitical life in Japan is not novel (especially to many of my Japanese colleagues), but the primary purpose of this book is to point to what I believe are important linkages between various areas of inquiry: public/private distinctions, state/individual relations, bureaucratic structures, moral education, political legitimacy, and "common sense." A secondary item on my agenda involves a commentary on the intellectual discourse that has been used to understand Japan. The thrust of this commentary is of a demystifying sort, to place some of the intellectual idiom that is commonly employed to understand Japan in, what I hope, is a clearer light. Specifically, I examine the meaning of "culture" and how "ritual" and "rationality" are actually synonymous in important respects.

CAVEATS

My discussion about the importance of a bureaucratic mentality in Japan must be placed in proper context. First, I am not offering another theory about the "Japanese miracle," or why "Japan, Inc." works the way it does. Nor it is about some impending economic disaster – perhaps a mutation of over-rationalization – about to sink the island of Japan. Rather, my goal is different: to delineate, in the broadest strokes, the connections, often implicit, between personhood, cultural conceptualizations, and nation-statehood. My arguments about a rationalized/ritualized life are meant to offer clues, not conclusions, about Japanese society.

Second, I am certainly not arguing that a bureaucratized mentality is unique to Japan. The bureaucratic ethos, as an aspect of modernity, can be found everywhere, though in different guises and to varying degrees. The point of this work is to illustrate how certain paradoxes about Japan become clearer if it is understood that Japan's social life is notably bureaucratic (i.e. ritualized and rationalized).[6] Whether or not Japan is more bureaucratic than some other place depends, of course, on which place it is being compared with and in what way the two places are being compared. Also, I am not arguing that a bureaucratic ethos is necessarily bad, or that it is worse in Japan. The reader is encouraged to make such comparisons and judgments. For many, the words "bureaucratic" and "bureaucratism" conjure up all the Kafkaesque demons that afflict modern life: red tape; lost paperwork; clerks who see rules as ends in themselves rather than as means to an end; the problem of pinpointing decision makers in a Byzantine structure of rules and regulations; officials who seek jurisdictional expansion and pursue their own survival at the cost of the public good – none of these is unique to Japan. From making plane reservations to obtaining citizenship, modern organizations share similar procedures that tax the patience of individuals everywhere.[7]

A third caveat concerns a key debate in the political science and political economics of Japan, which has turned on the question of which is more powerful, the political parties and politicians or the state's ministries and mandarins. In this work, I will not attempt to answer this question directly, at least not in the conventional way. This is because I am interested in the style, assumptions, and understandings that guide the policy making and self-interested political maneuverings of *both* politicians and bureaucrats (indeed, anyone in a position of power in Japanese society). However, the fact that the latter term is a cognate of bureaucratic (as in bureaucratic ethos) is telling. At least relative to the United States, the label "bureaucracy" fits Japan quite well. This is also true, but at least arguably less so, for Western European nations. Those who argue that Japan's politicians are more powerful than its bureaucrats, in my opinion, seem to have missed an essential point about life in Japan: elected, appointed, and examination-selected officials all operate within a highly bureaucratized environment.

Here it is worth noting that this question – "who runs Japan, politicians or bureaucrats?" – is actually a relative of a host of other commonly asked questions about Japan's polity and economy (bureaucracy or democracy? authoritarian or free society? neo-Confucianist or liberal? centralized or decentralized state? socialist or capitalist? neo-mercantalist or open markets? managed capitalism or Anglo-American-style economy? developmental or regulatory state?).[8] Careful reading of the important works on such matters usually reveals that very few take absolute stands and most judiciously qualify their arguments, but in any case, these questions have acted as parameters for the debates about Japan and have fascinated scholars (particularly from the United States, where the "free market" is a sort of sacred given). Indeed, "Scholars who specialize on Japan are often deeply divided on the most basic issues, such as the contribution of government policy or market competition in Japan's economic growth" (Haley 1991: 4). In the media and at the popular level, these debates often degenerate into radicalizing dualisms, such as them/us, exotic/ordinary, and abnormal/normal (the latter term actually appears in political scientific writings and media editorials about the importance of Japan becoming a "normal" country). These debates employ terms that for many scholars act as convenient labels and idealizations. Their use also signals where one stands *vis-à-vis* the fundamental concepts and problems confronting Japanology. Is Japan radically different from other places? Or does it adhere to universal principles? Is one a member of the "Chrysanthemum Club" (apologists or defenders of the "Japan-is-special" school) or a "Japan basher"? Or, is one a "revisionist" (Japan is amenable to analysis like any other society) (*cf.* Prestowitz 1993)? Though these debates may seem stale to some Japanologists, this is not necessarily the case among non-specialists, who must live with decisions made by leaders (who are often informed by academics). Thus, the stakes are high for those whose image of Japan wins out. These debates bring us to the fourth caveat: this work is not about whether we should emulate or admire the achievements of the Japanese political system. Rather, it is about how the Japanese state (and by implication, its society) should be approached and understood. Thus, its focus is methodological, not judgmental. Accordingly, I would like to, as much as possible for the sake of intellectual inquiry, transcend the "Japan-is-normal"/"Japan-is-unique," "Japan-is-to-be-admired"/"Japan-is-to-be-criticized," and "learn-from-Japan"/"Japan-should-conform" arguments.

The fifth caveat concerns the two senses in which I will be using "bureaucracy": the first sense refers to the *characteristics of modern organizations* as elucidated by Weber. These characteristics apply to large businesses, armies, civic groups, and religious groups, as well as to state machinery. All modern societies, of course, are bureaucratic to some degree, but in relative terms, I contend, Japan is highly bureaucratized. The second sense refers to a *type of government.* Of course, all governments (being large organizations) are bureaucratic, but not all governments should be described as bureaucratic polities. Japan has – at least *relative* to other industrialized countries that regard themselves as liberal democracies – a bureaucratic polity; its political practices and philosophy are deeply rooted in the idea of government administered through bureaux and departments. This is not to deny its democratic impulses any more than to state that the United States is democratic and therefore lacks a governmental bureaucracy. The point is that relative to places with which Japan is usually compared, it is best characterized as a bureaucratic polity. Of all the G-7 powers, it comes closest to what may be called a "bureauarchy." In any case, it should not be surprising that the highly bureaucratized nature of Japanese society is in no small way related to its state bureaucracy. There is still a third sense of bureaucracy, which is derogative, and to quote Crozier means "the slowness, the ponderousness, the routine, the complication of procedures, and the maladapted responses of 'bureaucratic' organizations to the needs which they should satisfy, and the frustrations which their members, clients, or subjects consequently endure" (1964: 3). This work is not primarily concerned with this latter meaning.

One last caveat concerns the admittedly vague feel to "bureaucratic ethos," a term that may scare away my more hard-nosed political science and political economy colleagues. The meaning of "bureaucratic" does not require elaboration at this point, but what does "ethos" mean? This term is usually defined along the lines of "the character or attitude peculiar to a specific culture or group." It is a conceptual relative of what is commonly called culture, and as such is contoured by political forces. There is nothing mystical, and certainly nothing apolitical, about my use of ethos. In scholarship on Japan, "culture" (and any other term that smacks of mystical explanations) has become entangled within a web of misunderstandings, nationalizing ideologies, myths of modernization, orientalizing, and self-orientalizing projects (see Chapter 2).

THE ROLE OF INVISIBLE INSTITUTIONS

Polities are conventionally examined as systems composed of structures, commonly called institutions that represent, reflect, or are somehow manipulated by elites and non-elites for certain ends. However, these institutions – political parties, cabinets, ministries, legislatures, etc. – are only the most obvious manifestations of political processes and practices. Though such structures cannot be ignored, to focus on them exclusively prevents an understanding of the nature of power.

Specifically, the "institutional" approach, whatever strengths it may have, all too often encourages a rather simplistic notion of that most fundamental ingredient of power: legitimacy. Often, legitimacy is regarded as a given, or vaguely related to ideas about nationalism, economic progress, or other abstract political philosophies. Legitimacy, in fact, is sometimes thought of as a species of "common sense," whose ability to work legitimizing magic is later examined in Chapter 2. But legitimacy is anything but commonsensical, and it "is not an abstract principle but an established and elaborated accounting theory that links situations and structures to collective purposes" (Meyer *et al.* 1987: 36). Although official institutions and nationalist ideologies are certainly good places to start to look for the roots of legitimacy, I contend that political ideologies have two aspects: (1) an explicit and obvious ("visible") aspect; and (2) an implicit and indistinct ("invisible") aspect. A substantial part of legitimacy is to be found in the "invisible side" of ideologies, or what may be called "invisible institutions." The latter are institutions because they are to a large degree structured, systematized, and shared, and invisible because they exert their influence on our behavior for the most part unawares. Many of these invisible institutions, which are usually unquestioned, implicit, and uncontested, are actually supports for the more explicitly agreed-upon parts of an ideology. "Invisible institutions" are the subjective substructures that glue a society together through which any political system can maintain its control.[9] Individuals support the state through invisible institutions of thought that form internalized legitimizing. Bureaucracy, with all its hierarchies, categories, formalities, and other rationalizing forms, often structures subjectivities unawares. This is why it "is one of those phenomena people only notice when it appears to violate its own alleged ideals, usually those concerning a person's place in the social scheme of things" (Herzfeld 1992: 3). That bureaucracy goes largely unnoticed only enhances its power, since it is shielded from close scrutiny.

Taken together, self, society, and state constitute an edifice. But if state and society are the structures, then the self is the foundation upon which the former are built. And if there are foundations (often overlooked or assumed in political studies) that support the structures of sociopolitical life, there are even less talked about places than the foundations. These places, deep below the foundations, are the caverns where the most implicit and taken-for-granted notions dwell. To be more technical, these notions are nonconscious ideological constructs (*cf.* Freud's proverbial "iceberg"). The caves (or, the invisible institutions) are often connected by tunnels hallowed out by sociopolitical forces, and it is the task of the researcher to discover these tunnels and mine the unspoken knowledge stored in them. In this book, this hidden knowledge constitutes the important linkages between areas of inquiry that need to be explicitly exposed: public/private distinctions, state/individual relations, bureaucratic structures, moral education, political legitimacy, and "common sense." If this approach is evaluated as "unscientific," then it would be fair to judge other more conventional political scientific works as naively scientific.

Proposing the existence of invisible institutions provides us with a place where the necessary labor is carried out by sociopolitical forces that have an interest in building their own supports. Any society must be substructurally grounded within each individual member. Invisible institutions grant us a more sophisticated (though messy) view of power relations than what may be termed the "billiard ball view" of politics, in which social actors merely react to greater force in a political force field. The billiard ball view of politics fails to acknowledge the encyclopedic range of information a social actor requires to function in the sociopolitical arena.[10] It also pays scant attention to how most of this knowledge is nonconsciously instilled, worked, and reworked. This point is significant, because any sociopolity is a daily creation, legitimized by a referendum of economic productive practices, minor civilities, and state-confirming duties. The relationship between macro-structures and individuals is not one of simple cause and effect but a much more complex and subtle one in which structures and social actors co-constitute – not cause – each other.

SOCIETY IN THE SELF

In many ways, then, this book is about where state and subjectivity meet, and this is where the cultural psychological aspect of this work enters. I am interested in how culture (i.e. what is learned about social structures, political relations, and economic interests) contours psychology, or of how society – or more specifically, the state – is placed in the self. For my present purposes, "psychology" designates a cognitive style that emphasizes "rituality": a predilection for standardization, formalization, and reliance on predetermined procedures which permeates various areas of Japanese social existence. I attempt to answer why so much of Japanese social life may be characterized as ritualized. High levels of rituality may be seen as rooted in the very "rationalized" policies of Japan's politico-economic elites. In other words, centers of power, by virtue of rationalizing socio-economic structures, may also be said to "ritualize" these structures. A large degree of rationalization bolsters a particular psychology (namely, a cognitive style that tends to ritualize). This cognitive style does not just offer social actors procedures that facilitate the accomplishment of certain tasks; it also shapes their perceptions about their environment. My interest is not so much in any *particular ritual*: rather, I am interested in the high levels of *rituality*, the tendency to regulate, routinize, and conventionalize behavior. Also, because Japan's politico-economic elites put their version of society into the self (e.g. moral education, scientific knowledge, national identity), the former may be said to utilize individual minds for specific purposes. "Perhaps it could be better said that the structures of mind are not so much the imperatives of culture as its implements," and in order to appreciate the role of cultural psychology, "it will be necessary to situate the human mental equipment as the instrument rather than as the determinant of culture" (Sahlins 1976: 122–3).

OUTLINE OF CHAPTERS

In Japanese studies, scholars and non-scholars alike have spun a confusing web around the word "culture" (and "tradition"). In Chapter 2, I disentangle this web, a necessary task if we are to appreciate some of the more subtle operations of power in Japan. As Smith notes, culture, as anthropologists usually understand the term, does not mean "tradition" (1992: 14). "Culture" and its uses must be clearly understood for another reason: discussing how elites in late nineteenth-century Japan and Germany implemented their politico-economic designs, Johnson writes that they developed and propagated ideologies "to convince the public that the social conditions in their country are the result of anything – culture, history, feudalism, national character, climate, and so forth – other than political decisions" (1995: 47).

In Chapter 2, I also clarify what I mean by rationality, rituality, and "common sense." It is upon these concepts that the arguments of this book rest. An examination of these terms is intended to clear up some intellectual misunderstandings that, in my estimation, plague studies of Japan. It is essential to explicate these terms – especially "common sense" – since, as I show in later chapters, they are the building-blocks that make up political legitimacy *and* academic methods. There is nothing commonsensical about "common sense," and there is a rationality to rituality that may not be obvious to those unfamiliar with anthropological understandings of the purpose and effects of rituals (which as social practices do not reflect but rather construct sociopolitical relations). An understanding of how rituality in Japanese social life is

actually a form of rationality demystifies the enigmas in Western political scientific studies of Japan. Also in Chapter 2, I offer examples of
how rationality itself is best understood as a cultural construction, and
I offer snapshots from Japanese social life that illustrate high degrees of
rationalization. As I argue in later chapters, rationality is actually a
conceptual thread that is sewn into the fabric of Japan's sociopolitical
life, connecting public/private distinctions, state/individual relations,
bureaucratic structures, moral education, political legitimacy, and
"common sense."

A few commentators on this work have noted that it could be
strengthened by using a more "comparative" approach. These commentators have apparently missed Chapter 3, where I look at Japan
using a decidedly Euro-American notion: civil society. It is in this chapter
that I raise the issue of how private/public distinctions and "civil society" should be considered in the Japanese sociopolitical context. I do
not attempt to describe all the aspects of Japan's version of a civil
society but rather to delineate its basic conceptual map and show how
this map is very much drawn by rationalizing priorities of state structures and economic interests (which are treated in Chapters 4, 5, and 6).
I attempt to show the mutual supports of personhood, group formation, and nation-statehood. After all, to quote Bennett, "The evolution
of the social and economic forms of the contemporary state is less
mysterious than the question of how, in the apparent absence of binding spiritual routines, members can display such sentiments as patriotism, loyalty, national identity, and belief in the virtue and inspiration of
the civic order" (1979: 107).

State structures and economic interests, via rationalization, are
intimately bound up with rituality in Japan. All societies have rituals,
walls of conventionalized activities that separate, bring together, and
pattern the social traffic of individuals and groups. In Japan, these walls
of rituals are particularly high and thick. In Chapter 3, I attempt to
answer why these walls are so important in Japanese society by investigating an idiom (*uchi* [inside]/*soto* [outside], *ura* [hidden]/*omote*
[exposed], and *honne* [real intentions]/*tatemae* [façade]) that is usually
regarded as timeless and unique to Japanese culture. I argue that,
whatever its historical origins, this idiom, due to high levels of rationalization, is clearly highlighted in modern Japan. This is because these
"traditional" divisions are expressions of a bureaucratic ethos that
functions as social classificatory and hierarchizing mechanisms, sharply
delineating social domains and effecting rationalized practices, economic and non-economic. Because differentiated private (society)
and public (state) spheres in Japanese society are lacking in the

Anglo-American sense, individuals must use ritualized practices to sustain private/public distinctions. In Chapter 3, I also discuss how rationalization produces a standardized feel to a set of norms that are found in many spheres of Japanese social life. In Chapter 3, I also touch upon how law and the media relate to Japan's version of civil society.

Japan's postwar success, however it is judged, "is the result of state–society relations that are utterly different from what Anglo-American democracies think of as the norm" (Johnson 1995: 8). In Chapter 4, I point out important features of Japan's governmental organization that indicate a bureaucratic blurring of state and society. Politico-economic elites maintain indeterminate social spaces between private and public domains, and for their own benefit, exploit such spaces. I delineate the machinery that serves the state's interests and those of economic elites. In particular, I examine the role of "para-state organizations" (e.g. special corporations) and advisory councils.

Perhaps the clearest example of the bureaucratic blurring of state and society is "administrative guidance." Though usually associated with economic policies, this key practice actually describes a remarkable amount of government policy in Japan and evidences the lack of a neutral "public space" that buffers the private sphere from state action. In Chapters 6 and 7, I provide examples of how educational authorities, which view schooling as much a moral-instilling as a learning experience, administratively guide educational policies.

In Chapter 4, I also examine how historically central state structures have controlled the peripheral areas' attempts to rationalize local political arrangements. In the same way that civil society buffers the individual from too direct state intervention, it may be stated that local autonomy grants the local citizen protection and a sense that central officialdom is only one type of authority among many. But if a sense of "publicness" is not strongly rooted, then there is little justification for regarding local government as a layer between the central state structures and the individual.

Chapter 5 concerns the mythologies of state and legitimacy, specifically the belief that rationality equals bureaucracy equals state equals legitimacy. Much of legitimacy is built through one of the greatest functions of bureaucratization: classification. In this chapter I examine how the construction of national identity ("Japaneseness"; another type of "common sense") bureaucratizes nationalism (a topic also treated in Chapters 6 and 7). Related to this nationalizing project are the Japanese language, the symbolism of the emperor, and how a version of equality reinforces "Japaneseness." I also touch upon the state structures that categorize and construct gender, another naturalized and essentialized example of "common sense." I also describe how elite interests have developed a "strategic economy" (Huber 1994) that has hierarchized, classified, and regimented key economic sectors of the Japanese socio-economic landscape, so that state goals equals rationality equals economic "common sense."

In the next two chapters, I narrow my focus and discuss how the state and its values are placed in the self. In Chapter 6, after describing how Japan's educational system is rationalized by strategic economic interests and state goals, I offer a portrait of the institution – i.e. the Ministry of Education – that reproduces the ideology of rationality needed to train students to accept a society of hierarchies, categorizations, and routinizations. Through schooling, these rationalities become "common sense." The Ministry of Education not only attempts to instill an ideology of rationality; its very internal structure and relation to external organizations are highly rationalized. In other words, it is patterned after a strategic three-tiered model: (1) high command (goal-setting organs, the ministry's secretariat); (2) intermediate linking institutions (ministerial bureaux and divisions, boards of education); and (3) tactical level, or the local socializing units (individual schools). In this chapter, in order to demonstrate that there has been and still is a definite ideology of state-directed economic expansion rooted in the Meiji period, I trace the institutional lineage and development of the present-day bureaux and divisions in the Ministry of Education.

In Chapter 6, I pay particular attention to state interests in "lifelong learning," "social education," and formal education. The latter is a massive "ability-testing device" that shapes and selects future workers. Moreover, I examine state-authorized educational organizations (education-related special corporations and authorized juridical persons) that reinforce Japan's strategic schooling and socialization. I also discuss the role of the Agency for Cultural Affairs (an external organ of the Ministry of Education) in building "Japaneseness" and "managing culture." To conclude this chapter, I describe the how internal organization of schools – which are the tactical units charged with turning out "good Japanese workers" – has been structured by state goals.

Chapter 7 is a continuation of the previous chapter. Here I examine moral education as the state's attempt to inculcate its vision of civil society. Thus, this chapter describes a link, via moral education, between state and self. I examine state-published texts about how to teach moral education. These texts, which have an exhortative tone, actually advocate a rationalizing/ritualizing ideology (e.g. hierarchizing, classifying, formalizing social relations). Thus, moral education may be viewed as linking notions of civility (how to relate to others), rationality (performing economic practices for future employment in an appropriate fashion), "common sense" (notions about behavior that are "natural") and what it means to be a good person (national identity; i.e. "Japaneseness"). Specifically, I examine how the state would prefer to see "school, neighborhood, and home" work in tandem to socialize children (an example of the state attempting to permeate the private social sphere), the meaning of administrative guidance in the educational context, and how to make "morality visible."

In Chapter 7, then, I examine the core values of moral education that build a sense of rituality and rationality which govern Japanese notions of civility and economic arrangements. I focus on how pedagogic methods and school activities "ritualize" experience, further bolstering individual subjectivities that formalize, routinize, and compartmentalize the social landscape, thereby constructing a rationalized view of the world necessary for operating in a hierarchical, highly ordered, and well-organized social system. To do this, I investigate how repetition, emotion, and participation in ritualized activities naturalizes a sense of morality and ensures that moral instruction becomes a "total" education. Values expressed in moral education texts underlie concepts and support public/private distinctions (described in Chapters 2 and 3) and support state structures (treated in Chapters 4, 5, and 6). In short, moral education upholds a bureaucratic ethos.

In the final chapter, I offer some important lessons from Japanese society. These lessons are intended to be methodological in spirit, rather than morally evaluative. Whatever one may think of over-rationalization, racialist thinking, or a civil society free from too much statist interference, an examination of these issues illustrates some of our misunderstandings of what should be investigated more carefully. Rigorous intellectual investigation need not preclude moral judgments, but in the interest of expanding the social scientific discourse, we should not allow the latter to hinder our research agendas. The first lesson concerns what happens in a society that is over-rationalized. Much has been written about how the successes of Japan's bureaucracy and rationalized social life have resulted in unprecedented prosperity and power. In this last chapter, relying on media accounts of how the Japanese sociopolity responded to the great Hanshin earthquake, I provide some examples of the darker side of the bureaucratic ethos. There are many places to look for the excesses of too much bureaucratization, of course, but a sudden disaster on a large scale clearly exposes a sociopolity's strengths and weaknesses, especially the condition of its civil society. I also offer some final thoughts about Japan's civil society and its incestuous relation to the state, and suggest why present-day nationalism, being largely premised on a racially essentialist view of "being Japanese," weakens the creation of public space. Finally, I suggest why we need to "de-orientalize" our understanding of Japan (since it presents Western social science with a number of sticky methodological problems) and eschew academic methodologies premised on natural–scientific paradigms.

2 Demystifying a discourse

The misuses of "Japanese culture" and the production of rationality

THE ABUSES AND MISUSES OF CULTURE

"Culture" is a word that inevitably crops up in any discussion of Japan. It is a word so bound up with Japanese studies that any serious observer of Japan is well advised to come to terms with its uses and abuses. For many Japanese (as well as non-Japanese), this word refers to their "unique" tradition, a collection of customs and beliefs found nowhere else. For some non-Japanese scholars committed to conventional political scientific and economic research, culture is a charming but less important variable, or perhaps a catch-all category for matters that cannot be investigated "scientifically." For other scholars, aware of the misuses of culture, it is a code word for cleverly disguising or justifying unfair practices and exploitation in Japan. And for yet other scholars, culture means something else; knowledge that is acquired, negotiated on a daily basis, and used to interpret and construct sociopolitical relations and realities. Here I will attempt to disentangle these many meanings of culture found in discussions of Japan and argue that unless they are all clearly understood, researchers and anyone else with a vested interest in Japan run the danger of ignoring the subtle and nuanced operations of power in Japan. There are many works in political science and political economics that mention "culture." However, for the sake of space, I will focus on one recent work (Reed 1993) that explicitly tackles the issue of culture in Japanese studies and, in my estimation, is representative of common misconceptions about its anthropological meaning.[1]

The first point to be made is that, as in Japanese, "culture" has several meanings. The first (culture as art) refers to artistic pursuits or intellectual endeavors, usually of a refined nature. The second definition refers to the particular traditions, knowledge, and institutions associated with a particular group, often geographically defined (culture as ethnicity). The third meaning (culture as knowledge), which subsumes the first two definitions, is a social scientific concept whose precise definition has been and is still hotly debated. Here I will not treat the numerous definitions offered in the literature. Below, what I mean by culture in a political context will become clear, but for now I provide a provisional definition, in two words, that everyone should agree on: "something learned," or more specifically, the arts, beliefs, customs, sociopolitical institutions, and all other products of human creation and thought developed by a group of people at a particular time that is learned. Stating that culture is learned actually entails a host of key axioms that have already been introduced in Chapter 1: the unquestioned, implicit, and uncontested nature of invisible institutions; how these institutions link different bodies of knowledge (e.g. public/ private distinctions, state/individual relations, bureaucratic structures, moral education, political legitimacy, and "common sense"); and how these bodies of knowledge are tied together without an individual necessarily being aware of it. In any case, social structures, political relations, ideologies, and economic interests, being learned, are cultural, and are inextricably related to how society – or more specifically, the state – is placed in the self. This view of things may be too messy for some, but culture and its concrete expressions such as symbols (or political myths) are difficult to dissect precisely because "they are such basic components of everyday perception." But culture, symbols, and political myths "are like the lenses in a pair of glasses in the sense that they are not things people see when they look at the world, they are the things they see with" (Bennett 1980: 167).

Distinguishing the aforementioned definitions of culture may seem elementary, but it is surprising how many scholars conflate these different meanings. Moreover, everyday usage of the term "culture" in Japan often merges culture as art, culture as ethnicity, and culture as socially acquired knowledge. In the next several sections, I continue to disentangle the various uses and abuses of "culture" in Japanese studies.

CULTURE AS ESSENCE

It is not uncommon for some Japanese to point to traditional or fine arts as examples of their own culture, and then, unreflectively, move the discourse from culture as art to culture as ethnicity, eliding two distinct definitions. This semantic shift is not insignificant, because any object or custom, no matter how trivial, suddenly acquires an ethnic and nation-defining power. Like people anywhere, most Japanese are proud of their culture's traditions. Some are so proud, in fact, that they are more than happy to tell non-Japanese just how special and "unique" their society is. The "Japanese-culture-as-unique" line of thought (e.g. four seasons, eating raw fish, Japanese language, sleeping on floors, using chopsticks, and Japanese rice[2] are commonly reported as "unique" examples of Japanese culture) at first glance may seem innocuous, even quaint, to the more cosmopolitan, but it possesses an ideological thrust that is insidious and far from being necessarily innocent. After all, the "uniqueness of the Japanese" (often meaning "superiority") was a prewar fascist and racist slogan, used to justify imperialism, enslavement, and war atrocities. Today, non-Japanese (especially non-whites) living in Japan often receive treatment that is blatantly discriminatory. Such treatment is often justified by invoking some "unique" feature of Japanese culture. When Japanese legitimize, defend, or explain some trait as being due to the "uniqueness" of their culture they are often engaging in a form of cultural essentialism (among Japanese scholars, *bunka honshitsu shugi*), which, simply put, means to obfuscate (or to be kept unaware of) some belief or behavior's intimate relation to political plays or economic interests.[3] Concealing the political side of belief or behavior is a means to posit a "truth" that is immune from critical scrutiny, so that people often come to accept a certain tautological determinism; i.e. "Japanese act that way because they are Japanese" (a circular argument prevalent among Japanese students I taught). "Culture, no less than biology (and perhaps implicitly because of it), is seen as destiny" (Herzfeld 1992: 9). A deterministic view of culture, of course, short-circuits intellectual analysis and bolsters sociopolitical and economic arrangements.

Cultural essentialism may be referred to as "culturalism." Bestor's study of the cultural dynamics that sustain and give identity to an urban neighborhood in Japan is pertinent here. He uses the term "traditionalism": "the manipulation, invention, and recombination of cultural patterns, symbols, and motifs so as to legitimate contemporary social realities by imbuing them with a patina of venerable historicity" (1989: 2). According to Bestor, traditionalism is a "common Japanese cultural device for managing or responding to social change" (*ibid.*: 10). Traditionalism and culturalist explanations are both attempts to add legitimacy to present-day social and political arrangements by constructing and reshaping conventions (*cf.* Hobsbawm and Ranger 1983).[4] Portraying Japan as "unique," whether by Japanese or non-Japanese, is sometimes phrased in a such a way that one is forced to take untenable positions on what cultural differences mean in Japan. Often, one is asked to agree with either: (1) Japan is different or somehow unique and thus not amenable to typical social scientific modes of analysis (the "special-category-for-Japan" argument); or (2) Japan is the same as any other society (here, "society" often implicitly means industrialized liberal democracies) and is amenable to conventional social scientific modes of analysis (i.e. political economic). To agree with (1) is to accept a proposition that violates key social scientific principles and espouse dubious notions about "Japaneseness." For many, accepting (2) all too often means that any differences between Japan and other places are somehow insignificant. Differences are epiphenomenal, usually of a residual, or "cultural" variety.

Remarkably, especially at the popular level and in the media, the notion that Japan (like all sociocultural systems) is in some ways similar to and in other ways different from other societies is infrequently placed on the table of intellectual debate (though many works in the political and economic fields, which often take a comparative view, are correctives to this tendency). But it is worth asserting (no matter how obvious, especially to some Japanese scholars) that the ideas of classical thinkers, so often evoked to explain social phenomena in other places, work just as well in Japan. Conceptualizations such as Durkheim's organic/ mechanical solidarity (1966), Tönnies' *Gemeinschaft* (community)/ *Gesellschaft* (society) (1957), Michels' "iron law of oligarchy" (1959), and Weber's rationalization and disenchantment (1978), whatever their currently perceived failings, shed light on the Japanese experience of modernization, economic expansion, centralization, urbanization, and bureaucratization. Though Mills's writings focused on America, his ideas on elitism (1956) have relevance to Japan (particularly, its often noted triad of business circles–bureaucrats–politicians), and even Parsons's thinking on the social changes (brought about by shifts from affectivity to neutrality, particularism to universalism, functional diffuseness to functional specificity, ascriptive to achievement orientation, and collectivity to individual orientation) (1951) may serve as a useful theoretical point of departure. Also of relevance here are Elias' ideas on individualization and the domestication of emotions (1978, 1982, 1983) and Foucault's studies of disciplinary institutions (1973, 1975, 1979, 1980). Their approaches chronicle the increasing power of both socialization and state machinery to monitor and manage the mind and body (both as individual persons and units in populations).

Another point that deserves attention is that, once the term "cultural" is injected into any discourse about Japan, critical analysis is sometimes derailed because some, Japanese and non-Japanese alike, automatically equate cultural analysis with an extreme form of "cultural relativism," so that "if x is defined as cultural, it is not amenable to social scientific investigation and it would be unfair to judge it." This is why so-called "revisionists" are often charged with failing to understand Japanese culture and are sometimes accused of "Japan bashing" and advocating a subtle form of racism.[5]

Some Japanese like to talk about their rich cultural heritage and traditional arts because it is a tactic to draw attention away from what are perceived as their society's less than admirable traits (such as bureaucratism). This is an overly cynical view, of course, if taken in all situations. However, it would be naive to believe that, at more official levels, there is no conscious effort to have non-Japanese focus on Japan's culture as art rather than culture as knowledge as a means to distract attention away from how power is organized in Japan.

Another form of essentialism, very much related to culturalism, is historical essentialism (or historicism): rooting present practices in the past while ignoring present-day realities. Researchers interested in "culture" are often charged with ignoring social change, since those making the charge accept the myth that "culture" means "ahistorical." For example, Reed notes that "culture does change, though slowly. But culture is also a drag on change, a factor resisting change" (1993: 39). Fukushima writes that "Because culture is a matter of ethical habit, it changes very slowly – much more slowly than ideas" (1995: 40). Consequently, many are surprised when told that most anthropologists assume that culture is a daily creation, spun into existence by social actors with practical intentions, and that very few anthropologists would agree that culture is a nation's unchanging core of values or a static "coherent whole" (*cf.* Reed 1993: 32) (Ruth Benedict is usually brought up here as an example of anthropological studies on Japan).[6]

Like cultural essentialism, historicism does not encourage useful analysis. The key question that historical essentialism ignores is why certain practices and beliefs are *still* in place. In Japan, common examples of historicism include: "Japanese are like that because we lived in a closed country (*sakoku*) for so long," and "because Japan was never conquered or ruled by a foreign power, Japanese have trouble dealing with foreigners" (the American Occupation does not figure in this latter analysis).

An important essentializing distinction of the historical variety turns on the Meiji Restoration of 1868. Pre-Meiji Japan was closed, pre-modern, feudalistic, and somehow "very Japanese." But after 1868, Japan had been pushed by internal strife toward reform and opened up by Commodore Perry's "black ships." Japan started on its path toward modernization, shed its feudalistic legacy, and became, to a limited degree at least, "less Japanese." Another significant historical point is Japan's defeat in 1945. Before and during the Pacific War, Japan was ultra-nationalistic, militarized, and anti-democratic, a warmongering nation that fanatically deified the emperor, but after that war, it became demilitarized and democratic and "adopted" a "peace constitution" (i.e. it was imposed by the American Occupation authorities) whose Article 9 renounced war. The emperor announced that he was not divine and Japan became a peace-loving country. The prewar/postwar distinction has been used to essentialize the values needed to mobilize the Japanese workforce for economic reconstruction. At the same time, it has also been used to preclude national-level examination and recognition of Japan's wartime atrocities and ignore historical continuities, both negative and positive, between prewar and postwar periods. The prewar period, in fact, has become "abnormal," while the postwar period is "normal," precluding the former era from historical analysis and critical reflection.

Essentialist explanations of Japan, whether of the cultural or historical variety, are driven by an orientalizing discourse (originating outside Japan), self-orientalizing discourse (originating within Japan), and faith in "modernization," "convergence theory," and high-speed economic development.[7] Both Japanese and non-Japanese alike are pulled into this identity-defining dynamic. These discourses have established dichotomies that shape Japanese national identities and characterize much scholarship on Japan. Taken together, these discourses postulate an essentialist "Japaneseness" and "non-Japaneseness," and in concrete terms, operate using an exclusionary/inclusionary symbolism that sets up a tight logic of binaries; if Japanese are x, then foreigners are not x, and if foreigners are y, then Japanese are not y. Japanese often apply this logic to the United States, a nation that has had such a profound impact on their country in modern times. But as Reed correctly points out, many misconceptions result from comparing Japan with only the United States; "on many dimensions Japan and the United States are the two most different of all industrial democracies." In terms of political and economic organization, Japan does not seem so unusual if it is compared with most Western European nations. Major misconceptions also result from comparing "Japanese reality to Western ideals instead of Western realities" (1993: 6).

An important word in the Japanese self-defining project that deserves commentary – incessantly heard in media reports, government pronouncements, and among average Japanese – is "internationalism" (*kokusaisei*). This term is part of a complex nationalizing discourse that compares and contrasts self with Other, ironically highlighting what it means to be a Japanese.[8] If anything, "internationalism" often conceals a complex discourse of nationalizing tendencies. Regardless of the benefits that a real "internationalism" might afford, this term is often appropriated by politico-economic elites for rather different ends. The discourse about "internationalism" ideologically mirrors an immense body of writings ranging from the scholarly, semi-scholarly, and popular, to the silly, and deals specifically with "being Japanese." The consumption of these writings constitutes "a minor national pastime" (Befu 1993: 109). Usually referred to as *nihonjin-ron* (theories about the Japanese), Mouer and Sugimoto point out the less innocent impact of this huge body of literature as something "used as an ideology to enhance the interests of those in control within Japan." More specifically, theories about what it means to be Japanese are used for the "maintenance of social order at home" and "the promotion of Japan's economic interests abroad" (1986: 169–88). Examples of the latter point are the well-known stories about trade barriers against the foreign importation of skis (Japan's snow is different), beef (Japanese have longer intestines), and rice (its unique spiritual significance in Japanese culture).[9]

Scholars who research Japan are confronted with a tenacious discourse operating at the folk level and in academic writings about Japan's "unique culture" and other myths. This discourse is made stronger by the *nihonjin-ron* literature. It is notable that even today, some non-Japanese scholars still carelessly refer to the Japanese people, their language, and culture as "homogeneous," failing to recognize the political implications of such statements and reproducing an essentialist idiom, indicating that scholars have become entangled in the official myths of Japan. Below are some common examples of the identity-constructing discourses:

Japaneseness	Non-Japaneseness
Japan	other societies (usually Western)
Japanese culture	"internationalized"
Japanese spirit	"Westernization"
pastness	presentness
tradition	modernity
Japanese morals	technology
spiritual wisdom	materialism
homogeneous	heterogeneous
closed society	open societies
classless society	class-based societies

Here it should be noted that during the 1960s and 1970s, thinking about Japan's modernization (which for many meant convergence) were reinterpreted.[10] Whereas some had regarded Japan's feudalistic and "traditional" modes of social organization as obstacles to its modernization, the "Japanese tradition was redeemed and proclaimed a uniquely suited vessel for modernization by a new school that developed around the 'unique Japan' hypothesis" (McCormack and Sugimoto 1989: 4).[11]

Another key identity-building dichotomy is ritualism/rationalism, which brings us to the theme of this book. A number of other meanings are subsumed under these two terms, such as hierarchical/egalitarian, emotional/logical, and groupism/individualism. Such terms are commonly invoked to explain human relations and business dealings in Japan versus those in the West. The former are "wet" and warm, while the latter are "dry" and cold; Japanese prefer amicable understandings and consensus, but Westerners like calculating dealings and contracts; Japanese are comfortable with sympathetic silence, while Westerners enjoy hard-nosed negotiation.

THE "NON-CULTURAL" CULTURAL ARGUMENT

Many researchers confuse or conflate cultural analysis with what should be called a "culturalist" argument. But sometimes, even those who recognize the distinction between a valid social scientific concept and an essentialist discourse still view the former with suspicion. Because many anthropologists use culture as a shorthand for socialized knowledge about sociopolitical and economic processes (and other forms of knowledge), the richness, complexity, and sheer extensiveness of what this term implies is often lost on those unfamiliar with anthropological assumptions and argot. It is interesting (if not puzzling) how many deny that they are using "culture" in their analysis when in fact they are. Many assume that culture, as a variable, can somehow be factored out of their analyses. Such thinking fails to recognize that, because culture is knowledge, any human endeavor – from running a ministry, drafting laws, voting, selling stocks, raising a family, to washing cars – requires culture. In the next section, I examine some of the other myths surrounding the meaning of culture as knowledge and why political analyses can profit from utilizing this concept.

CULTURE AS A RESIDUAL CATEGORY

One common misconception is that the intellectual tools used to under-stand small-scale, non-literate, and "primitive" groups are inadequate for large-scale, industrialized, and "modernized" societies. Concomi-tant with this view is that there are essential differences between exotic "simple" and the more familiar "complex" societies. However, as far as determining the relations between political institutions and the way people think, small societies possess just as much sociocultural com-plexity as the largest nation-states (*cf.* Douglas 1986: 21–30). Thus, as Herzfeld notes, "It is though we confronted two different worlds: sym-bolic analysis is appropriate for the soft definitions of religion and ritual, but the real world of government organization calls for sterner approaches," and the implications "are sometimes bluntly ethnocentric: 'traditional or primitive societies' have 'ritual' where the industrialized West enjoys the benefits of 'rationalism'" (1992: 17).

But the most egregious misunderstanding of culture as a social scien-tific concept, entangled with the misconceptions above, is the view that it is simply apolitical.[12] Both anthropologists and political scientists search for power in society. At the risk of simplifying, the latter have usually focused on governmental structures and their official links to other sec-tors of society. Often, the point of a political scientific endeavor is to compare and contrast governments or their component parts from dif-ferent nations. The danger with such an approach is that any similar function of parts is often mistaken for evidence that there are political institutions (e.g. legislatures, executive organs, leaders, judiciaries, par-ties, bureaucracies) that, for analytical purposes, can be abstracted from their local sociocultural moorings. All one has to do to discover their common function is to shift through all the cultural layerings. This is why some believe that "culture is unlikely to be an important explanation for things of concern to comparative social scientists" (Reed 1993: 74).

As a rule, most anthropologists are suspicious of any study that pos-tulates transcendent, idealized political institutions ripped from their local contexts. There may be similar governmental institutions from around the world, but on closer inspection there are undoubtedly dif-ferences that, as subtle as they might be, should not be sacrificed on the altar of political scientism.[13] Their functions may be similar but is very doubtful that they are the same. Comparative approaches in themselves may be useful for certain purposes, but if carried out carelessly they may distort the goals, motivations, and less obvious projects of a socio-polity. Also, while certainly not ignoring officialdom, anthropologists are sensitive to the danger of uncritically accepting what is "officially" designated as the "political" in any society, because sometimes the "political" is not necessarily very politicized, and by the same token, the supposedly "non-political" is politicized. The assumption that "real" power resides in the institutions, organs, and agencies of government, or that power is best measured and understood as economic clout, ignores the insidious nature of power. Besides the political and economic varieties of power, there are other forms that are just as important: everyday social relations, non-institutionalized groupings, various organized movements, gender roles, interpretations of the past, and the sociopolitical uses of "tradition," "culture," and "language."

Another misconception concerning culture that should be discarded is that is merely "expressive." Culture does not "reflect" a more real reality. Culture, like Durkheim's social facts, is real, and as such, constructs our definitions of reality. Not only does it do things to people, but people also use culture to do things. For example, consider values (a conceptual cousin of culture), another slippery and much maligned concept. Like culture, values are agreed-upon facts. Admittedly difficult to put into empirical terms, they nevertheless exert a powerful influence on social life that any serious account of human nature cannot ignore. Values are emotionally charged beliefs about how people should act toward one another. They have two aspects: (1) as cultural desirables, as ways of behaving that people find desirable for themselves and others; and (2) as tools, as the means by which social actors obtain certain things. This is the pragmatic, strategic side of values, and consequently relates to political concerns. Related to the strategic use of values is their use as categories of thought, as ways of classifying, ordering, and thereby evaluating the behavior of others and oneself.

The idea that culture is the epiphenomena of more real and solid economic and political processes – the smoke rising from the fire and heat of politics – leads to statements such as "A reliable interpretation must start with the basic dynamics of human society and add the cultural context later" (Reed 1993: 105). The notion that the cultural context can be added later – like the top layer of the wedding cake with the lowest layers representing the materialistic base and the second layer the social structures – is simply reductionistic. While it may sometimes be useful to speak metaphorically of culture in this way, such a perspective persuades us to regard culture as merely "expressive" or "symbolic," in contrast to "instrumental" and "substantial." Here it is worth quoting Sahlins:

At first glance the confrontation of the cultural and material logics does seem unequal. The material process is factual and "independent of man's will"; the symbolic, invented and therefore flexible. The one is fixed by nature, the other is arbitrary by definition. Thought can only kneel before the absolute sovereignty of the physical world. But the error consists in this: that there is no material logic apart from the practical interest, and the practical interest of men in production is symbolically constituted. The finalities as well as the modalities of production come from the cultural side: the material means of the cultural organization as well as the organization of the material means.

(1976: 207)

Some consider culture as a residual "variable" whose factoring into analysis detracts from parsimonious explanations of "real" social behavior. Thus, we have statements such as "Direct cultural causation of major economic, political, or social changes is improbable" (Reed 1993: 75). Culture, however, cannot be converted into a variable, the leftovers of a social system picked clean by sharper methods.[14] The view that culture "adjusts to physical, social, economic, and political realities" (*ibid.*: 32) reifies culture into a ghostly presence. Anthropologists have a different understanding of culture; it transmits, builds, connects, and in a very important sense, *is* those realities. This is true for the more obvious as well as the less apparent activities and practices, and for such things as an "economic basis," which is "a symbolic scheme of practical activity – not just the practical scheme in symbolic activity" (Sahlins 1976: 37). In Japan, for example, colorful neighborhood festivals, annual sports days, seasonal gift exchanges, etiquette, *aisatsu* (prescribed sociolinguistic behavior), and daily rituals may appear innocuous enough at first glance, but these activities and practices construct politicized cultural realities and are embedded in larger sociopolitical structures.

Some attempt to dichotomize "culture" and some more "real" reality, usually of an economic or political variety.[15] Note Reed's attempt: "At an aggregate level of analysis, culture represents the values shared by a group, and structure represents the relatively constant or repetitive situations people find themselves in. Sometimes the situation dominates and the question of values hardly enters the equation" (1993: 28). Such a naive objectivism misses the point that there are no such things as "situations" minus human interpretation (i.e. culture). Because there is so much overlap between individual understandings – and between different cultural definitions of situations – many assume that there is a "reality out there" distinct from culturally informed perceptions. However, there are no situations that are not interpreted by social actors. In this sense, situations or structures are provisionally agreed-upon definitions of reality; i.e. they are cultural products. The argument is often made that if overlap in belief produces so much agreement, there is no practical reason to be concerned about the marginal areas where there is no overlap. However, such an approach prematurely rejects much information that might be useful and perpetuates a false view about the role of culture in constructing human nature. Analyses based on convenient approaches may make neat models, but they do not necessarily and adequately portray social realities, which in any case display more disorder, contradictions, and multiplicity than the more "scientific" approaches seem ready to admit.

Reed continues the naive objectivist argument by stating that "our most basic beliefs do not come from socialization but from our own experiences." Such thinking fails to note that all human experience is mediated via socialized understandings. To argue that socialization cannot explain why political systems fail to create perfect citizens (*ibid.*: 30–1) is to misunderstand the very concept of socialization as commonly used. Individuals utilize instilled understandings for a variety of purposes and in a creative fashion that, while not denying the effects of socialization, proves only that it occurs imperfectly and with unexpected results. Very few social scientists equate socialization with passive acceptance of what one is taught. Usually implicit in the usage of "socialization" are the numerous resocializations and desocializations that individuals are exposed to throughout their lives. Socialization, after all, occurs on a daily basis. New knowledge is constantly acquired, integrated into older knowledge, and deployed to tackle various problems.

THE PROPER USES OF CULTURE

What are the advantages of a political analysis that utilizes the culture concept (or phrased differently, symbolic analysis)? One advantage is a more contextual perspective.[16] Many (but not all) political scientific studies look at the big picture, at things from a distance. In contrast, political anthropology has traditionally focused on the small picture and has preferred to look at things from ground level. These differing perspectives produce remarkably different views and understandings. For example, it is easy to assume that the same behavior results from the same belief. But this is an unwarranted assumption. Different beliefs may generate the same behaviors, but a top-down view, or one that relies too heavily on polls, questionnaires, and statistical studies, may fail to come to terms with more complex motivations. Institutions and organizations are daily constructions that are incessantly negotiated by social actors, and culture points to many things that "institutional" approaches miss:

> The sweeping bird's eye view of indices of economic productivity, technological innovation and bureaucratic efficiency reveals very little about the state of human rights, freedom of expression, equality among people, and the general quality of Japanese life. To examine the life conditions and lifestyles of ordinary men and women with respect to these areas, it is necessary to develop a "worm's-eye" perspective.
>
> (McCormack and Sugimoto 1989: 7)

Using the culture concept gives the researcher the tools to ferret out hidden hierarchies, nuanced relations, and subtle complexities. The strength of the anthropological approach is in its recognition that power does not dwell only in official institutions, but is disguised as, concealed behind, hidden in, and symbolized as innocuous activities, affairs, and relations. Cultural analysis helps researchers to understand how culture as knowledge is depoliticized and culture as art politicized. Because a social actor's cultural knowledge is encyclopedic in range, cultural analysis allows the researcher to make connections between sites of social interaction that are not always obvious. Thus, Williams notes that since Japan is a complex society, "the longer a professional researcher spends *in situ*, studying, observing and thinking about Japanese politics, culture and history, the more he will find in the methodology of Malinowski, Evans-Pritchard and Lattimore his preferred approach" (1996: 24). Unspoken associations and linkages between spheres of sociopolitical life that more top-down, institutional-centered approaches gloss over become visible through a cultural approach. In this book, I look for the linkages between public/private distinctions, state/individual relations, bureaucratic structures, moral education, political legitimacy, and "common sense."

There are, then, limitations to focusing solely on governmental institutions as the only "real" loci of power. Even the most innocent things – folk art, festivals, language use, and other apparently innocuous matters and practices – deserve close scrutiny because it is precisely through many of these that the most cherished and solidly rooted notions of Japaneseness, gender relations, and other concepts operate. These notions work hard at supporting larger and more obvious structures, ideological and institutional. "It is the transformation of people as they adopt the symbols of the state and the transformation of the state as it incorporates symbols from society – both seemingly 'non-political' processes – that an anthropology of the state can illuminate" (Migdal *et al.* 1994: 14). Symbols of the state may be obvious – e.g. flags, anthems, seals, etc. – but symbols of society may be less obvious. However, the latter can be just as potent, just as notions of "rationality" and "common sense" are also symbolic in operation and content.

> All these types of practical reason have also in common an impoverished conception of human symboling. For all of them, the cultural scheme is the *sign* of other "realities," hence in the end obeisant in its own arrangement of other laws and logics. None of them has been able to exploit fully the anthropological discovery that the creation of meaning is the distinguishing and constituting quality of men – the "human essence" of an older discourse – such that by processes of differential valuation and signification, relations among men, as well as between themselves and nature, are organized.
>
> (Sahlins 1976: 102, italics in original)[17]

At this point, I summarize my argument so far and list three main reasons why some researchers have become suspicious of "culture": (1) they associate culture (as a social scientific concept) with Japanese attempts to explain or excuse certain behavior or portray their society as "unique" (culturalist arguments); (2) they equate culture with the fine arts, folk traditions, religious rituals, and the past, matters which are assumed to have very little to do with the "real" world of hard-core politics and economics; and (3) they have a naive idea of how the concept of culture is used by anthropologists and often imply that culture is an apolitical concept. They deny they are using culture in their analysis when in actuality they are. But as Smith makes clear, "There is no aspect of the political economy in which culture is not implicated, for it is the context in which all decisions are made." Indeed, the very concepts "politics" and "economy" are cultural constructs (1992: 15).

THE FALLACY OF "COMMON SENSE"

I once asked a class of Japanese students to write an essay about the role of manners in Japanese society. More than one student equated the term "common sense" (*jōshiki*) with manners in ways that for me were not commonsensical. When I asked them to explain how manners were related to common sense, I learned that as manifestations of morality, manners were a type of common sense that included obeying the orders of school club superiors (*senpai*) and bowing to them, using proper speech when appropriate, and not littering. When pressed for other examples, many students mentioned removing shoes and announcing "*tada ima!*" ("I'm home!" literally, "now") when returning home, trying hard not to stand out when among friends, looking studious while in the classroom, and for women, wearing make-up when in public. While not unknown to people outside Japan, some of these examples of "common sense" do not necessarily seem commonsensical.

There is an obviousness, naturalness, and practicalness to common sense that affords it an unquestionable authority: reality so hard that it cannot be taken apart ("immethodical," to use Geertz's inelegant but trenchant term).[18] Its firmness, in fact, provides daily life with a surety and comfort that we take for granted. This certainty comes from massive agreement between people, making it highly "accessible" (Geertz 1983: 85). However, like all agreements – contracts, covenants, treaties, and other promises – it can be broken. It can, in fact, be dismantled. The belief that common sense is woven out of more real and reliable facts on which everyone unquestionably agrees (as opposed to culture, which is learned and differs between groups), is a quaint but fallacious proposition whose dismantling has been a leitmotif of the social sciences.[19] Thus, Reed's puzzling remark that "While not denying a major role to socialization, I argue that one important aspect of culture is common sense, what people learn from their own experiences" (1993: 73) misses the point that there is no such thing as presocialized, acultural experience.[20] The obviousness, naturalness, and practicalness of common sense are qualities bestowed upon things, not qualities that the world inherently possesses. "Common sense is not what the mind cleared of cant spontaneously apprehends; it is what the mind filled with presuppositions . . . concludes" (Geertz 1983: 84).

Because notions of publicness, civility, morality, rational behavior, and human nature are to a large degree rooted in common sense, an understanding of the tacit nature of common sense is germane to much of what I examine in this work. Like many forms of truth, the tacitness of common sense protects it from critical analysis, thereby affording it staying power. Consequently, if common sense is

> as much an interpretation of the immediacies of experience, a gloss on them, as are myth, painting, epistemology, or whatever, then it is, like them, historically constructed and like them, subjected to

historically defined standards of judgment. It can be questioned, disputed, affirmed, developed, formalized, contemplated, even taught, and it can vary dramatically from one people to the next. It is, in short, a cultural system, though not a very tightly integrated one, and it rests on the same basis that any other such system rests: the conviction by those whose possession it is of its value and validity.

(ibid.: 76)

THE RELIGION OF RATIONALITY

My use of "rationality" deserves comment. By this term I mean a particular style of reasoning that is culturally grounded and historically specific. This does not mean, therefore, that there exists a universalistic mode of human thought that has as its opposite "irrational" thought (popularly used to characterize children, "primitives," the "insane," and anything that does "not make sense"). In Japan, understandings of "rationality" (*gōrisei*) are congruent with Western notions (though not perfectly so; see Mutō below), and this term is basically used in the same way that many Westerners do: to describe efficient socio-economic relations and practices.

Rationality is also commonly synonymous with the ability to reason, good sense, and logic, and it is the basis of our folk philosophy that colors so many of our deepest assumptions about how to view the world. There is something comforting, in a way difficult to articulate, about the meaning of "rationalism": the theory that the exercise of reason provides the only valid basis for action or belief. As such, rationality is a close relative of common sense. The Latin root of rationality is *ratio*, meaning "calculation," whose many connotations (ration, measure, standardize, prearrange, control in a predictable manner) link it to its use among economists: "the methodical attainment of a definitely given and practical end by means of an increasingly precise calculation of adequate means" (Weber in Gerth and Mills 1958: 293). Another useful definition is the "processes by which explicit, abstract, intellectually calculable rules and procedures are increasingly substituted for sentiments, tradition, and rule of thumb in all spheres of activity" (Wrong 1970: 26). Still another definition that captures how most scholars use the term is the one offered by Meyer *et al.*: "the structuring of everyday life within standardized impersonal rules that constitute social organization as a means to collective purpose" (1987: 24).[21]

Rationalization, regardless of its universally understood reasonableness and commonsensical nature (rooted in modernity's projects of statism, capitalism, and positivism), has a variety of meanings, local permutations, and historical manifestations. In the case of Japan, rationalization, as a definite concept, was borrowed from Germany after World War I in order to improve technological and organizational efficiency and to strengthen management's control over labor. After the war, rationalization "has proved an ideologically potent and semantically slippery rubric for reform of everything from work rules and school texts to kitchen design, traffic flow, and dietary habits." It has become implicated in "the professionalization of roles, the bureaucratization of institutions, and the systematization of procedures" (Kelly 1996: 606). According to Mutō, rationalization (*gōrika*) "conveys in the Japanese context a peculiar degree of thoroughness, intensity, and refinement whereby the buildup of new production capacities, application of new technological methods, restraints on organisation of labour, and enforcement of new kinds of labour control devised to preempt and decimate workers' power are organically linked" (1986: 118–19). But whatever the culture-specific meanings of rationalization, it undergirds economic philosophies on both the left and right, from liberal democracies to Marxist states. This is because rationalization is deeply rooted in understandings on a par with positivism, practicality, progress, and materialism, commonsensical cosmologies that have driven capitalist and communist economic projects alike. Part of the faith in rationality stems from the belief in the inherent goodness of production (another tenet that undergirds a range of contemporary economic philosophies), so that in industrialized societies

> the economy is the main site of symbolic production. For us the production of goods is at the same time the privileged mode of symbolic production and transmission. The uniqueness of bourgeois society consists not in the fact that the economic system escapes symbolic determination, but that the economic symbolism is structurally determining. . . . In other words, the cultural scheme is variously inflected by a dominant site of symbolic production, which supplies the major idiom of other relations and activities. One can thus speak of a privileged institutional locus of the symbolic process, whence emanates a classificatory grid imposed upon the total culture.
>
> (Sahlins 1976: 211)

Therefore, the modes of production and the sociopolitical structures that manage them are sacred and beyond doubt. Thus, "the idea of

organizational reason is itself a symbolic construct with powerful ideological appeal," and bureaucratic formalism "places rationality above
and beyond mere experience, transcending the particularities of historical time and cultural place" (Herzfeld 1992: 18–19). Of course, the
details and particulars of production are often questioned, improved,
and further rationalized, but even those who decry the excesses and
dangers of capitalism (on both the left and right) nevertheless have faith
in the catechisms of a positivist rationalism, so that the merits of production are transmuted into a "commonsense" view of things with all
the authority of any ancient cosmology. That there are other societies
where economic activity is *not* the primary site of symbolic production
may seem quaint to some, but the fact that kinship or religious systems
can equal economic activity in symbolic generative power does illustrate the culturally contingent and constructed nature of economic
rationalization.[22]

In the next two sections I examine why it is useful to look for rituality
in rationalization, and the rationalization in rituality, rather than offering tidy definitions of these concepts. In this way, a certain synonymy
between rituality and rationality may be revealed. Furthermore, there is
a political aspect to recognizing the synonymy between rituals and
rationality. Power relations are placed in the foreground once it is
understood that terms that have become staples in the discourse on
Japan – consensus, cooperation, harmony, loyalty, and ritualized
behavior – are better described as control, coordination, management,
compulsion, and regulated behavior. As Haley points out, "The
repeated references to conformity and collective, cooperative, or collusive behavior in descriptions of Japanese society nearly always refer
to examples of collective efforts to induce or compel conformity"
(1991: 180).

THE RATIONALITY OF RITUAL

Rituality and rationality – especially for my political science and
political economic colleagues – may at first glance appear antithetical.
For many, the former is associated with "expressive" ceremonials,
religious rites, and other "non-rational" events that are incongruous
with an economically powerful, technologically advanced, and post-
industrial society such as Japan's. Ritual is just mere social ornamenta-
tion. Such a view, of course, suffers from the positivist assumption that
ritual is somehow irrational, inefficient, non-secular, and unconnected
to the "real" problems of social existence.

Rationalization, on the other hand, is usually associated with "instrumental" and "practical" activities that concern "real" problems of social existence and economic subsistence. However, I contend that despite their differences, rituality and rationalization sometimes share important commonalties: simply, both may facilitate the sociopolitical processes of cooperation, control, communication, and centralization. Like rationalization, ritualization at times advances efficiency and production. Rituality and rationalization, of course, are not necessarily the same thing, nor can rituality be reduced to rationalization, or *vice versa*. But for my present purposes, both rationality and rituality designate a package of activities and processes: standardization, formalization, and routinization that advance the above-mentioned sociopolitical processes.[23]

In the social scientific literature, rituals have been associated with tradition, the "expressive," and the religious. Rationality has been associated with modernity, the "instrumental," the secular. Rituals and rationality at first glance may seem incompatible, but these two concepts, as already mentioned, share common characteristics (hierarchizing, categorizing, formalizing, and routinizing). Consider Tambiah's definition of ritual, which is "constituted of patterned and ordered sequences of words and acts . . . whose content and arrangement are characterized in varying degree of formality (conventionality), stereotypy (rigidity), condensation (fusion), and redundancy (repetition)" (1979: 119). And Kertzer notes that "Ritual action has a formal quality to it. It follows highly structured, standardized sequences and is often enacted at certain places and times that are themselves endowed with special symbolic meaning" (1988: 9).[24] These definitions adequately describe rationalization just as well, and they characterize the bureaucratic mentality. There are other common features, such as a concern for precedent and procedure and the co-opting of smaller social units into larger ones or, probably more commonly, individuals into collectivities.

Weber linked rationality and rituals in a religious context when he noted that "Ritual has corresponded to rules and regulations, and therefore, wherever a bureaucracy has determined its nature, religion has assumed a ritualist character" (in Gerth and Mills 1958: 283). He also noted that the individual's quest for salvation outside hierocracies (i.e. contemplation, orgies, asceticism) "has been considered highly suspect and has had to be regulated ritually" (*ibid.*: 283). The significant word here is "regulated." And if there is one word that captures a central theme in Japanese social life, it is *chōsei suru*, which means to regulate, adjust, control, coordinate, correct, reconcile, or tune. All

industrialized societies are rationalized and consequently bureaucratized to some degree, but Japan offers a conspicuous example of the
bureaucratized society, where corporate culture, government, and the
mental maps required to navigate through daily life are all highly
rationalized and bureaucratized. That diverse spheres of social life
and practices are rationalized should not be surprising, because the
"general cultural effects" of the "rational bureaucratic structure of
domination" develop "quite independently of the areas in which it
takes hold" (*ibid.*: 240).

THE RITUALS OF RATIONALITY

All societies have rituals, symbolically informed patterns of practice
that reveal a society's fears, fault lines, and points of tension. They are
multi-purpose, dynamic social practices, constructing, deconstructing,
and reconstructing social groupings and organizations; indicating and
reinforcing group boundaries; signaling and strengthening status; and
marking socially significant transitions (rites of passage). All of these
functions may be found anywhere, though particular societies
emphasize certain ones more than others, and, it may be argued, some
societies (such as Japan) have a tendency to ritualize social life.

However one defines ritual, it is necessary to make the point that like
the term "culture" (see above) we should not assume that rituals reflect
social structure and activity. Like culture, ritual is constitutive, not
expressive of power relations. Its expressivity is its instrumentality. Ritual does not merely disguise, refer to, or ornament the workings of
power; rather, ritual constitutes sociopolitical structures. As Bell notes,
ritual practices do not exist "before or outside the activities of the rite,"
but "are themselves the very production and negotiation of power relations" (1992: 196).[25] Or, phrased differently, "ritual systems do not
function to regulate or control the system of social relations; they *are*
the system" (*ibid.*: 131, italics in original).[26] The same is true for symbolism. Speaking of political symbolism, Kertzer notes that "Far from
being window dressing on the reality that is the nation, symbolism is the
stuff of which nations are made" (1988: 6). This is especially pertinent
for the study of nation-states, since "Living in a society that extends
well beyond our direct observation, we can relate to the larger political
entity only through abstract symbolic means. We are ruled by power
holders whom we never encounter except in highly symbolic presenta-
tions." This is why, according to Kertzer, the argument that "symbolism
and ritual play important roles in the political process in Western

societies flies in the face of much received wisdom. Yet, far from arguing that politics becomes less encrusted in symbol and myth as a society grows more complex, I suggest that a case could be made that just the reverse is true" (*ibid.*: 8).

Japanese social life has often been described as permeated by rituals, formality, and ceremony.[27] The question of why there is such a high degree of rituality in Japan becomes easier to answer once it is understood that what is usually referred to as ritualistic behavior in Japan is described just as well by rationality. Simply stated, for many Japanese, rituals are regarded as a very rational way to organize social life. In Japan (as in other places to varying degrees), sociolinguistic practices that clearly mark group boundaries and status, workplace and school entrance/exit events, highly formalized social roles, standardization of knowledge needed to move up the socio-economic ladder, and highly ceremonialized politics are considered convenient and appropriate measures that ensure smooth social relations and operations. Despite their apparent non-practical (even impractical or "irrational") nature, there are, at least from the social actors' point of view, clear purposes and reasons behind the enactment of all these rituals. Labeling them as ritual may convince one about the time-honored traditions and specialness of one's society, or it may take the edge off the calculating coldness of a highly industrialized and competitive society. But the rationalizing features of these practices cannot be ignored.

MODERNIZATION IN JAPAN: THE CULTURAL PRODUCTION OF RATIONALITY

Here I should emphasize that I am not arguing that rituals can be reduced to rationality in the sense that all human behavior can ultimately be explained as utilitarian, reasonable activity. Rationality, like rituality, is a cultural production (as is "common sense") intimately linked to historical developments and modernization, and no reductionistic explanation can account for its complexity. Rationality is part of the doctrine underlying the faith in the inherent goodness of economic production, modernization, progress (*cf.* Nisbet 1980), and concomitant sociopolitical organizing practices and ideologies, which are all linked in modern nation-states, jointly subsumed under the rubric of "common sense."

In the following sections I offer some quotidian examples in order to introduce the procedure-oriented tone (i.e. rationalized/ritualized) that characterizes so much of Japan's *kanri shakai* (managed society) which,[28] according to some, suffers from the state's cult of procedure and precedent, resulting in *kajō kanri* (over-management).[29]

Calculating the contractual relationship

The contractual relationship, based on abstract, calculable rules and procedures rather than on particular customs, tradition, or sentiments, greatly expands the bureaucratic operations of commercial, govern-mental, and other networks. Popular portrayals of Japan often dismiss the significance of contractual relationships, stressing emotional bond-ing in forging relationships in the business world. This "Japanese way" contrasts with the "dry" or calculated relationships that, for many Jap-anese, characterize Western societies. There is also the popular belief that Japanese prefer unspoken communication and heart-felt trust rather than clearly explain contractual understandings. But the salient role that written proof and regulations play in Japanese daily life repudiates these myths.[30] For example, even well-established individuals in Japan are asked to provide letters from guarantors (*hoshōnin*) when renting apartments or transacting major business deals,[31] and the role of go-betweens (*baishakunin*) is not just to maintain face if negotiations break down between two parties but also to act as a handler of suspicious unknowns.

Concepts often trotted out to portray the "wet" (emotional) aspects of Japanese social life – e.g. *ninjō* (human feelings), *giri* (obligation), and *on* (debt) – are actually based on notions of reciprocity and instrumentality (Mouer and Sugimoto 1986: 216–19). There is, in fact, an emphasis on contractual relationships that can be traced back through Japanese history: "thinking of people as replaceable and there-fore expendable modules over the centuries" has resulted in a "lucid understanding of functional relationships, the ability to deal with abstractions and to see other persons not sentimentally as particular or otherwise irreplaceable units, but as units of labor or as numbers of votes which are interchangeable and can be utilized to accomplish one's own goals" (*ibid.*: 231).

Rationalizing and record keeping

The importance of contractual relationships is reflected in the great number of written records. All bureaucratized societies, of course, keep written records. However, "the important difference is one of degree: the greater frequency with which Japanese keep these kinds of written record, and the attention given to making entries in a correct or standard manner" (Mouer and Sugimoto 1986: 217). Engagement books, electronic notebooks, budget books, and a high number of well-stocked stationery stores indicate a great concern for recording and managing information.

In Japanese businesses, government offices, and other institutions, *ringishō* (written memoranda) are utilized. Requests, suggestions, and anything else that requires official involvement must pass through the *ringi* system, in which a formal document or form is written up and then circulated from the bottom of the organization to the top. A person in each level of management affixes his or her seal to the document as it moves up the hierarchy to indicate agreement, objection, or at least acknowledgment. Fiske refers to this practice as a "concurrence system" in which the permission of superiors is sought. "By getting concurrences, information of an action is spread around and *de jure* agreement is achieved." Some call the *ringi* system a method in "CYA (covering your ass)." Because everyone has been involved, no one can be blamed individually for any particular action (1994: 100).[32]

Behavior at the workplace is regulated through filling in *shimatsusho* (written explanation) to apologize for being late or some other minor mistake. There are also applications for permission to take a day off from work (*kyūka negai*), and special forms for vacations, on which one must indicate where one is going and the reason. For serious offenses, there are *hansei-bun* (written reflection on what one did wrong), used by companies, schools, police, and government offices.

Commercialized traditional hobbies are highly rationalized and hier-archized, and proof of accomplishment is symbolized by plaques and certificates representing levels of proficiency. In many martial arts, rank (*dan*) are assigned indicating levels of mastery (Mouer and Sugimoto 1986: 218). Note the rationalized features of Japanese leisure behavior and the way economic practices are interwoven with leisure: (1) clearly prescribed norms of leisure behavior for people of certain age groups, or at least a tendency to ascribe certain activities to people of the same age; (2) leisure behavior that is clearly differentiated by gender; (3) a preference for group activities; (4) a tendency to regulate leisure behavior; (5) a tendency to transfer work attitudes to leisure activities, so that leisure becomes an extension of work; and (6) a tendency to devote much of one's free time with people from the same workplace (Linhart 1988: 305).

The stress on contractual relationships is also apparent in a pre-occupation with rules and regulations. Though there is much discussion about the lack of clearly defined job descriptions and agreements between employee and employer, companies provide written materials that explicitly define a worker's rights. However, considerably more space is devoted to a worker's responsibilities and obligations. Every aspect of the employee–employer relationship is spelled out:

> Work is an area where regulations seem to proliferate. Upon enter-
> ing a company, new entrants are required to sign a contract, and to
> submit a résumé, a certificate of health, a diploma, their official
> transcript, additional proof that they have graduated, a signed
> pledge, a personal guarantor's statement, written evidence of a
> clean criminal record and a photograph. They are usually given a
> book of over 100 pages which spells out the company's regulations
> (*shūgyō kisoku*). Again the extent and the detail would startle most
> foreign employees. Many Western firms have some regulations, but
> employees seldom read them, even when they are asked to sign a
> sheet saying that they have. In Japan employees are often required
> to memorize them and are sometimes even examined on them. In
> addition to *shūgyō kisoku*, employees are also given various texts
> on bylaws and procedures: how to wear the company pin, how to
> bow, what phrases to use with customers, how to position one's feet
> when standing, various particulars about singing the company song
> and attending morning ceremonies, the dos and don'ts of eating in
> the cafeteria, etc.
>
> (Mouer and Sugimoto 1986: 255–6)

The concern with clearly outlining an organization's philosophy and regulations extends beyond the business world. Other groups – schools, religious groups, civic associations – often have detailed charters that formalize and standardize the role of members.

Other important documentation comprises technologies of surveil-lance and control. Though recent public pressure have put some restric-tion on their use, the family register (*koseki*) and residential registry (*jūmin tōroku*) are parts of an elaborate file system that records previous addresses, marriage particulars, convictions, and other information. Formerly, Japanese who traveled overseas were required to fill in a resi-dence card at the nearest Japanese embassy.[33] Neighborhood police boxes (*kōban*) gather information about local residents through forms and visits, which are sometimes followed up with phone calls. The infamous *naishinsho* (confidential report on students) at schools ensure that behavior is carefully self-regulated, since its contents may deter-mine a student's future. "The control mechanism here is not shame, but rather the threat that the door to upward mobility will be closed to them" (*ibid.*: 258). All this documentation, which taken together comprises a monitoring machinery that is omnipresent, inculcates the sense that one's actions will affect someone else (*ibid.*: 239–42), and significantly, that one's behavior is constantly being watched.

Rationalizing, recording, checking, and rechecking results in bureaucratization so that transactions produce considerable paperwork.[34] A good example is renting an apartment. The red tape is inordinate (as is the expense; various kinds of expenses make up a package of about six months rent – and in some places twelve – demanded before one even moves in). On top of this, a renter must present a letter from a guarantor for security reasons.[35]

As for bureaucratic red tape, Woronoff notes that it is hard to discern the purpose of certain kinds of paperwork except to give the bureaucrats more work:

> Noteworthy aberrations include a MITI [Ministry of International Trade and Industry] form containing forty questions about the specifications of every single boiler operated by large companies. Another required each car rental office to report the date every vehicle was rented, to whom, the destination and the time and place of return. And one set of regulations spawned a whole industry. The Ministry of Transport required inspection of every car every two years and, as of the tenth year, annually. This *shaken* [car inspection] was very costly and time-consuming for car owners and yet not very effective. For cars could be specially adjusted to pass the tests. Meanwhile, local authorities apparently spent nearly half of their time processing paper work related to subsidies from the national government.
>
> (1986: 147)

The emphasis on contractual relationships and written records "produce[s] an atmosphere in which it is very difficult for groups to form spontaneously" (Mouer and Sugimoto 1986: 227). Indeed, far from spontaneously forming out of consensus, group affiliation in Japan is instrumental and roles within a group well defined (*ibid.*: 215).

Japanese, like people in all industrialized societies, devote a considerable amount of attention to scheduling, segmenting, and classifying time. The sociopolitical and economic advantages of rationalizing temporal relations are obvious. There are many examples of clearly partitioning time in Japan; its public transportation system is world famous for its punctuality; the Japanese themselves display an aversion to tardiness and dress according to a strict seasonal schedule; and there is a strong general awareness about how the seasons – the Japanese archipelago is often characterized as "unique" because of its four seasons – should be reflected in food and other things. Perhaps this is why "Japanese seem to be offended by lapses in nature's schedule." Japan's Meteorological Agency uses the cherry trees at Yasukuni Shrine to determine the official cherry blossom season, and "Once the official season has been announced, all Tokyo trees are expected – like all school children – to appear in appropriate dress." However, "For the past several years efforts have been made to force cherry trees at the National Showa park . . . to fall in line with the official blossom schedule." Thus, "Attempts to speed up the lackadaisical blossoms have included building windbreaks, covering the ground with black vinyl sheets and reflecting sunlight with aluminum boards" ("Unnaturally natural," DY 30 March 1995: 8). And in 1995, the Meteorological Agency decided not to declare the starting and ending days for the rainy season. According to the agency, "since the rainy season is a seasonal phenomenon, it is unreasonable to declare certain dates as the starting and ending points." This announcement is significant, because it affected the opening of beer gardens and beach resorts, as well as changes in regional governments' disaster prevention systems. According to one official, "It was awful when it rained after the declaration (saying that the season had ended)" ("Weather agency to stop predicting rainy season," DY 11 February 1995: 2).

Standardization and accentuation

Standardizing, stereotyping, and conventionalizing ensure that commands are easily understood and readily disseminated, thereby strengthening lines of authority. It is not surprising that in many businesses – both large and small – there is much talk of the importance of *tōitsu suru* (standardizing or unifying) working procedures. Furthermore, conformity, *à la* Foucault, secures unhampered vigilance (one thinks of open offices and assembly lines).[36]

One subspecies of formalization is accentuation, or the highlighting or essentializing of certain features. This makes the environment easy to "read," and hence predictable, controllable, and operable. An example of accentuation is the tendency to clearly mark, label, and explain. Taped commentaries – incessantly run – are heard in train and subway stations, parks, amusement centers, and other public places, greeting, teaching, informing, and warning visitors. This had led one observer to describe Japan's "nanny culture": "It is a nation filled with talking machines that supply senseless or downright stupid information to one of the world's most well-educated populations. Everything from trains to trucks to vending machines has an obsequious word of thanks or warning for the Japanese and foreigner" ("Inane messages symbolize nanny culture," DY 14 June 1995). "The incessant repetition of the announcements, prodding people to behave in a prescribed way, smacks of a scene from a science fiction novel." At train stations,

> One might say that such detailed instructions show great concern for safety and station employees' devotion to their work. But I say that the incessant instructions on another level are a manifestation of a desire to regulate people, treating us as primary school students.
>
> ("Incessant, noisy warnings treat public like kids,"
> DY 5 December 1994: 8)

Or perhaps, one observer notes, "the recordings are a comfort by giving the appearance of order and organization everywhere citizens go – on the subways, in the stores and on the streets. And if there's one thing the Japanese love, it's order" ("Inane messages symbolize nanny culture," DY 14 June 1995).

In some rural areas, public address systems announce the time (this is usually done three times: morning, noon, and evening), and in certain places, advise children to return home around supper time. The best example of formalized accentuation are food samples, displayed in almost all restaurant windows. These samples, whose likeness to the real thing is often extraordinary, constitute a well-developed art form. Another example of visual accentuation is seen in nightly news programs, which employ a heavy dose of subtitles. Reporters often rely on superfluous visual aids, and sometimes, as they relate the day's news events, peel off posters, revealing to the eye what the ears hear. Sometimes it appears as if anything verbal needs to be substantiated by visual props, and vice versa.

Rationalizing roles

Establishing formalized and fixed procedures makes for clearly defined social and work roles and permits personnel, resources, and information to be mobilized quickly and manipulated for certain purposes. Routinization grants social actors their predefined scripts. Moreover, precise definitions ensure that information is easily processed and managed. In Japan, each individual is expected to possess a *bun*, or part, which has a predetermined set of norms, social ideals, and assumptions. In order to denote how a *bun*-holder should behave, the auxiliary adjective *-rashī* (like) is suffixed to nouns. This adjective modifies nouns, so that a "woman-like woman" (*onna-rashī josei*) is a "feminine woman" or a "student-like student" (*gakusei-rashī gakusei*) is a "studious student." This adjective possesses an adverbial form, as in "be a man" (*otoko-rashiku shiro*; literally, "do like a man"). The use of this adjective is notable because it often seems to merge fact with value, description with norm, the real with the ideal, so that "since x is Y-like, X must therefore be Y." Another way to put it is that a certain *bun* has an inner essence that a *bun*-holder must manifest through appropriate behavior. In this way, a sort of social typecasting is effected, thereby naturalizing, essentializing, and legitimizing cultural expectations, gender definitions, the social structure itself, and "common sense."

In Japan, there is a close association between ritualized routines and group membership. This is why knowing the "right" way of doing something – especially if it involves commitment and group participation – is important in countless spheres of Japanese social life. Navigating through Japanese social life requires mastering the appropriate knowledge for various prescribed scenes and sets.

Guiding behavior

Directions, instructions, and injunctions, of course, are evident in any society, but their ubiquity in Japan is noteworthy (later, I will discuss the state's unofficial attempts at guiding behavior: "administrative guidance" [*gyōsei shidō*]). Not only do directions have an inordinate amount of detail, but the "regulations are invariably worded to specify not what one may do but what one may not do." What would seem to be commonsensical to the average person is often written out in mind-numbing detail: "People are either not given much credit for thinking or taking initiative on their own, or it is simply assumed, perhaps correctly, that they have their own values and will go off and do something else" (Mouer and Sugimoto 1986: 246). Note the example of something as innocuous as coin lockers, "which at bus and train stations in the United States have a simple set of pictures explaining their operation, in Japan have posted on each door a list of a dozen or so stipulations for their user, including sub-paragraphs telling him or her that corpses should not be left in the locker and that the management will not be responsible for anything lost or damaged in the lockers" (*ibid.*: 247).

Experiencing frames and framing experience

Form, formal patterns, and proper forms (*kata*) predominate, especially in the traditional arts (*cf.* Buruma 1984: 70). Indeed, attuned to routines, regulations, and rules, Japanese acquire a tendency to ritualize experience and perceive matters in a "framed" manner (McVeigh 1994b: 63–5).[37] Thus, knowledge acquisition and learning become formulaic, conventionalized, and pre-packaged.

In Japan, bookstores devote entire sections to etiquette manuals that instruct readers on how to act during weddings, funerals, parties, first introductions, and other public events (*ibid.*: 58). Ceremonials are broken down into *shikijidai* (a ceremony's sequence), so that they are clearly segmented into "openings," the "event" itself, and "closings." These temporal divisions theatricalize the event and inform participants of who and what is privileged in the performance. Knowing about these divisions comes from performers, participants, and organizers having a "sense of ritual" (see Chapter 7).

CONCLUSION

I have attempted to delineate the sociopolitical foundations of a psychology by providing examples of its procedural, prescriptive, and formulaic tendencies. Observers of Japan should recognize that rituals are not feudalistic, quaint social customs, or traditional leftovers from another time. Rituals – entering a school or company, voting, attending a rally, protesting, singing the national anthem, politely interacting with neighbors – have an instrumental aspect that may not always be obvious to those who readily divide behavior into "instrumental" and "expressive," and then focus on the instrumental as somehow more "real."

Myths about uniqueness and homogeneity need to be dismantled, and the political functions of historicism need to be exposed. The politicized aspects of life in Japan are often disguised by a litany of terms referring to "groupism," "consensus", "harmony," and "cooperation." What many observers fail to recognize is that the evocation of these favorite descriptions is often a ritualized attempt to maintain hierarchy, a response to simmering conflict, or a suppression of any differences that may incite envy, a powerful sentiment too often overlooked in observations on Japan.

3 The bureaucratized self

Public, private, and "civil society" in Japan[1]

THE PROBLEM OF "CIVIL SOCIETY"

Does Japan have a "civil society" in the Western sense of the word? Is there a non-state "public space" in which autonomous individuals act for the collective good while self-serving, private interests are suspended? These are not easy questions, but whatever qualifications, complexities, or subtleties one may raise in an attempt to answer them, the meaning of "public" in Japan, as in any other place, is not insignificant, because it is intimately related to questions of state legitimacy, selfhood, and taken for granted assumptions about sociopolitical relations and economic practices. In this chapter, I contend that it is misleading to assume that a "civil society" or "public" in the Euro-American (specifically the Anglo-American) sense of the word exists in Japan.[2] I do not claim that there is no sense of collective interest in Japan, nor do I contend that some type of "public" or "civil society" is lacking in Japan. However, I do argue that the ideological supports of collective life in Japan are different, and that we should apply terms such as "civil society" or "public" – as usually understood – cautiously in discussions of Japan. But before proceeding, one caveat. The word "civil society" – like "democracy" – has a strong evaluative tone of a positive nature. But civil society can also be understood in a non-evaluative way, and it is in this sense that I employ the term: as a social region positioned between state and society.

Stated simply, my contention is that in Japan, rituality and staged formalities take the place of a neutral public space. The lack of a clearly defined public space encourages a social theatrics of formalized etiquette in Japan that mediates personal encounters and defines identities. Rituality in Japan results from the confluence of core values that encourage in many situations (but not all) group dependency rather than self-autonomy, empathy rather than impartiality, and hierarchy rather than egalitarianism.[3] Human relations are conceived as best realized through concrete and particularized connections rather than as being managed through abstract and transcendent rules.

In order to introduce this chapter's topic, I first discuss the meaning of "publicness." This inelegant term is needed because the word "public" carries connotations that are not universal. Although I discuss Euro-American notions (i.e. civil society and public) throughout this chapter, this is done not to imply that Euro-American notions about social order are ideals to which others should aspire; rather, I do so because it provides us with a certain perspective or reference point from which Japanese values can be better appreciated (I save my more judgmental tone for Chapter 8).[4] Then, I turn to an intellectual cousin of publicness, "civil society." Next, in order to lay the specific cultural groundwork, I investigate what publicness denotes in Japan by furnishing an index of key concepts – which function as the conceptual substructural building blocks of Japanese sociopolitical life – that delineates a highly ritualized sense of civility.

THE MEANING OF "PUBLICNESS"

Though "public" is a slippery and multi-faceted concept, most would agree that all societies have rules for dealing with others, strangers, and non-kin. Publicness arises when a group realizes that cooperation benefits everyone: "The public is a generalized self in the form of the other" (Moore 1984: 27). More specifically, when a group begins to produce an economic surplus, a segment of the population or a set of rules becomes necessary to appropriate the surplus. This may lead to a sense of publicness, as may the development of institutions to settle internal conflict and resist external threats (*ibid.*: 15). Certain societies, due to sociopolitical forces (population density, urbanization, stratification, economic complexities), have culturally expanded and elaborated publicness and equipped their members with specific sociopsychological tools needed to navigate through a social landscape peopled with others, outsiders, and unknowns that they must confront on a daily basis.

For the sake of argument, it can be stated that "public" has three meanings: (1) anything related to or for the collective interest and open to communal use; (2) institutions associated with state authority or officialdom; and (3) a socially recognized and organized forum where an individual's opinions, interests, or self may be readily and freely expressed in front of a collectivity that safeguards such expressions.

Euro-American political philosophy has conceptualized the third type of publicness as "civil society", which is often associated with a sociopolitical environment within which individualism is fostered and a set of institutions that guard the individual from officialdom or infringements by the collective.[5] In this sense, "public" does not refer to the group; instead, it refers to freedom from the group, a protective zone within which the individual is secure. It is an area that may be used to mediate disputes, defend rights, effect political changes, or facilitate social exchanges, wanted and unwanted. It is essential to point out that the third meaning of public may conflict with the second meaning: i.e. the public may be utilized by an individual as a institutional buffer in the face of governmental infringement. The third type of publicness, which for my purposes may be referred to as "civil society," is the topic of the next section.

CIVIL SOCIETY AND COMMON SENSE

"Civil society" is a concept so basic and interwoven into the Euro-American political experience that it is often taken for granted. It is, in fact, a type of social "common sense."[6] Thus, many seem to assume that all democratic, "modernized" nation-states possess "civil society." But civil society is anything but commonsensical; it is in fact quite historically specific. Its origins can be traced to political philosophers of eighteenth-century Europe, though there are many theories about what civil society actually is. Giner notes that there are Lockean, Hegelian, Hobbesian, Marxian, and Gramscian (I would add de Tocqueville's) conceptualizations.[7] However, they all refer to a sphere of social existence separate from the state, though some did not consider it free from state interference (1995: 304).[8] Much could be said about civil society, but for my present purposes it suffices to state that this term "can be applied to all those social relationships which involve the voluntary association and participation of individuals acting in their private capacities," and it is "a coming together of private individuals, an edifice of those who are otherwise strange to one another." Significantly, civil society is "clearly distinct from the state. It involves all those relationships which go beyond the purely familial and yet are not of the state" (Tester 1992: 8), and is largely based on "the symmetric reciprocity of strangers" (*ibid*.: 41).[9] Over time, the Euro-American tradition gradually invested (in principle, if not always in practice) each individual "with the same intrinsic value purely as a human being regardless of societal position."

Most would probably characterize societies that have civil society as also possessing a limited government that is elected and accountable; the rule of law; a market economy; numerous voluntary associations; and unhindered public debate. However one chooses to define civil society, it has performed a dual role in Euro-American states, both connecting citizens to and protecting them from government. In some respects, civil society and the state are mutually reinforcing (Figure 3.1).[10] It is important to point out that civil society is not synonymous with society (as is often implied in the literature); nor is it merely a residual category for social structures or forces that cannot be labeled governmental. In the Euro-American tradition, civil society has acted as a normative consensus that allows the communication, contestation, and sometimes the resolution of competing perspectives. Its power resides in its ability to provide a common discourse.

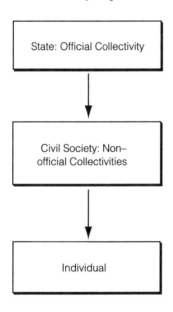

Figure 3.1 Euro-American polities: the relation between the state, civil society, and the individual

THE IDEA OF PUBLICNESS IN JAPAN

The term "civil society" (*shimin shakai*) "translates only poorly into the Japanese language" (Williams 1994: 165), and Japanese and non-Japanese alike lament the lack of "public spirit" in Japan. Starting in the prewar period, Japanese scholars belonging to the Marxist-influenced "civil society school" (*shimin shakai-ron*) have argued that Japan lacks a civil society. Associating the latter with liberation from feudalistic socio-economic relations, they have often equated "civil society" with democracy and equality, and they asserted that capitalism developed in Japan without a healthy civil society. The most famous representative of this school of thought was Maruyama Masao (1964). Though scholars such as Uchida Yoshihiko argued that postwar American-instituted reforms did spur the development of civil society to some degree, its underdeveloped nature paradoxically allowed Japan's exceptionally rapid economic development (*cf.* Uchida 1981, 1985; Hirata 1987).

All the attributes usually associated with civil society are evident in modern Japan. Democratic institutions; a media with a large readership; a relatively open market of ideas and commodities; residents' movements (*jūmin undō*), citizens' movements (*shimin undō*), and other collectively organized activities and groups (usually prefixed with *kai*, meaning "group" or "association") certainly indicate some type of "publicness" or "civil society."[11] If "publicness" is defined as "the capacity to put oneself in another person's position, to identify with other persons" (Moore 1984: 27), then Japan does possess a type of public interest. However, we should be wary of carelessly assuming that civil society in the Euro-American mold exists in Japan, where the lines are drawn differently between public and private spheres – and significantly for my argument – there are indeterminate social spaces that Euro-American political thinking would find questionable.[12] As Williams points out, "Whatever hopeful resonance the word 'public' may evoke in the English ear, it must be stressed that 'government of the people, by the people, and for the people' is not a Japanese administrative tradition. At best, the Confucian bureaucratic tradition is about paternalistic benevolence, not power-sharing with the masses" (1994: 111). This is perhaps why the type of "civic virtue" needed to encourage and sustain popular outrage over scandals is lacking (Abe *et al.* 1994: 206):

> Even in regard to today's younger generation, so unblushingly self-absorbed in their affluence, one may doubt whether there is any inclination toward a social order based on individual autonomy. In that the subjective creation of objective norms by individuals who are either repressed by collectivities *or* hedonistically self-absorbed is impossible, there is an eerie continuity between the prewar and postwar eras.

> (*ibid.*: 210, italics in original)

In a manner that many Euro-Americans would find surprising, Japan's bureaucrats often act as if they were responsible for the ethical fiber of the average Japanese. This is why "Japanese public policy aims to affect people directly. The contrast with the Western approach, which stresses impersonal objectivity (administrative fairness) and indirect influence on economic actors via marketplace regulation, reflects a different state philosophy" (Williams 1994: 71).[13] This issue is related to how the Japanese state is paradoxically characterized as both weak (often attributed to factionalism) and strong. In modern Japan, the state has struggled with "other political actors, whether interest-group-corrupted politicians, romantic idealist with a weakness for political violence or grasping businessmen keen to line their own pockets at national expense." Consequently, from the perspective of the bureaucrats, the state must be strong to get anything accomplished (*ibid.*: 25). This is why, in contrast to Euro-American political philosophy, the state sometimes sees its role as merging, not separating, the state and society.

Haley argues that the state is weak in Japan (lacks coercive power), but that it possesses great authority and is effective because it relies on an autonomous and cohesive society to carry its demands (1991). Consider his observations about law in Japan:

> The inability of the formal legal system in Japan to provide effective relief, to impose meaningful sanctions, thus tends to buttress the cohesion of groups and the lesser communities of Japanese society and to contribute to the endurance of vertical, patron–client relationships. The use of private mediators, reliance on banks and other large-scale enterprises, the role of *yakuza* [gangsters] and organized crime all fit this pattern of conduct. The features of postwar Japanese society so often labeled as vestiges of a familial, neo-Confucianist, or feudal past tend upon closer examination to have been adaptations of social controls, legitimated perhaps by traditional symbols and ideological claims, designed to satisfy a basic need for security against risks the state is unwilling or unable to provide.
>
> (*ibid.*: 180)

According to Haley's "command-without-coercion" thesis, the role of Japan's bureaucracy is distinctive, not because of its size (which is relatively small) nor its influence *per se*, but because of its "conjunction of broad, seemingly limitless authority without, however, even a relatively normal degreee of coercive legal powers" (*ibid.*: 143). I would add that the Japanese state's reach is enhanced by a general preference for a bureaucratic ethos in Japanese sociopolitical life. Haley may be right when he states that "There is in fact no evidence to support the widespread belief that bureaucratic influence is any greater in Japan than in other developed parliamentary democracies. Once again, we confront a persistent and underlying myth" (*ibid.*: 142), but this myth is kept in place by perceptions and shared convictions about the range of state powers. More than administrative regulations, laws, and direct contact between citizen and government, it is the general rationalized and ritualized tone of Japanese society that sustains the bureaucratic ethos, both in its state and non-state varieties.

Civil society has many functions, but in Euro-American societies one of them is to legitimate and guard personal beliefs and opinions from unwarranted interference. I contend that the lack of a strong civil society that buffers the private sphere from state action (as in Euro-American societies) enhances the power of Japan's bureaucrats, who, in the words of Isomura and Kuronuma, administer "for the sake of the citizenry," but not necessarily with the "participation of the citizenry" (1974: 11) (Figure 3.2).

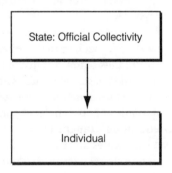

Figure 3.2 Japanese polity: the relation between the state and the individual

There are, of course, other social forces that buffer the individual Japanese from the state, and my description admittedly suffers from being too abstract and simplistic. In the next chapter I discuss advisory councils, administrative guidance, and special corporations in order to provide concrete examples of state–society relations in Japan.

A WALL OF DENSE RITUAL

Above I suggested that in Japan, staged formalities erect thick walls of rituality, taking the place of an impartial public arena. In this section, I examine the idiom used to discuss these ritualized practices. These terms (especially *uchi/soto, honne/tatemae, ura/omote*) are employed by scholars of Japan and average Japanese alike to describe sociopolitical behavior and self-presentation in Japan. Though not always explicitly stated in the academic literature, use of these terms often implies that they are somehow unique to Japanese culture. Sometimes, these terms are positively associated with Japan's "traditional culture," or negatively, as premodern, feudal remnants. However, whatever their historical origins, the social uses of these terms are in fact quite modern. In this chapter, I argue that, regardless of a certain idiom found only in Japan, the terms referred to above point to sociopolitical dynamics that are not "uniquely Japanese" and can be found anywhere. Though they are specific to Japan in some respects, there is a danger of exoticizing these concepts, which have counterparts in other sociopolitical orders. Thus, in order to demonstrate that Japan's supposedly "unique" ritualized society is amenable to analysis, I inject some observations from Goffman that correspond to notions found in Japan.

The divisions (sharply delineated social domains) that the Japanese terms cited above describe are social classificatory mechanisms posited by state-sponsored political and economic interests, and as such, are expressions of a high level of ritualization in Japanese social life. This ritualization is actually part of sociopolitical and economic rationalization and bureaucratization. As I show later, a link between these concepts and the state is found in "moral education" taught in schools. This is an example of how the state actively advocates an ethnomorality of rituality, thereby strengthening socio-economic rationalization. Thus, the idiom I dissect below is not rooted in pastness but is shaped by modernity; it is not ahistorical "tradition" but very present practices; and it is not depoliticized "customs" but politicized socio-economic relations and structures. Regardless of the premodern ring of such terms as "groupism," "collectivism," and "cliquism," these social phenomena are as contemporary as they are "traditional." These terms (the words sectionalism, fragmentation, and atomization basically carry the same significance), in fact, are describing social processes produced and reinforced by a bureaucratic ethos. The discourse I analyse below, a product of a bureaucratized social landscape, is firmly anchored in social forms that induce people to separate clearly personal self from public persona.

There is no one Japanese term for "public" that captures the sense of a neutral space in which the individual may stand alone, detached from commitments and yet safeguarded by codes of civility.[14] Nevertheless, the Japanese language does possess a number of words that approach what is usually called "public" in the Euro-American sense (and its counterpart, privacy). In order to appreciate how the domain of others, unknowns, and the unfamiliar is conceived, I list and comment on the conceptual coordinates that Japanese employ to navigate through their social landscape. These terms are meant to be a glossary of sorts, and the careful reader may want to refer back to these terms while reading Chapter 7 on moral education.

Ōyake   Significantly, this word originally referred to the imperial family. It could also denote official authority or governmental powers, and has associations of high-sounding purpose, order, fairness, and the collective good. *Ōyake* did not mean public in the sense of a social space that protected the individual from civil disturbance or state authority, but represented a "primary fraction" (i.e. the imperial family) among a group of competing political powers and institutions. Though *ōyake* has lost its original meaning of imperial family and acquired the sense of "public" since the war, "the old '*ōyake* spirit' still pervades the Japanese mentality" because the government is afforded much power *vis-à-vis* the people (Doi 1986: 44). Indeed, behind any surface similarity with "public" lurk the old rigors of imperial hierarchy and official power" (Williams 1994: 70). Currently, *ōyake* is used to mean public in the sense of officialdom or "to make public" (*ōyake ni suru*). It is also used adverbially (*ōyake ni:* "publicly").

Kō   This word, written with the same ideogram as *ōyake* and often carrying the same denotations, is a prefix for dozens of compounds, conveying "public," "communal," "open," "official," "legal," "governmental," or anything or anyone exposed to the collectivity. "The word '*kō*' conveys a specifically illiberal weight which is untrue of the English word 'public'" (Williams 1994: 111). *Kō* is part of the commonly used *kōshū* (the public; literally, "public multitude"), which is used to describe anything available to public use, such as *kōshū denwa* (public phone). *Kōkyō* (literally, "public together") is very similar in meaning to *kōshū* and signifies "community" and prefixes many words, such as *kōkyō toshokan* (public library). *Kōeki* (public benefit) is another commonly used word, as in *kōeki jigyō* (public utilities). *Kōyō* (public use) means "for official use" in a business setting, as opposed to "private use" (*shiyō*). Here it is pertinent to point out that "public spirit" is *kōtokushin* (literally, "heart of civic virtues") or *kōkyōshin*. These words are rarely heard in everyday speech and for many Japanese possess an abstract feel, though they do appear in moral education materials.

The next several words are commonly heard in everyday speech. Notably, these terms possess a sense of being observed, monitored, and scrutinized by others, and lack the more positive meaning of a social space where one can theoretically feel protected by impartial and universal civil codes.

Seken This is probably the most commonly heard word used to describe "public." Lebra defines it as the "surrounding world of community consisting of neighbors, kin, colleagues, friends, and other significant persons whose opinions are considered important" (1984: 338). This word may mean those who are immediately present and known, or it may mean those who are more distanced from oneself. It is used in many idioms and may mean the local community, society, or the world at large. *Seken* is often associated with rumor and gossip (*sekenbanashi*) or one's reputation (*senkentei, senkenguchi*). What one wears, does, and says are carefully observed by the *seken*, which strongly denotes "being watched" (Mouer and Sugimoto 1986: 239–40), as in *seken no me* ("the eyes of the *seken*").

Hitome Literally meaning "the eyes of people," this term often suggests being seen by those immediately around one. A sense of what it means can be gleaned from the idioms it appears in: "to attract attention" (*hitome o hiku*); "a conspicuous place" (*hitome ni tsuku tokoro*); "in secret" (*hitome o shinonde*); and "to avoid observation" (*hitome o sakeru*).

Hitomae This is similar in meaning to *hitome* and literally means "in front of others," though *hitomae* often carries a stronger connotation of being in front of unknowns. The idiom "to keep up appearances" (*hitomae o tsukurou*) provides a sense of what it means.

Soto (or *yoso*) This term prefixes many words and means out, outside, non-domestic, public, exposed, or anything to do with the unknown, strangers, and others. In an economic, commercial setting, it may refer to customers (*cf.* Quinn 1994: 63–4).

Omote This is another important term (which shares the same meaning and ideogram with *hyō*). Used in many compounds, it means front or surface, but it may refer to anything exposed to public attention, legitimate, and it sometimes means dignified, formal, or even dramatized. It appears in phrases such as "putting up a front" (*omote o tateru*), "keeping up appearances" (*omote o tsukurou*), and "keeping up a façade" (*omote o haru*). *Omote* corresponds to Goffman's "front," the accentuated area or activities of impression, or "that part of the individual's performance which regularly functions in a general and fixed fashion to define the situation for those who observe the performance" (1959: 22). In Japan, however, "fronts" seem to be more explicitly thought about and discussed.

Tatemae   This term means stated policy or the rules or conventions that have been established and agreed upon by a group, and it often refers to attempts to create an atmosphere of amiable consensus through public play-acting. More negatively, *tatemae* may mean pretense or façade. What one really feels in one's heart is not necessarily important; rather, what one is judged on is the degree to which one attempts to support the feeling of amiable consensus. "Ritualism" and ritualistic conformity are often linked to *tatemae*, which entails the "preservation internally of nonconformist values and beliefs while outwardly conforming to established behavior patterns" (Koschmann 1978: 20). *Tatemae* corresponds to Goffman's "working consensus," for which a person

> is expected to suppress his immediate heartfelt feelings, conveying a view of the situation which he feels the others will be able to find at least temporarily acceptable. The maintenance of this surface of agreement, this veneer of consensus, is facilitated by each participant concealing his own wants behind statements which assert values to which everyone present feels obliged to give lip service.
>
> (1959: 9)

Tatemae "can also refer to bureaucratic red tape, that is, official rules and procedures that are bypassed to expedite matters" (Kyogoku 1993: 59–60).

Just as it is difficult to capture in one Japanese term "public," it is also hard to gloss "private." However, there are a number words that come close, and an idea of what publicness means in Japan can be gleaned from examining words for the personal and private.

Shi   This word is commonly used to form compounds that denote the personal and privileged, though it often carries a sense of the illicit that the English word "private" lacks. Many of the compounds prefixed by *shi* concern things secretive, hushed, and selfish.[15] It may be used to refer to irregular dealings, personal feelings, or private desires. It is written with the same character as *watashi* (or more formally, *watakushi*), one of the many words in Japanese meaning "I" or "me." Recently, the English-derived *puraibashī* is often used to refer to the private.

That privileging the personal is a novel notion in Japan – a notion supposedly on the increase among the younger generation – is evident in terms such as *mai kā* (my car) and *mai pēsu* (my pace). Also, employees who do not devote enough time to work are accused of harboring thoughts of *mai hōmu* (my home) or *mai hōmu shugi* (my home-ism), reflecting how the workplace is often given more weight than family affairs and the consequent tensions between corporate demands and personal concerns.[16]

Uchi   This is an extremely important term (which shares the same meaning and ideogram with *nai*) and is the counterpart of *soto*. It means inside, internal, informal, familiar, concealed, or private. It is used as an adjective to indicate oneself, family, house, group of play-mates, workers, school, company, or even one's nation.[17]

Ura   This is another significant term (which shares the same meaning and ideogram with *ri*) and is the counterpart of *omote*. It means back, reverse side, but it may refer to anything hidden from public attention, privately allowed, and it sometimes implies practical, efficient, informal, or flexible. *Ura* corresponds to Goffman's back region, backstage, or the area or activities that are suppressed because they might discredit the fostered impression. The backstage is "defined as a place, relative to a given performance, where the impression fostered by the performance is knowingly contradicted as a matter of course." Thus, "It is here that the capacity of a performance to express something beyond itself may be painstakingly fabricated; it is here that illusions and impressions are openly constructed" (1959: 111–12). And, "Since back regions [*ura*] are typically out of bounds to members of the audience, it is here that we may expect reciprocal familiarity to determine the tone of social intercourse. Similarly, it is in the front regions [*omote*] that we may expect a tone of formality to prevail" (*ibid.*: 128).

Minkan This word, basically meaning "among the people," is used to mean private, popular, or civil in the sense of unofficial, not under government control, as in *minkan jigyō* (private business). It is also used to refer to civilian (non-military).

Honne This is the counterpart of *tatemae* and means one's true opinions, personal thoughts, or real motive (literally, it means true tone or pitch). A word with the same meaning is *honshin* (literally, "original heart"). *Tatemae* and *honne* should not be thought of as opposites, since they mutually define each other. Indeed, the existence of *tatemae* legitimizes *honne*, so that "*tatemae* conceals *honne* even as it represents *honne*" (Doi 1986: 35–40).

The expressions *seken*, *hitome*, *hitomae*, *soto*, *omote*, and *tatemae* all strongly imply that a public gaze confronts people once they leave a group or their inner circle of family or friends. Such an awareness regulates behavior and shapes subjectivity and self-expression, and supports a sharp distinction between inner (*uchi*, *ura*) and outer (*soto*, *omote*) social settings. In Euro-American cultures, however, the basic unit of society has been the individual, who stands alone in spaces either open (public) or closed to observation (private). Thus, "inner" and "outer" – while certainly not unknown in Euro-American contexts (as Goffman has demonstrated; 1959) – do not carry the same social weight.

Lebra's insights into how *uchi*, *soto*, *omote*, and *ura* dynamically interact, resulting in "three domains of situational interaction" (1976: 112), are relevant to the topic at hand.[18] Below, in order to conclude this section on publicness in Japan, I briefly describe these domains.[19]

1   Intimate situations (*uchi-ura*). Among family and friends people consider themselves equal, so rank loses importance. Togetherness, emotional attachment, and spontaneity characterize intimate situations. Free from the observations of rationalizing and ritualizing hierarchies of school, workplace, and the outside world (*seken*), individuals express their true opinions (*honne*).[20]
2   Ritual situations (*soto-omote*). In direct contrast to intimate situations are settings that demand visibly rationalized forms of self-presentation. In such situations, hierarchies carefully scrutinize behavior: bodies are put in uniforms (most notably in schools, but also in factories and among "office ladies," who inevitably wear uniforms), language and posture are monitored, movement is regulated, and *tatemae* is judiciously employed in order to erect walls between authority figures, non-kin, and strangers. Ceremonial

occasions (weddings, funerals, formal gatherings, etc.), the work-place, a chance encounter with an acquaintance on the street, and meetings of some kind all elicit ritualization to some degree (*cf.* Lebra 1976: 120).[21]

3   Anomic situations (*soto-ura*). Japanese are noted for their very civil and courteous behavior, and on Japan's streets, there is a general sense of cleanliness, orderliness, and safety. It is perhaps accurate to state that many Japanese are not impolite in public, but it is also true that neither are they very polite toward strangers. This is not to pass judgment. The sense of security and orderly civic traffic found in Japan is commendable, and the Japanese manner of passing through public space is just as effective as any that this author has observed in Western cities. But if we are to understand Japan's sociopolitical dynamics, we must look beneath the surface of social interactions, and upon closer inspection (particularly in the urban areas), the subtle differences in Japan's public life with those of Euro-American societies become evident. If ideally (and I emphasize "ideally") the public in Euro-American societies are spaces in which grids demarcate agreed-upon routes traveled by individuals who temporarily leave their privacy behind, in Japan, the public is a somewhat more disordered place where atomized individuals take their privacy with them and try their hardest to coolly disregard others. Abe *et al.* note that "'Freedom,' in con-temporary Japan, is less a value to be realized through the unremit-ting efforts of human beings than it is simply a condition in which people are living tranquilly by coincidence" (1994: 210). Perhaps the same could be said for the Japan's civil society.

Long-time foreign residents in Japan are apt to comment on the lack of politeness in Japan's busy public spaces. Perhaps the most common complaint concerns commuters refusing to give up seats for handi-capped or the elderly on trains and subways (or worse, occupying spe-cial seats designated for such people). Congregating near subway or train doors, thereby blocking those attempting to board and exit, is another common inconvenience. Perhaps the most irritating are cyclists – often mothers loaded down with groceries and children careering through busy intersections, down narrow alleys, or around tight corners – who recklessly weave in and out of crowds. One observer, struck by the inattention (and occasional rudeness) of cyclists, pedestrians, and commuters to each other's personal space, notes that "Even if other people see us when we get really close, they are indifferent to our fate" ("Japan deals body blow to personal space," AEN 12 June 1996: 6).

58 *The nature of the Japanese state*

Some "pushy, rude, and selfish" middle-aged and elderly females have earned the appellation *obatarian*, a combination of *oba* (old woman) and *batarian* (battalion) (the latter word is associated with a horror movie about carnivorous aliens).

There are other signs indicating that in Japan, the public is a place where one carries personal space (i.e. does not give way to others unless told to do so by recorded announcements, station attendants, police, or authority figures) into a no-man's land populated by out-group (*soto*) others. Men can frequently be seen, sometimes in broad daylight, urinating in public (*tachishōben*; literally, "standing piss"). Vomit on train floors or in stations is not an uncommon scene at night, along with inebriated drinkers sprawled on the ground with faces flushed, the result of corporate culture's use of alcohol to relieve workplace stress. My most vivid memory of public transportation in Japan is of waiting a few times each week at my college's bus stop while several junior high school teachers pleaded with raucous junior high school students (the females were the more boisterous) to board a public bus. Every day the bus driver would patiently wait the ten to fifteen minutes required to board the students. The teachers, who struck me as infinitely tolerant, were dispatched daily by the school to the bus stop to handle the troublesome students. The problem was simple: students would refuse to sit next to anyone they did not know, thereby standing and taking up valuable space, and they would not move away from the door, because they wanted to be near the exit when reaching their destination.

If for many Japanese intimate situations involve "insiders" (*uchi*) and ritual situations involve "outsiders" (*soto*) but require *tatemae* practices and face-maintaining maneuvers, there are situations that cannot be clearly defined as inside or outside. These are ambiguous social spaces, between family and non-kin group-regulated settings. It is in these areas, described as anomic by Lebra (1976: 112), that an individual regards someone as an "outsider" but feels no need to maintain face, since there is no ritualizing hierarchy observing behavior and thus no rules to uphold.[22] It may be argued that, ideally at least (again, I emphasize "ideally"), there are no anomic areas in Euro-American conceptions of the social landscape. Rather, as the basic unit of society, the individual is expected to move between different settings. All space between intimate and non-intimate situations is recognized as an arena regulated by agreed-upon codes of conduct. In Japan, however, it is the group setting (whether intimate or ritualized) that establishes the rules. Any space between these groups is incidental to the groups themselves, a sort of marginal area unregulated by significant social concerns.[23]

Now that an index describing the contours of the Japanese social landscape has been furnished, we can better appreciate its landmarks, boundaries, and the preferred routes Japanese will follow to traverse their sociopolitical landscape. Six points demand attention and elaboration in order to appreciate how Japanese society conceives of and organizes publicness:

1 the social functions of *tatemae*;
2 vulnerability and shame;
3 empathy as facilitator of social relations;
4 the role of hierarchy;
5 two versions of self; and
6 group boundary maintenance.

The social functions of tatemae

If a politically and economically complex society lacks a culturally sanctioned sphere where an individual's opinions, interests, or self may be readily expressed before a collectivity that safeguards such expressions, then certain social practices will be needed to facilitate exchanges. In Japan, *tatemae* is employed to construct a type of publicness and thereby serves a similar function to that of public institutions in Western societies; i.e. *tatemae* serves as a collectively agreed-upon neutral or buffer area where the individual is, in a certain sense at least, protected from others.

Vulnerability and shame

If there is a sharp division between inner/backstage (*uchi-ura*) and outer/forestage (*soto-omote*) settings but no mediating social buffer zone (public), we should expect individuals to feel exposed when confronted with unpredictable social situations. It is not surprising, then, that many Japanese refer to their "shyness" (*hazukashī*) as a people. Shyness, in fact, is used to explain the many Japanese characteristics, such as their modesty or their reluctance to express opinions (my students' favorite excuse for not participating in class). *Hazukashī* is actually a term rich in implications, since it may also mean ashamed, disgraced, or embarrassed. An emphasis on being shy makes sense in a society where ethics are often equated with etiquette, since breaches in manners, besides eliciting embarrassment, may also cause shame. In such a context, shyness may be better understood as the fear of inadvertently disgracing oneself by not playing one's role in a society where conformity to culturally sanctioned norms is highly valued. The cultural desirable of shyness/shame/embarrassment is part and parcel of other values such as "face" and "reputation."

Empathy as social facilitator

If staged formalities (*tatemae*), rituals, and etiquette are employed to maintain the face of others and preclude social *faux pas*, it becomes difficult to know another's true intentions (*honne*). Consequently, social actors are burdened with discerning each other's thoughts. Because individuals are reluctant to express their thoughts directly, unwrapping the etiquette-packaged messages forces individuals to concentrate on sympathizing with others; i.e. anticipating what others are thinking. Consequently, an individual will be forced to consider carefully what others are thinking and feeling. This is why "empathy" (*omoiyari*) becomes important in a society that lacks an open arena where people may present selves in a relatively unguarded manner (public). *Omoiyari* has two interrelated meanings: (1) to sympathize with another; (2) but in order to sympathize effectively, one must be concerned about what others are feeling and experiencing to the point of anticipating their wishes (Lebra 1976: 38–49). In order to express empathy, one should be constantly searching for any clues about what others are thinking. One should also guard against unintentionally slighting or causing another to lose face. Thus, the role of etiquette is to prevent careless offenses. There is the sense that "the impression of reality fostered by a performer is a delicate, fragile thing that can be shattered by very minor mishaps" (Goffman 1959: 56).

The role of hierarchy

Occupying one's proper social station is also part of the strategy used to prevent social contretemps. Thus, Japanese have a tendency to signal clearly their social status (via proper attire, sociolinguistic behavior, and other forms of etiquette). Manners preclude upstaging those with more status.

Two versions of self

If an individual moves between two predefined social spheres – one under the watchful scrutiny of others, where staged formalities are called for (*soto-omote*), one that is charged with intimacy (*uchi-ura*) – then it is not surprising if two distinct styles of self-presentation result. One is performed in front of others according to the conventions of the out-groups, while the other is relatively spontaneous and is expressed to intimates of the in-group.

Japanese stand between the strong ties of the intimate group and the more formalized demands of other groups, both contouring the self. "The formalization of ritual often appears to involve a distancing within actors of their private and social identities" (Bell 1992: 216).[24] This distancing has been described by Bachnik ("personal emotions/social constraint") (1992); Lebra ("empathetic self" and "presentational self") (1992: 106–11); Rosenberger ("discipline and distance/spontaneity and intimacy") (1989); and McVeigh (spontaneous, private self expressed to intimates, and an observed self, performed in front of others according to predefined conventions), who links this oscillation of self to the ubiquity of ritual in Japan (1994b, 1997a). Without a protective zone (public) that is both free from the formalized demands of the *seken* (observing others) and the strong ties of the intimate group, self-presentation oscillates between two poles.

A self socialized to balance itself carefully between personal wants and collective demands, not surprisingly, resorts to "ritualism" or "ritualistic conformity," which "entails the preservation internally of nonconformist values and beliefs while outwardly conforming to established behavior patterns" (Koschmann 1978: 20). This socio-psychological phenomenon is not unique to the Japanese, though the heavily bureaucratized landscape of their society makes it salient. Investigations of the self in Japan (such as those just cited) are useful and certainly view the self as existing in a web of sociopolitical relations. However, we would do well to remind ourselves that the webs within which selves are found are spun by larger forces (i.e. state and economic interests; examined in Chapters 4 and 5) that shape and subsume more immediate and local contexts and idioms.

Group boundary maintenance

If the individual feels pulled between an array of groups – some demanding formalized performances, others requiring more personal expressions – then society is perceived as an aggregate of well-sealed boxes. Leaving one box and entering another requires care, since the space between them is perceived as asocial and anomic, and is not an area in which one would usually want to become stranded. Consequently, particular groups with specific interests are privileged over an all-encompassing collectivity composed of individuals with common interests (public in the Euro-American sense).

The focus on the group, in fact, is the most noted characteristic of

Japanese society. The Japanese social world can be understood through the many terms used to talk about cliques or factions (*batsu*). There are factions formed through kinship, marriage, and extended families (*keibatsu*). There are also political factions, academic cliques, factions of military officers, and regional or hometown factions. By establishing a set of rules, rather explicit at times, that all members are expected to follow, the group itself takes on an identity and acts as a source of authorization for the individual. Learning the ways of the group is more than just a matter of acquiring practical information, since the acceptance of a certain way of doing things, often different from the way the same thing is done in another group, symbolizes one's affiliation to the group and acceptance of its authority.[25]

Maintaining group boundaries forces one's attention on consensus, and a value that hopefully and closely follows, cooperation (*kyōryoku*). Cooperation and consensus are important for maintaining fronts and allowing the group to execute its tasks effectively and obtain its goals. Ideally, members of the same group work together and form a "team," a "set of individuals who co-operate in staging a single routine" (Goffman 1959: 79). Each group is under pressure to put on "team performances" during which individuals must behave according to the group's norms, since "it would seem that while a team-performance is in progress, any member of the team has the power to give the show away or to disrupt it by inappropriate conduct" (*ibid.*: 82): "consensus may often be a public façade, but then façade counts for a great deal in Japanese life" (Buruma 1984: 221).

THE JAPANESE LEGAL TRADITION AND PUBLICNESS

How does Japan's legal tradition relate to its conception of civil society? It is worth quoting Haley's description of the Chinese legal tradition, in which Japanese law is rooted:

> There was no developed concept separating "public" and "private" spheres of activity to contain state authority. Instead, private activity was in effect those areas that the state chose to exclude from its regulatory reach rather than a realm to which its authority could not extend. Traditional Chinese thought did recognize a dichotomy between "public" and "private," but these terms, imperfectly defined, were used more to differentiate more valued, "higher" official concerns, as represented by imperial

authority from intrinsically base, selfish, personal interests and behavior.

(1991: 27)

Unlike Western legal traditions, there was no concept of private law or rights. Laws were either administrative or penal (*ibid.*: 11). "Neo-Confucianism imperatives of loyalty and filial piety precluded any conception of a litigant's assertion of a claim as a legal right to be enforced by a neutral arbiter" (*ibid.*: 83). Modern Japan has inherited this tradition, and law, rather than being primarily a code to judge the individual impartially, often appears to be disciplinary and didactic in spirit. Because law is not considered to exist in a sphere separate from the state (i.e. the judiciary and administrative branches are not clearly distinguished in practice), those who are prosecuted are almost always convicted.[26] Once the state machinery aims its sights on a perceived wrongdoer, a guilty verdict appears to protect and enhance the legitimacy of the state. The lack of a neutral arena, in which even the state itself may be judged, precludes the American tradition of an activist judiciary. In fact, "the Japanese government has attempted to prevent the development of litigation into an effective and ongoing vehicle for social change" (Upham 1987: 18). Moreover, in Japan legal regulations seem to discourage active political participation among citizens. Though practices such as voting, campaigning, and local and neighborhood political activities play an important role in Japan, the Public Office Election Law, with its highly detailed restrictions on the length and practices of campaigning (e.g. door-to-door canvassing is illegal), seems to "prevent candidates from making an appeal to the voters on the basis of a political platform." Thus, "A candidate's legal campaign activities are effectively limited to riding around the district in a sound truck, repeating his or her name over and over and asking the people for their votes." Also, given the restrictions (which are routinely violated), "the voters are relegated to the passive role of judges in a beauty contest – direct participation in campaigns is practically impossible" (Abe *et al.* 1994: 146–8).

One interpretation of Japan's particular approach toward politicking is that it prevents the formation of a public space in which politics can be carefully and objectively debated. Though voting rates are high in Japan (higher than in the United States), voting itself requires very little initiative, and in Japan all citizens are registered automatically when they turn 20; "for most Japanese voting is the *only* way in which they participate politically" (*ibid.*: 155, italics in original).[27] Around election time, political hopefuls can be seen standing on trucks in front of train stations (sometimes surrounded by pretty women), desperately pleading with passers-by. This sort of politicking seems to be an attempt to appeal directly to peoples' hearts, rather than an account of one's policies via a public arena:

> A typical campaign consists of politicians repeatedly shouting their name, party affiliation, and other slogans through loudspeakers. . . . Cruising neighborhoods or busy intersections in mobile vans, sometimes with as many as four attached speakers, their sheer decibel level forces the public to listen. They are so loud that they often can be heard for miles.
>
> ("Noise a deafening problem in Japan," AEN 2 May 1996: 5)

There is rarely a discussion of policies, though lately TV political debates have become more common. There has also been a recent increase in the number of *tarento* (celebrities) and sports stars being elected to the Diet's House of Councilors, and in 1995 two former comedians were elected as governors of Tokyo and Osaka.

THE MEDIA AND JAPAN'S VERSION OF PUBLICNESS

What are the implications of Japan's type of publicness for the media?[28] The Japanese media are generally characterized as being good at enumerating facts but are criticized for not tying them together and often lack critical analysis. Indeed, there is a bureaucratic feel to much of the news, which often becomes an exercise in announcing listings, classifications, and details, which are left unconnected. The function of the media in Japan often appears to be one of sheer neutrality. There is reporting of different angles with an unquestioning attitude, to be sure, but it is a neutrality shorn of investigative and inquisitive journalism. There seems to a strong concern for reporting news that satisfies everyone and for avoiding stands that might offend anyone (Abe *et al.* 1994: 195).[29] According to Satō, Japanese journalism has lost its mission, which ideally should be to act as a watchdog and criticize the authorities when necessary. Instead, the mass media do not criticize but simply report facts (1994). There are, however, important exceptions to this studied distance from events, as when the fallout from a political scandal becomes so odious that its implications cannot be ignored (or, as suggested by the conspiratorially minded, when certain elites feed information to the press in order to discredit enemies), or when non-Japanese reporters pick up on a story and Japanese reporters follow suit.[30]

The nature of Japanese media cannot be understood unless the role of the 400 or so *kisha* (press clubs) is taken into account. These reporters' organizations, which are often criticized for practising self-censorship, are connected to ministries, political parties, police, industrial associations, and "everything and everybody, in short, that help make Japan go round" (Van Wolferen 1989: 94). *Kisha*, which had their origins in the prewar period, when censorship was official, are exclusive and many are closed to non-Japanese reporters and have developed an "institutionalized symbiosis" between journalists and elite power brokers (*ibid.*: 94). Many argue that *kisha* have been co-opted into political structures and placed in a hierarchy with reporters subordinate to officials, their bureaucratized in-group/out-group mentality resonating with the lack of a clearly demarcated neutral arena (i.e. a social space detached from official structures in which information is objectively reported). Others refer to *kisha* as "news cartels."[31] Indeed, the homogenized nature of Japanese reportage has led many to conclude that it fulfills the same function as the controlled media in socialist countries.[32] Real information is gathered by journalists on their *yomawari* (literally, night rounds; i.e. visiting officials) and is often reported in "weekly magazines" (*shūkanshi*) rather than the major dailies. In the media – like so many other things in Japanese life – there seems to be a distinction between official (*tatemae*) news and the more frank (*honne*) (or gossipy) facts reported by weekly magazines.

Though the argument may be made that the Japanese media have been politically defanged, it does not necessarily follow that elites do not use them for their own purposes. Though the NHK (*Nihon Hōsō Kyōkai*; Japan's publicly supported but not government-run broadcasting company) appears non-partisan and unbiased, it does support state policies in subtle ways. Krauss argues that it does this by presenting information in such a way that the public receives the following impressions:

1 *salient state*: the state is omnipresent, so that society and economy are "rarely portrayed as having a 'life of their own' ";

2 *administrative state*: "input" actors (e.g. politics, parties, interest groups, protest movements) are given far less coverage than the "output" of the bureaucracy or bureaucratically appointed councils;

3 *state as ritualized rule maker*: the bureaucracy is depicted as making rules for society, not implementing them;

4 *impersonal state*: individual bureaucrats are not presented. Rather,

bureaucrats are shown together in groups at meetings, maintaining individual anonymity;

5   *state as paternal, active guardian*: the bureaucracy is portrayed as the active guardian of people, so that it is the ministries, and not the media, that appear as the public's watchdog.[33] Ritualized activities, such as "press conferences," are used symbolically to reassure the public; and

6   *the image of state as conflict manager*: the state is neutral, standing above selfish politicians.

(1996: 118–19)

This last point is particularly pertinent here, because it points to an equation about political legitimacy that reads: state equals rationality equals the common good. Such a formula does not factor in the need for diversity and debate (i.e. a strong civil society): "Bureaucracy is anti-political because it cannot recognize the legitimacy of conflict, seeing it as a temporary aberration to be dealt with through elaborated administrative techniques" (Ferguson 1984: 20).[34]

News that would cause an uproar in other industrialized societies often results in only a faint murmur in Japan.[35] For example, the Japanese public seemed surprisingly indifferent to North Korea's test-firing of a missile into the Sea of Japan in the summer of 1992, and considering the international repercussions, the media downplayed the event. At other times, what the Japanese media decides to cover is simply bizarre. For several days in the spring of 1994, the nightly news and newspapers were dominated by coverage of an unfortunate duck that had been wounded by an arrow. Newscasters, with serious faces, interviewed those who discovered and aided the duck, explained diagrams showing how the duck had been rescued, and kept the nation abreast of the latest developments.

The entertainment side of the media also plays a role in depoliticization. Kogawa refers to Japan as a "manipulated society" and discusses the politically managed nature of Japanese popular culture. Though the mass media and a large-scale information industry seem to disseminate a "friendly" face, they are actually manipulating subjectivities by creating an atmosphere of political apathy (1989: 54–66).[36] Abe *et al.* note that

dramas and documentaries that aim at social critique are not welcomed, and mindless dramas and movies filled with sex and violence form the mainstream of programming. One cannot say that this sort of TV entertainment has any particular political influence *per se*, but, insofar as it does not provoke criticism of the social or political status quo, it serves to reinforce this status quo.

(1994: 193)

STANDARDIZING VALUES

An investigation of any society usually reveals a set of key concepts distributed among different social settings and spheres, affording a degree of cultural coherency. But if a high degree of such cultural coherency is found in a large-scale society, then the researcher should be on the lookout for the political implications and managing centers of such congruence. This has been a theme in my own research, and I have been struck by how a remarkably similar normative idiom – advocating a bureaucratized social landscape of hierarchy, social categorization (i.e. groupism), and standardization (i.e. consensus) – appears in diverse settings (McVeigh 1994a). This idiom is shared by the moral beliefs of a new religion (McVeigh 1991a, 1991b, 1992), the values female junior college students are taught while training to be "office ladies" (McVeigh 1995b, 1996a, 1997a), and government publications on how to conduct moral education in schools (McVeigh 1995a). This idiom is also implicated in the ritualized ethos of daily life (McVeigh 1994b). Regardless of their diversity – in terms of group goals, social setting, and other variables – there is basic agreement between these three social settings concerning a theory of how human relations should be. Thus, whether searching for spirituality, training for employment, or developing personal character, we find expressions of local versions of a more diffused and general view of human nature in Japan. In the most simple terms, the basics of this ethnomorality dictate that people should be emotionally dependent on others in hierarchical and group-centered relationships, and they should symbolize their devotion to the hierarchy and group through expressions of etiquette and *aisatsu* (sociolinguistic behavior). The average Japanese finds this common moral idiom quite understandable, acceptable, and even desirable.

What does the existence of a common idiom of values suggest? I believe it indicates that a high degree of bureaucratization exists in various Japanese social settings. The values so frequently cited in the literature are products of hierarchizing, classifying, formalizing, and co-opting practices (not a historical hangover from the feudal past). A familiar repertoire of values is used to stratify individuals, clearly mark in-group/out-group boundaries, and standardize behavior. There are many sites (companies, schools, families) that propagate these values,

though I would suggest that they dance to the same tune set by the
Japanese state and its drive toward economic rationalization and sociopolitical management. Thus, regardless of the particular social setting,
similar values are strategically deployed for different ends. There is wide
agreement on language and meaning, but differing opinions on what
should be said and why.

CONCLUSION

In coming to terms with Japanese society, Euro-Americans should
avoid assuming that its sociopolitical fabric is understandable if viewed
through the same conceptual prism they use to understand their own.
Regardless of any superficial similarities, the foundations of Japan's
civil society are different. In the Euro-American tradition, civil society,
while in many ways a public endeavor, is nevertheless privately and
spontaneously inspired. In Japan, however, civil society is in many
respects state-centered and induced.

If we speak in the most general terms, "society" in Euro-American
conceptions is conceived as an all-encompassing community composed
of individuals who move about in a buffer or "public" area that fills the
gaps between islands of private domain. This public space nurtures a
civil society, or publicness, that is distinct from the state (Figure 3.3).
Japanese society, however, may be conceived as being composed of
numerous small "societies," each with its own subculture and particular
rules. It sometimes seems as if the bureaucracies encourage pockets
(*uchi*) of privacy because they are suspicious of collectivities coalescing
that might come between the state and the individual citizen, a sort of
"divide and rule" strategy. Though interest groups exist in Japan in
great numbers, "there is no theory of pluralism that legitimates their
political activities" (Johnson 1982: 49). Consequently, "civility" – rather
than being a code that maintains personal inviolability while not in the
private domain – is primarily a matter of managing the movement
between these many societies. The focus is on maintaining clear boundaries between in-groups (*uchi*) and out-groups (*soto*), and fostering
impressions and practices (*tatemae*) that expedite inter-group traffic.
Areas between groups are ambiguous (Figure 3.4). Because this
"semiprivate/semipublic" area (the area between groups) is socially
ambiguous, groups must clearly carve out and continually reinforce
their perimeters in order to define (or as the case may be, defend) themselves. This is why passing between groups demands entrance and exit
rituals symbolized by elaborate sociolinguistic codes. Thus, rather than

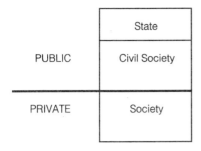

Figure 3.3 Euro-American societies: the relation between public and private

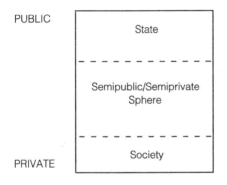

Figure 3.4 Japanese society: the relation between public and private

complex codes of behavior designed for a neutral, mediating space, navigating the Japanese social world requires boundary-clarifying practices. Thus, the necessity for proper introductions, without which, "businessmen, government officials, libraries, and schools are often inaccessible" (Haley 1991: 181–2).

The liminal nature of the semiprivate/semipublic sphere invites incursion and appropriation of this space by politico-economic elites for their own interests. In its attempts to realize its ends, the state sometimes sees its role as merging, not separating, the private and public spheres.

In the next chapter, I provide concrete examples of how politico-economic centers – through ritualizing practices and rationalizing policies – exploit the ill-defined nature of the interstices between society (private) and state (public).

4   Japan's government
The bureaucratic blurring of state and society

In this chapter I provide concrete examples of how state and society are linked in Japan. After outlining the basic structures of state and their rationalizing functions, I examine the bureaucratic ethos that permeates Japan's political system. Then, I discuss how "para-state organizations" occupy an ambiguous area between private and public and related issues. I also examine the role of "advisory councils" and how the state penetrates society through "administrative guidance." Finally, I examine how the bureaucratic center attempts to reign in local government through rationalizing policies.

JAPAN'S GOVERNMENTAL BUREAUCRACIES: RATIONALIZING STATE AND SOCIETY

In this section, I introduce some key conceptual markers in order to provide the bearings necessary for navigating Japan's political landscape. These markers were put in place by historical circumstance and sociopolitical expediency, and for my present purposes, the Meiji Restoration of 1868 will be my historical starting point. This was when a self-selected group of Japanese patriots, witnessing the political domination and commercial exploitation of other Asian nations, embarked on an ambitious enterprise of nation building to protect their homeland from foreign incursion. According to Samuels, even today it is *fuan* ("insecurity") that guides (1994: ix). This anxiety has been generated by a general perception that Japan is a poor country surrounded by nations with suspicious intentions, and in order to survive it has to develop, improve, and promote its industries.[1] General insecurity is one of the prime ingredients of what has become known as the "capitalist developmental state."[2] "Enrich the nation, strengthen its arms" (*fukoku kyōhei*) and "develop industries, nurture enterprises" (*shokusan kōgyō*), and "catching up and surpassing the West" (*oitsuki oikose*) became the rallying cries of a nation in the making. Though such slogans may now sound out of date, their spirit at least has been institutionalized in state structures that in no small measure shape everyday practices. Japan's crash course in nation building was realized by bringing non-Japanese mentors to Japan and sending study missions abroad to learn from other countries on how to "catch up with the West."[3]

Given the pre-Meiji Confucian legacy of bureaucracy and hierarchy, it is not surprising that Japan's elites sought to realize the policy ends of "revolution from above" through bureaucratic means.[4] It is significant that the first governmental institutions set up by the new Meiji government were the ministries, preceding a constitution, parliament, and political parties. These ministries, established to guide Japan along the path of modernization, were designed to be free from political influence and pressures and firmly under the control of the ruling elite, or the "elder statesmen" (*genrō*).[5] Over the years, recession, depression, and war enhanced the bureaucrats' power.

Though Japan's defeat in World War II saw the dismantling of the more abusive aspects of its bureaucracy, many argue that there are important continuities between the imperial officials (*tennō no kanri*) and the national officials (*kokka kōmuin*). Johnson contends that, at least for the greater part of the postwar period, the ministries have had fewer rivals for power than did the prewar bureaucracy (1975: 13). In fact, "The bureaucracy did not really come into its own until defeat and occupation destroyed the military" (*ibid.*: 14). Indeed, the Allied occupation seems to have enhanced bureaucratic power by not purging many of the prewar bureaucrats. Tsuji notes three other important reasons: (1) the Allies administered the Occupation through indirect government; (2) the belief that the bureaucracy was politically neutral; and (3) the lack of experienced politicians in postwar political parties (who could check bureaucratic power) (1964: 109–25).

Though there is a lively debate in the literature about how powerful the ministries (specifically those concerned with economic matters) actually are at present, few would disagree with the observation that "Japanese policymakers sought to maintain the aroused state of wartime national emergency in peacetime. They sought not only a peacetime equivalent to war, but to reverse the outcome of the war by peaceful means" (Williams 1994: 118–19).[6] Whether one accepts this assessment or not, the "key aspects of postwar Japanese society took place during the 1930s ... when there was a strong emphasis on rational, comprehensive planning at the national level" (Allinson 1975: 88). The fifty-five-fold increase in the Japanese economy between 1946 and 1976 (Johnson 1982: 6) and its "plan-oriented market economy" must be understood from the Japanese leaders' perspective: "economics as defense."[7] Japanese economic policies were designed under the banner of nationalism (*cf.* Marshall 1967), and for much of the Japanese politico-economic elites, the world market has been viewed primarily as something to be conquered and controlled, with profits being a secondary concern.

Being a late industrializer and following a developmental path, it is not surprising that Japan has been characterized as a "goal-oriented society" or "goal-achieving culture," and "this fundamental orientation (determine the goal, then set about achieving it) influences all aspects of Japanese social practice" (Williams 1994: 11, parentheses in original). What is significant for my present argument is that the ministries have set the pace, tone, and standards not just for the more obvious aspects of modernization, but also for the rationalized, bureaucratized, and ritualized resonance of daily life in present-day Japan. I also contend that Japan's bureaucracies have taken advantage of and sustained sociopolitical arrangements that do not always distinguish clearly between public (state) and private (society) interests. Thus, much of Japan's bureaucratic power rests on its ability to segment, fragment, and categorize society (gender, interests, regional, national, etc.) as it sees fit, thereby weakening state–society distinctions.[8]

The national government of Japan is divided into legislative (National Diet: composed of the House of Representatives and the House of Councilors), judicial, and executive branches. As I discuss below, in theory the legislative branch formulates policy, though it is the executive branch (i.e. bureaucracies) that more often than the latter writes the laws. The administrative branch is headed by the cabinet, comprised of the prime minister and ministers of state. Directly under the cabinet are the Cabinet Secretariat, Cabinet Legislative Bureau, and the National Defense Council. Also under the cabinet are the National Personnel Authority and the Prime Minister's Office. The latter are composed of agencies (*chō*), which though they have lower status than ministries (*shō*), are represented by their respective heads on the cabinet.[9]

The Management and Coordination Agency (*Sōmuchō*) (which is larger than the Ministry of Foreign Affairs) and the National Personnel Authority (*Jinjiin*) deserve mention as the agencies that oversee ministerial operations. The latter, established by the National Public Service Law, is an autonomous body modeled after the US Civil Service Commission. These two agencies administer civil service examinations at the national level; manage personnel; plan and develop the administrative system and procedures; oversee the government's organizational structure; coordinate certain programs falling under the jurisdiction of more than one ministry or agency; administer the national public pension programs; and conduct government statistical studies.[10]

It is important to note that these agencies of the Prime Minister's Office are staffed by personnel from the ministries (listed below), where the government's policy-making center of gravity is located. Officials from the ministries are posted in the agencies for short periods, where they act as "spies" for their home ministries (as a ministry official nonchalantly explained it to me), thereby protecting their own interests. But what is significant for our present purposes is that the staffing of the Prime Minister's Office by the ministries results in a transfer of bureaucratic mind-set, habits, and policy responses to other sections of the government, ensuring that administration via bureaux impairs government by legislation. It is notable that many politicians are former bureaucrats, and between 1947 and 1972 all but one prime minister were ex-bureaucrats (Kim 1988: 4).

The ministries

For all its strengths and accomplishments, the Japanese bureaucracy is relatively small and inexpensive compared with those of other nations.[11] For all their power and prestige, the buildings of the ministries themselves are surprisingly unimpressive. The old buildings suggest a no-nonsense, bare-bones operation, and their gray or dark brick exteriors house halls cluttered with boxes and small offices whose desks are overloaded with documents. Though guards are posted at the entrances, security appears rather lax. In some ministries, office etiquette is unexpectedly informal even among high-level officials, with colleagues knocking on doors and poking heads in before being granted permission to enter.

Many Japanese perceive bureaucrats as dedicated civil servants who, unlike elected politicians, are unsullied by dirty power plays and corruption.[12] Unlike Diet members, who devote themselves to local, narrowly defined issues, bureaucrats have the nation's interest in mind. On the other hand, many Japanese criticize bureaucrats for usurping legislative power and, like people everywhere, complain of official inflexibility, red tape, and administrative arrogance, and like bureaucrats everywhere, it sometimes appears as if they are not concerned with "rational efficiency, but individual and organizational survival" (Britan 1981: 11).[13] Nevertheless, there is a deep respect for bureaucrats, who are usually regarded as the *crème de la crème* and credited with supervising Japan's meteoritic rise to prosperity. Many dealings with bureaucrats, it should be noted, are mediated through *chinjō* (petition, appeals) and *chinjōdan* (petition groups), encouraging an attitude of dependency on officials and diminishing open political processes. The major criticism leveled at bureaucrats is that because they cannot be voted out of office, they cannot be held accountable for their actions.

For Weber, rationalized political organizations are governmental bureaucracies, and all the characteristics of modern bureaucracy as described by Weber are readily found in Japan's ministries: (1) a division of labor based on functional specialization; (2) a well-defined hierarchy of authority; (3) a system of rules covering the rights and duties of employment; (4) as system of procedures for dealing with work situations; (5) an impersonality in interpersonal relations; and (6) an apparatus of promotion and selection based on technical performance (*cf.* Kim 1988: 15). As in most Western democracies, Japan's civil service is based on three principles: (1) personnel are selected on merit, largely determined through civil service examinations; (2) employment in the public service is secured even if the national administration changes; and (3) "civil servants are expected to be responsive to the current elected leaders, regardless of which political party holds power" (*ibid.*: 1). As I discuss below, this last characteristic is debatable in the case of Japan.[14]

Koh lists nine important characteristics of Japan's bureaucrats. The first is the degree to which Japan's top bureaucrats may be described as an elite. Japan's civil service examinations are the most rigorous among the industrialized democracies, and those that survive the competition tend to be among the best that Japan's educational system has to offer (1989: 252).[15] The second characteristic is that only those who have passed the higher civil service examination have a fair chance of being promoted to section chief and beyond, becoming "career" officials. In other words, one's future success depends to a large extent on mode of entry into a ministry. The third characteristic is the stress placed on seniority. Though merit is not ignored, age ranking is strict and shapes relations with one's colleagues. The fourth characteristic is the large number of law graduates in the ministries. A law graduate is considered a "generalist," and the fifth characteristic is the predominance of generalists over technical specialists in the bureaucracy.[16] The sixth characteristic is the sectionalism and turf battles between ministries (the *shōeki* [interests of one's ministry] versus *kokueki* [interests of the nation] problem). These result in "waste of resources, duplication of effort, occasional paralysis of government action, and erosion of bureaucratic power" (*ibid.*: 256). The seventh characteristic is the importance of consensual decision making in the ministries, especially through *ringisei* (in which a formal document is composed and then circulated from the bottom of the organization to the top) and *nemawashi* (pre-meeting negotiations). The eighth characteristic is the privileged position of power that Japan's ministries enjoy compared with other bureaucracies outside Japan. The last characteristic is the retirement patterns of Japan's administrative elite. Although they are guaranteed lifetime employment, almost all retire early (mid-fifties, and some even earlier). Those who retire find employment in business, "para-state organizations" (see *amakudari* below), politics, or academia, where many still wield considerable influence (*ibid.*: 252–8).

There are twelve main ministries (Table 4.1), each consisting of a

Table 4.1 Japan's ministries (in conventional order)

Ministry	External agencies
Ministry of Justice (*Hōmushō*)	Public Security Investigation Agency
Ministry of Foreign Affairs (*Gaimushō*)	
Ministry of Finance (*Ōkurashō*)	National Tax Administration Agency
Ministry of Education, Science, Sports and Culture (*Monbushō*)	Cultural Affairs Agency
Ministry of Health and Welfare (*Kōseishō*)	
Ministry of Agriculture, Forestry and Fisheries (*Nōrinsuisanshō*)	Food Agency Forestry Agency Fisheries Agency
Ministry of International Trade and Industry (*Tsūshōsangyōshō*)	Patent Office Natural Resources and Energy Small and Medium-Scale Enterprise Agencies
Ministry of Transport (*Unyūshō*)	Maritime Safety Agency Marine Accidents Inquiry Agency Meteorological Agency
Ministry of Posts and Telecommunications (*Yūseishō*)	
Ministry of Labor (*Rōdōshō*)	
Ministry of Construction (*Kensetsushō*)	
Ministry of Home Affairs (*Jichishō*)	Fire Defense Agency

central organization (*honshō*), with some ministries having external agencies (*gaikyoku*) or other organs under their jurisdiction. All ministries have advisory councils (*shingikai*, discussed below), which research and deliberate on specific matters under a ministry's purview. Principal subdivisions within a ministry include a secretariat (*kanbō*) and several bureaux (*kyoku*). The latter are divided into *ka* (divisions) or *bu* (departments), and these are further divided into *kakari* (offices).

Each ministry is headed by a cabinet minister and a parliamentary vice-minister. They serve for a short time (hence the term "Minister What's-his-name") and are not chosen for their expertise. Rather, the top ministerial posts are "handed to up-and-coming politicians to make them look more important. Appointees tend to be mere ornamental figureheads, without much say. This explains why they are known derisively as the 'appendix' of the ministry" (Miyamoto 1994: 44). But even if they are competent or harbor plans for changing the way a ministry operates, they inevitably confront a bureaucracy that often regards their ostensible head as an intrusive guest or perhaps even a threatening outsider. The result is that, in general, ministers have minimal policy impact upon the bureaucratic structure that they supposedly head. For all intents and purposes, then, the administrative vice-ministers occupy the highest posts and wield the real power in any ministry. This is why politically appointed ministers must work with and through the administrative vice-ministers (*jimujikan*), who control the minister's access to lower-level bureaucrats and information. "The 'political master' [politically appointed minister] finds himself in the position of the 'dilettante' who stands opposite the 'expert,' facing the trained official [administrative vice-minister] who stands within the management of administration" (Weber in Gerth and Mills 1958: 232). This leads to what is called *gekokujō* (juniors making policy for seniors). Besides the ministers themselves, a prime minister must also face an entrenched bureaucracy, whose interests often differ from the head of state. Though there are exceptions – Yoshida, Satō, and Kishi, and more recently Tanaka and Nakasone have left their marks – most prime ministers have had little impact on bureaucratic policy making.

Ministries are well known for their territorial consciousness (*nawabari ishiki*) and inter-ministerial turf battles are a constant variable in Japan's polity. Thus, to diminish a ministry's jurisdiction in any way is the "cardinal taboo governing the lives of all active-duty officials" (Johnson 1975: 7). Because everything is connected to everything else in a post-industrial society, the chance of trespassing on other ministries' jurisdiction is on the rise. While other governments have strengthened central controls to deal with complexities arising from socio-economic interdependence, Japan has been slow to respond to these problems, resulting in intensified conflict and increasingly fragmented authority (Campbell 1984). However, there is the argument that sectionalism restrains bureaucratic power:

> If "the government" of Japan were actually a highly coordinated set of agencies, its powers could be applied with overwhelming force. Instead, partly as a result of sheer ambition for status and partly as a result of divergent interests within the society itself, there is intense rivalry and jealousy among the ruling agencies and their personnel. In competing for power, they tend to neutralize one another's authority to some extent. It is this offsetting effect, rather than the absence of specific powers of internal control, and also "rule by personalities" as opposed to "rule by law," which provides the degree of freedom in Japan's peculiar species of enterprise economy.
>
> (Hollerman 1967: 160–1)

The strength of bureaucratic power, however, should not be exaggerated. It is also important to note that during the 1970s, the ministries have lost power *vis-à-vis* the Diet, opposition parties, local governments, consumer movements, and the courts, so that there was a general fragmentation, decentralization, and debureaucratization of government power (Pempel 1987a: 285–6).[17] Nevertheless, we should be wary of "the tendency to equate diminution of power with loss of power" (Prestowitz 1988: 238).

Bureaucratic culture

The most sought after jobs in Japan are in its ministries. Though the pay is not overly generous and selfless dedication to the ministry is expected, the high status and coveted prestige more than compensate for any monetary rewards available in the private sector. Because the Ministry of Finance controls the government's purse strings and thus possesses budgetary authority over the other ministries, positions here are the most sought after. Other prestigious ministries are International Trade and Industry, Construction, and Foreign Affairs.

In theory, ministry positions are opened to anyone regardless of sex, educational credentials, and socio-economic background. In reality, most officials are male, from the best schools, and though there are many examples of those making it to the top through perseverance, over time the greater financial resources of the upper classes have increasingly facilitated their ability to place their own in the higher echelons of administrative service. A disproportionate number of bureaucrats are graduates of the nationally established and very prestigious University of Tokyo (thus the appellation *kanryō yōseijo*; "training school for bureaucrats"), especially its law department, which is known for designing curricula that prepare graduates for the civil service examinations. Other schools whose graduates are well-represented in the ministries are the University of Kyoto (also nationally established) and several private universities, such as Keio and Waseda. The University of Tokyo was originally established to train future government officials, and along with the other top schools, has traditionally been a source of dedicated civil servants.

There are two types of national civil service examination. The first (non-career) is for lower-level civil servants, and those who pass it cannot be promoted beyond division chief. The other examination (career), which fewer examinees sit for, is more difficult and comprehensive. Those who pass have a chance to be considered for promotion beyond division chief all the way to vice-minister. After the examination, candidates must sit through a series of interviews at the ministries, which choose new employees from the pool of successful examinees.[18]

Ministry officials are divided into "generalists" (*jimukan*) and "specialists" (*gikan*), with the former ranked higher than the latter. In many ministries, specialists are restricted to middle-ranked positions. Only the Ministry of Construction allows specialists to be promoted to the vice-ministership.[19] High officials are overwhelmingly male. However, a recent minister of education was a woman, and a few posts, such as the chief of the Women and Young Worker's Bureau in the Ministry of Labor, are usually reserved for women.[20]

Those who enter a ministry each year belong to the same *dōki* (literally, same period). Because university education provides little useful knowledge, members of a cohort serve an apprenticeship that is lengthy and comprehensive. Employees are rotated to different positions within the same ministry (*sotomawari*, going around the track), and some are sent overseas for further training. The purpose of rotating bureaucrats from section to section is not to acquire technical knowledge, but to meet others and to cement relationships, thus developing institutional *esprit de corps*. Some bureaucrats are loaned to other ministries or agencies, though this is considered merely temporary and their primary allegiance is always to their home ministry. Employees rise through the ranks at about the same rate during the first ten or twenty years, but then after that they are gradually sorted out and only a few make it to the top posts, for what is called the elite course (*erito kōsu*). Those not on the elite course settle down in one section, do not circulate as frequently, and become "walking dictionaries" or "human encyclopedias" (*iki-jibiki*) (Johnson 1982: 63).

The career hierarchies in the ministries are strict, and employees advance through the ranks in the same way that military officers do. This reflects the prime importance of age grading (*nenkō joretsu*), respect for seniority (*nenji sonchō*), and senior–junior (*senpai–kōhai*) relationships. As they move up the ranks, they not only acquire skills but also are socialized to be loyal and obedient to the organization. "Recruitment, socialization, and promotion practices encourage each official to internalize the ministry's official and unofficial values as his own." Such practices are specifically designed to foster "inside/outside," "we/they" (*uchi/soto*) distinction, enhancing organizational cohesion and normative integration (Campbell 1989: 120). Because the organizational pyramid becomes narrower at the apex, there are fewer positions at the top. Thus, at a certain point in their collective career, a cohort practises *dōkisei zennin yūtai* (all classmates voluntarily resign together), and only a limited number are promoted to ministry-level and bureau-level spots (*shitei-shoku*: designated positions).

The Management and Coordination Agency administers a performance evaluation that examines sixteen personal qualities. Some of these qualities are cheerfulness (*meirō*); impartiality (*kōsei*); decisiveness (*kadan*); positiveness (*sekkyokuteki*); logicality (*rironteki*); rationality (*risōteki*) (*sic*: *risōteki* is usually glossed as idealistic); obedience (*sunao*); gentleness (*onwa*); high-spiritedness (*kigai*); precision (*chimitsu*); and scrupulousness (*kichōmen*). These traits are marked with A, B, C, or D. This system has been criticized as imprecise and emphasizing personality characteristics, not work performance. Furthermore, employees are not shown the results (Kim 1988: 12–13). These qualities offer a view of what is valued in the ministries, norms required to function in a bureaucratized setting.

Though there is variation among the different ministries, in general

> it is highly irregular to leave work at quitting time, and that it is not uncommon to work until midnight or even spend the night at the office when the budget is being drawn up. If they work in the Budget Bureau of the Ministry of Finance, they should also expect to work Sundays and holidays from September through December. The conscientious public servant will easily put in 200 hours of overtime a month.
>
> (*ibid.*: 45)

Within ministries, relations between ministry-level officials and bureaux vary from ministry to ministry. In some ministries, the central staff may be very powerful, but in others, one or two bureaux may dominate the rest. In other ministries, several bureaux may be equally influential and pay little attention to the ministerial staff (Campbell 1976: 15–16).[21]

A theater of politics

Previously, I introduced several important concepts useful for appreciating Japanese sociopolitical processes. These include *omote* (outer, in plain view) versus *ura* (inner, hidden from sight); and *tatemae* (official line, stated policy) versus *honne* (real intentions, actual practice). These concepts legitimate a commonly reported phenomenon in Japan: the clear separation of content from form, ruling from reigning, and actual power from formal authority. The "invisible" political processes occur in the *ura*, where the more consequential decision making transpires. "This extra-constitutional process is not illegal, since it is legitimized by the *omote* process" (Johnson 1980: 92).[22] In prewar times, the emperor legitimated those who actually wielded power, and in the postwar period, the authority of the Diet and majority party sanction the mandarinate (Johnson 1982: 35).[23]

THE BUREAUCRATIC ETHOS

There are two main schools of thought about who actually wields power in Japan. One school argues for "bureaucratic dominance" (*kanryō yūi*) and the other for "party dominance" (*seitō yūi*). This has been a persistent debate, though many scholars have come to view the issue as somewhat sterile, since bureaucrats may be powerful in a particular area, but in another area the party politicians may be more influential. There are no easy answers to this problem, of course, and one must first take into account a certain period and particular issue before reaching any conclusions. Campbell notes that "ideological" issues (moral education, teaching, textbook contents, administrative control of public school practices, constitution, government's relationship to religion, position of emperor) have been, to a large degree, influenced by right-wing Liberal Democratic Party (LDP) members. However, bureaucrats take the initiative toward other issues that do not interest politicians as much (foreign aid, diplomacy, community education, programs for the handicapped, broadcasting regulation, labor standards) (1984: 129–30). Furthermore, policy making is a complex process that involves negotiation, compromise, and balancing interests between different political actors, and it is too simplistic to assign one side too much power. Abe *et al.* note that "what evolved is less a rivalry than a process in which the respective powers and policy competences of the bureaucrats and the politicians are intertwined in every sphere of policy, resulting in a mutual infiltration and manipulation of civil service and ruling party" (1994: 127). In any case, the Japanese media carefully watches for any shift in power, reporting on *kankō seitei* (ascendancy of bureaucracy over politicians) or *seikō kantei* (ascendancy of politicians over bureaucracy). But no matter how the balancing act between the ministries and party politicians is described, *compared* with Euro-American polities, the Japanese bureaucracy (though not supposedly as much as it once did in the 1960s and 1970s) possesses considerable power.

In any case, the debate about who has the real power, bureaucrats or politicians, misses an essential point, which is that, regardless of who is in control, all members of the Japanese governmental elite operate within a highly bureaucratized political climate. Perhaps more so than in Euro-American polities, governing in Japan is basically an administrative, rule-oriented science rather than a legislative, deliberative art. Upham notes that "The economic bureaucrats and their business counterparts come from similar educational backgrounds, advance at approximately similar speeds, and rotate in and out of jobs having direct contact with each other's institutions" (1987: 167). This is probably true for almost all Japan's elites, who are socialized to believe in the benefits of rationalization, such as hierarchy, in-group/out-group distinctions, formalized roles, and other key tenets, such as the centrality of national values and state goals.

Consider how the non-ministerial organs of government have been bureaucratized. There are important alliances and networks between Diet members and bureaucrats, cliques are generally organized around ministries, and traditionally, the Diet standing committees and various divisions of the LDP Policy Research Council more or less corresponded to the jurisdictions of the ministries. Here it is worth noting that the LDP's factions (and, one would imagine, those of the newer parties) have become bureaucratized, "evolving from collectivities of individual politicians centered upon prime minister hopefuls into highly structured and institutionalized organizations" (Abe *et al.* 1994: 124).

Those who argue that Japanese bureaucrats possess a commanding position *vis-à-vis* Diet members point out that the Japanese Diet, in spite of its ostensible legislative functions, does not legislate. This is left to the ministries, which after the war, inserted an important clause into the Cabinet Act that permits them to propose bills. A similar clause in the Diet Act permits ministry officials to join legislative deliberations on their own proposals. The ministries, then, "write the laws, then write the interpretive ordinances, administer the laws, and handle most complaints from them" (Prestowitz 1988: 243). Bills, in fact, often include authorization of power to particular ministries or agencies. Instead of the "rule of law" (*hōchi-shugi*), the Japanese bureaucracy relies on "administration through law" (*hōritsu ni yoru gyōsei*) (Isomura and Kuronuma 1974: 11).

It is often asserted that politicians, understaffed and lacking the necessary expertise to draft legislation, are forced to rely on ministries to defend their positions. "We might even go so far as to say that a Diet session is a kind of ceremonial performance, to give people inside and outside Japan the impression that decisions are being made democratically" (Ueda 1994: 129). The Diet, then, may be thought of as an arena of *omote*, or a staged setting, where politicians pretend to debate issues that have already been decided by unelected bureaucrats. This is why Diet proceedings are characterized as charades. Johnson notes that "all cabinet members and officials have *sōtei mondō shū* (hypothetical question-and-answer booklets) in front of them, prepared by the ministries, and except for an occasional *bakudan shitsumon* (bomb question), everything is prearranged." This is why bureaucrats are referred to as *kuroko*, the kabuki stagehands – dressed in black in order to be inconspicuous – who assist actors during a performance (1980: 110). Miyamoto describes parliamentarians as "veteran actors" who read from scripts prepared by bureaucrats (1994: 41). "Bureaucracy naturally welcomes a poorly informed and hence a powerless parliament – at least in so far as ignorance somehow agrees with bureaucracy's interests" (Weber in Gerth and Mills 1958: 234). The upshot of all this is a legislature that "is little more than a branch of the bureaucracy" (Miyamoto 1994: 111).[24] However, to maintain the façade that the parliamentarians are in charge, ministerial officials refer to Diet members as *sensei* (a respectful term for teacher, mentor) (Johnson 1980: 110).

What, then is the Diet's role? Johnson states that it has a "mediating role" between society and state (i.e. the ministries), big business, and certain politicians (1982: 50). Also, Diet members, in order to reward those who elected them to power, deliver their local constituencies favors, and for this reason they are often criticized for privileging narrow, pork-barrel benefits over broader, national interests.

Lacking a neutral public space where opinions may be freely aired without concern for faction forming, political activity gravitates toward either a type of theatricalized politics (*tatemae, omote*), or *kuromaku* government (black curtain; i.e. behind-the-scenes) (*honne, ura*). When politicians refuse to perform "consensual" politics and cannot reach agreement behind closed doors, the absence of a neutral arena to hammer out differences leads to the breakdown of any type of cooperation. The result is immobilism or, from time to time, *rantō kokkai* (free-for-all Diet), incidents that raise suspicions about Japan as a "consensus society." In the past, "free-for-all Diets," in which fists, inkwells, or chairs are thrown, would sometimes appear on TV news, and commentators seemed to take pleasure in reporting on these parliamentary convulsions, repeatedly showing clips of guards intervening as Diet members mauled each other. Though changing, scholarship outside Japan has tended to focus on the Diet and parties, thereby obscuring behind-the-scenes, extra-parliamentary power plays. Party politicians themselves "overstate their weight in national affairs because it ameliorates their corrupt and often comic image to do so, but it is precisely this image that encourages the mass media to pay excessive attention to their petty feuds and larger failings." At the same time, "Bureaucrats stress the function of politicians because policy is easier to design and enforce when the real locus of state power is obscured" (Williams 1994: 37).

Bureaucratizing society

Modern bureaucracies segment, separate, classify, and rank members of society along economic, gender, generational, and regional lines (see Chapter 5). Such administrative engineering ensures that certain socio-political and economic goals are met. "State objectives are transformed into objectives of the department, and department objectives into objectives of the state. The bureaucracy is a circle from which no one can escape" (Marx in Tucker 1978: 24). The bureaucratic secret to success is to make top-level goals appear to be the same as subordinate interests, and to make central objectives identical to peripheral concerns. This is why each ministry (and a ministry's various subdivisions) conducts PR campaigns in order to portray itself to the public and media in a favorable light. As Campbell notes, the attempt to elicit public support is necessary for programs that require government expenditure. Ministries publish a steady stream of white papers and other documents, which are available at government publication centers and bookstores (1976: 22).

As in many other places, bureaucratizing society in Japan involves issuing permits, licenses, and certificates associated with every aspect of daily life. It also involves "administrative guidance" (*gyōsei shidō*), a term (discussed below) that describes an endless array of bureaucratic practices aimed at society and indicating high levels of state control and surveillance.

> Take, for example, the houses we live in. The houses themselves fall under the jurisdiction of the Construction Ministry, which issues detailed regulations governing form and structure. Most of the furnishings and household articles are manufactured according to the guidelines of the Ministry of International Trade and Industry (MITI), as is our clothing. Food is regulated by the Ministry of Agriculture, Forestry, and Fisheries; medications by the Health and Welfare Ministry; and art objects by the Cultural Affairs Agency. The water supply, sewage, electricity and gas, and telephone are controlled by Health and Welfare, Construction, MITI, and Postal Service respectively. If we step out into the garden, the trees and flowers we see are approved by Agriculture, Forestry and Fisheries, whereas any rocks in the garden are the responsibility of Construction. . . . The car, again, is MITI's. Of our pets or domestic animals, dogs and cats are the charge of Health and Welfare; cows, horses, and carp are controlled by Agriculture, Forestry, and Fisheries; and monkeys, goldfish, and tropical fish by Education. As for birds, pigeons are the responsibility of Postal Services; sparrows are that of Agriculture, Forestry, and Fisheries; and parrots that of Education.
>
> (Ueda 1994: 134)

PARA-STATE ORGANIZATIONS

In the previous chapter I stated that, compared with Euro-American societies, Japan lacks a well-developed public domain distinct from the government. This is why the government may even take the initiative of starting grassroots organizations (Campbell 1976: 25).[25] In Japan, organizations in what is called the "non-profit sector" in the West are under government or corporate supervision. Because non-profit public interest bodies focus on national rather than a particular group's interest, they are regarded as extensions of the government. And though there are autonomous citizens' groups, many lack official (ministerial) approval because they disagree with the government. Indeed, being independent from the government often seems to imply antagonism toward it (Ueno 1993). Many Japanese feel that policy formulation is a job for bureaucrats, not ordinary citizens. "Politics in Japan, therefore, is driven by a state bureaucracy with virtually no participation or involvement by those ostensibly charged with governing or the governed" (Ueno 1994: 4).[26] Furthermore, the bureaucracy is "judicially unaccountable" (Upham 1987: 199):

> It is not just informal actions that escape judicial scrutiny. Supervisory orders, permissions, approvals, or regulations within an agency or even among agencies and public bodies like *shingikai* [advisory councils], no matter how formal or final, are not reviewable because they are considered internal government behavior that does not directly affect the legal rights or duties of private citizens. Furthermore, administrative acts with general effect, such as agency plans or regulations, are not judicially cognizable unless they immediately and concretely affect a specific person's legal rights or obligations.
>
> (*ibid.*: 171)

Rather than a "citizens' sector" composed of privately administered, non-profit public interest organizations that monitor, scrutinize, and criticize government policies, "para-state organizations" occupy much of the social space between the individual and the authorities. Indeed, according to scholars like Okimoto, Japan has an "intermediate zone," a network of formal and informal linkages between state and society that acts as a "dual administrative structure." This structure, comprised of government-run enterprises, business associations, and informal connections, facilitates smooth government–business relations (1989: 152–4).[27] Note Okimoto's opinion about the strength of the Japanese state:

> Recognizing that the government consists not simply of central ministries but also of the much bigger but less visible stratum of intermediate organizations again helps to cast clearer light on the seeming paradox of Japan as both a minimalist and an interventionist state.
>
> (*ibid.*: 154)

Special corporations

A good example of para-state organizations are the ninety-two (as of 1995) "special corporations" (*tokushu hōjin*; literally, special juridical persons). These are institutionalized examples of how officialdom has attempted to cut a path through the semiprivate/semipublic sphere, thereby linking state interests with social needs. They are variously described as semi-governmental, semi-official, or quasi-administrative organs, and are regarded as both commercial enterprises and administrative organs. Whatever they are called, special corporations qualify as para-state organizations due to their ministry-ordained function. The following is a concise definition of special corporations (or as they are sometimes called, public corporations): [28]

> Public corporations are established by the national government, by special laws as instruments for activities required by the state, when particular activities are better managed in the form of a profit-making enterprise, when efficiency in performance is more likely to be produced by such an enterprise than under direct operation by the government, or when more flexibility in financial or personnel management is required than is normally possible under the laws and regulations pertaining to government agencies.
>
> (Tsuji 1984: 36)[29]

Though such enterprises are certainly not unique to Japan, their role and number in Japanese society are salient.[30] These are directly or indirectly under the control of some ministry and include well-known enterprises. There are two types of special corporation: those established by law, and those established by committees appointed by the government. In either case official sanction authorizes their existence and practices, though some organizations are more government-controlled than others. Some, such as Fujioka (1994a), consider special corporations – along with "authorized juridical persons" (*ninka hōjin*) – as forming government-controlled "networks." Still others see what may be characterized as conspiratorial designs behind official recognition and utilization of these organizations. Some special corporations (especially the type called *kōdan;* see below) borrow from the Trust Fund Bureau (*Shikin unyō-bu*) of the Ministry of Finance.[31] Others are self-sufficient, relying on public user charges. As of 1 April 1994, they employed 570,000 workers ("Coalition to urge govt to restrict amakudari," DY 10 December 1994: 16). Besides the centrally regulated special corporations, there are about 3,000 local public corporations that are controlled by local governments.

Special corporations vary in function and size and cannot be easily characterized. However, they are usually categorized into the following types:

1   the thirteen *kōdan* are government corporations engaged in construction work (e.g. Japan Highway Public Corporation);

2   the nine *kōko* are public finance corporations whose capital is supplied by the government (e.g. Housing Loan Corporation);

3   the seventeen *jigyōdan* are enterprises that, smaller than *kōdan*, engage in everything except construction (National Space Development Agency);

4   the three *kinko* and *tokushu ginkō* are public finance corporations whose capital is supplied cooperatively;

5   there is only one *eidan*, the Teito Rapid Transit Authority;

6   the twelve *tokushu gaisha* are mixed public–private joint stock companies and include Japan Airlines and Kokusai Denshin Denwa (international phone company), and the privatized Japan Railways, Japan Tobacco, and Nippon Telegraph and Telephone, which were formerly in category 8;

7   under the category of "others" are the thirty-seven *kumiai* or *kyōkai* (mutual benefit associations); e.g. Nihon Hōsō Kyōkai (public broadcasting company)); *kenkyūjo* (research institutes); *shinkokai* (promotion societies); and *kikin* (foundations; e.g. Japan Foundation);

8   a former type of special corporations were *kōsha*, which were primarily publicly owned utilities. Examples include the former Kokutetsu (Japanese National Railways, now JR), Nihon Denshin Denwa Kabushiki Gaisha (now Nippon Telegraph and Telephone or NTT), and Nihon Tabako (now JT). Though privatized in the mid-1980s, these corporations are still primarily owned by the government and have become members of category 6.

Though there were a number of similar enterprises in the prewar period, most special corporations were established after the war. Special corporations proliferated during Japan's heady period of economic growth: in 1955 there were 33, but by 1967 there were 113, with a slight decline during the 1970s (Tsuji 1984: 45). Some were set up by the Diet to get around bureaucratic resistance to reform; to overcome ministerial jurisdictional disputes; to expand bureaucratic jurisdiction; to expedite governmental tasks in a manner that was perceived to be more efficient than that of the ministries; or to provide employment for retired officials (*amakudari*; see p. 89).[32] There are many reasons for the establishment of special corporations, but their flowering illustrates how private and public elements are mixed in the soil of the Japanese politico-economic landscape. Special corporations, as para-state organizations, blur public/private distinctions and enhance the power of the ministries. This blurring is not merely academic, because special corporations are not accountable under any formal controls, and they have been criticized for being "deplorably secretive" about their finances and operations ("Finances of public corporations shrouded in secrecy," DY 9 December 1994: 16). They are also criticized for wasting tax-payers' money, and there are many cases in which an enterprise meets the criterion of being classified as a special corporation but is not legally classified as such.

There have been rumblings about the need to reform special corporations and many feel that they some have outlived their usefulness, while others interfere with the private sector.[33] According to one newspaper article, 75.2 percent of special corporations were headed by former high-ranking bureaucrats (see the following section on *amakudari*). The Ministries of International Trade and Industry and Agriculture, Forestry and Fisheries were the highest, with the Ministry of Finance not far behind. The Ministries of Construction, Transport, and Education were also popular (this survey does not include all types of public corporation, such as foundations) ("Amakudari still prevails," DY 14 August 1994: 2). In October 1994, ministries were asked by the Administrative Management Bureau of the Prime Minister's Office to submit suggestions for how special corporations might be abolished, reorganized, placed under private management (the profitable ones), or combined.[34] It is still too early to tell how the ministries and other parties will respond to reform attempts. However, given the vested interests in these organizations, the prognosis is procrastination, though minor reorganization will probably be carried out for appearance's sake.[35]

The space between state and society in Japan cannot be appreciated without mentioning "authorized juridical persons" (*ninka hōjin*). Similar in some ways to special corporations but created through the voluntary initiative of private persons, these legal entities are also under the auspices of the ministries, whose purpose is to promote activities of societal importance in the private sector, such as insurance, research, government-aided corporations dealing with business activities of local public entities, societies of certified professionals, and mutual benefit associations for public employees (Tsuji 1984: 36). There are other legally incorporated organizations that expect private companies to use their services, such as testing products and issuing licenses. Such organizations seem to be driven by a profit motive, and since their seals of approval carry a semi-official status, "requests" for testing cannot be easily turned down (see "Product 'testing' fees rack up huge profits," DY 6 May 1996: 2). The fact that these organizations are ostensibly for civic purposes and yet tied so closely to officialdom raises the question of to what degree a state-free civil society exists in Japan.

Amakudari

Many believe that special corporations have been established as enterprises to accept retired bureaucrats. True or not, many heads of special corporations are ex-bureaucrats, and as of 1 April 1994, 47.6 percent (397 out of 834) of full-time officers at special corporations were ex-bureaucrats ("Coalition to urge govt to restrict amakudari," DY 10 December 1994: 16). Because only one individual from a group that entered a ministry during the same year (*dōki*) can become an administrative vice-minister (in spite of the "vice" prefix, the most powerful position in a ministry), others in the same-year cohort are expected to retire.[36] But because retiring officials are still in their early fifties and receive less than generous retirement benefits, many "descend from heaven" (*amakudari suru*) into positions (selected by a ministry, not the retiring official) in the private sector or special corporations under their former ministry's jurisdiction. Others may run for the Diet (many postwar prime ministers and cabinet ministers have been ex-bureaucrats). Consequently, *amakudari* is "seen as a mechanism for extending bureaucratic influence over the Japanese economy, society, and polity" (Campbell 1989: 119). Officials fortunate enough to land particularly high post-retirement positions wield considerable power: "At this level the Western distinction between public and private loses its meaning" (Johnson 1982: 71).

Johnson notes that "*Amakudari* does not appear to reflect some kind of plot or stratagem to circumvent laws or to obtain unfair advantages. Its rationale is a reflection of circumstances that have confronted the nation in the past and that persist in lessened form to the present time." However, we must appreciate the sociopolitical milieu – the semiprivate/ semipublic domain – that invites *amakudari*. This placement of former officials ensures that the bureaucratic mentality permeates the elite decision-making centers, and is "one aspect of their implementation of so-called administrative guidance [discussed below]" (1974: 965).

Advisory councils

Another example of how the government exploits the interstices between state and societal domains are through the 212 advisory, consultative, or deliberative councils (*shingikai*) attached to national governmental bodies.[37] Legally, national-level advisory councils are established by Article 8 of the National Administrative Organization Act. However, each advisory council is created through a specific ordinance. Though in theory these councils afford a voice to citizens, they often function as para-state organizations. Advisory councils are created by and attached to a ministry, which may have several of these at any given time. Basically a postwar phenomenon, they are staffed by businessmen, academics, or specialists, and sometimes by representatives of consumer, environment, labor, or other movements and different societal concerns.[38] They are often criticized because their conclusions and "advice" are often scripted by ministry officials and their purpose seems to be to stamp a seal of approval on a ministry's policies.[39] Furthermore, "Whatever the precise nature of the *shingikai* action, it remains beyond legal challenge since no *shingikai* report, no matter how final and no matter what its role in industrial policy, constitutes an administrative disposition" (Upham 1987: 199). Advisory councils are also deployed as a "means of turf defense and image enhancement not only by each ministry but also by individual bureaus within ministries" (Abe *et al.* 1994: 40). This is not always true, and some councils actually debate and deliberate issues without being dominated by a ministry. Nevertheless, "To the extent that laws are scrutinized and discussed at all in Japan by persons outside the bureaucracy, it is done in councils" (Johnson 1982: 47).

Some advisory councils of the 1980s that were attached to the Prime Minister's Office (particularly under the guidance of Prime Minister Nakasone) gained in autonomy *vis-à-vis* the ministries. It was during the 1980s that a large number of "private consultative organs" appeared. Called "discussion groups" or "study groups," these were attached to the prime minister or other cabinet ministers. Private consultative organs "were criticized for existing in the shadows of the law and for blurring administrative responsibility." We should note that such organs "do not require parliamentary approval of their members, and their expenditures do not appear as separate items in the government budget" (Abe *et al.* 1994: 44–5). As such, "private consultative organs" are good examples of technically unofficial but *de facto* official organs.

ADMINISTRATIVE GUIDANCE

"Administrative guidance" (*gyōsei shidō*) is the most important term for understanding Japanese political philosophy and its distinctive practice of public administration and policy making. It is considered "the very core of postwar Japanese public administration" (Abe *et al.* 1994: 36) and is often used to characterize the advice or assistance that the government (usually a ministry) provides to corporations, private persons, and public organizations to realize what is thought to be in the national interest. Interestingly enough, currently, eight ministries have "guidance divisions" (*shidō-ka*) or include this term in a division's title, though most are in the Ministry of Health and Welfare. Business, special interest groups, schools (see Chapters 6 and 7), and local governments are all recipients of government guidance. When heard in an economic context, administrative guidance is considered an important policy tool of Japan's famous (or, depending on one's point of view, infamous) industrial policy. As a governing tool, administrative guidance (or some version thereof) is found in all governments, but such government assistance is notably salient in Japan, and though the ministries are not as officious as they once were, they still rely on directives to implement policies. "The reason is that the 'climate' of administration in Japan is favorable to administrative guidance" (Shiono 1984: 208). I believe that it is the lack of neatly demarcated lines between state and society that fosters this "climate."[40] Administrative guidance is an example of *kanmin yuchaku* (the growing together of the public and private sectors). *Kanmin* means "officials and people" and *yuchaku* is a medical term meaning adhesion, healing up, or union, or to have a cozy relationship. This term is "used in political discourse to mean specifically the cooperative relationship between the government and big business" (Johnson 1980: 97–8). Of course, there are thin lines between cooperation, collusion, and corruption, especially in Japan's construction industry.[41]

Administrative guidance has no legal definition, and the bureaucracies have their own rules and policies, which sometimes contradict formal laws.[42] The informal and opaque nature of administrative guidance makes it very difficult to debate it publicly, let alone overturn it. "Administrative guidance can be implemented as an interim measure until a law can be enacted," or it may be effected as an experimental measure (Shiono 1984: 207). Not being part of the nation's official laws, administrative guidance possesses a para-official authority, and companies that do not accept government advice may be denied licensing, permits, financial aid, tax incentives, or access to bank credit. Administration guidance gains its potency (and controversy) from its vague, informal status. Haley notes that

> In Japan informal enforcement is not *a* process of governing, but has become *the* process of governing. It is used to implement nearly all bureaucratic policy, whether or not expressed in statute or regulation, at all levels of government and all administrative offices. Japanese officials use informal enforcement to implement policy in

every conceivable situation from antitrust violations and price controls to regulation of financial institutions.

(1991: 63, italics in original)

According to Shiono, there are three basic types of administrative guidance. The first type, called regulatory, can be subdivided into two types: (1) "an administrative organ, even when it is vested with regulatory authority by law, frequently provides administrative guidance instead of resorting to its regulatory authority." In this situation, the administrative organs often point out illegalities to a certain party and request voluntary action before resorting to legal recourse (i.e. they issue warnings); (2) "an administrative organ can issue administrative guidance in order to bring about a desirable result from the standpoint of the welfare of the public, even when it is not vested with regulatory power." This latter type of regulatory administrative guidance illustrates its para-legal nature. The second type of administrative guidance is reconciliatory, which has the purpose of reconciling "conflicting interest between private persons." The third type is promotional or advisory administrative guidance: "An administrative organ issues promotional or advisory administrative guidance when it believes that the action induced will promote the public interest as well as benefiting private parties" (1984: 205–6).

The political culture of the Japanese government has its own special language and concepts through which governmental guidance (its legal and para-legal varieties) is administered.[43] There are two types of ordinance: cabinet (*seirei*) and ministerial (*shōrei*). These are directives for nonpolitical technical matters under the cabinet's or a particular ministry's jurisdiction. Memoranda or notifications (*tsūtatsu*) – of which there are four types – are simple directives for matters of even less import than those dealt with by ministerial ordinances. In descending order of formality they are: (1) ministerial orders (*kunrei*); (2) ministerial notifications (*tsūtatsu*); (3) internal memoranda (*naikan*); and (4) business correspondence *(jimu renraku)*. Only the first two are defined by law (though not necessarily legally binding), though all are treated as if they were legally binding (Samuels 1983: 44–5).

Though many would argue that Japan's postwar prosperity owes its success in no small measure to administrative guidance and the climate of public–private cooperation, others would claim that its effects have been exaggerated or misunderstood. Still others would label administrative guidance a form of bureaucratic bullying. Whatever position is taken, few would disagree that there are problems inherent in administrative guidance. Shiono lists four difficulties with bureaucrat-provided advice. The first concerns accountability: "it is not clear who assumes the ultimate responsibility for such guidance." There are no procedural rules or provisions for hearings. Nor are there any rules setting standards or substantive limits. Because "administrative guidance does not have any legal effect, private persons and business enterprises cannot seek to have a court invalidate it even when it is wrong." Second, because administrative guidance lacks procedural fairness, third parties may not know its contents. This is an example of how the public interest is not considered. Third, "despite the fact that administrative guidance is not based on statutory authority, it may work as if it were vested with regulatory power." That is, it acquires para-legal power. Finally, "over-dependence on the government may reduce the initiative of the private sector and eventually lead to excessive interference by the government in the private sector" (Shiono 1984: 212–13). Or in my own words, the government dissolves the boundaries between state and society.

BUREAUCRACIES AS RITUAL CENTERS

Debates about local government are premised on two interlocking concepts: (1) corporate autonomy – the power of local entities (prefectures and municipalities) to decide and administer a range of public policies on their own initiative with relative freedom from central supervision; and (2) citizen autonomy – the right of citizens to participate, directly or indirectly, in the formation of such policies. The nature of the Japanese debate about central versus local powers demonstrates that at a basic level of political philosophy and governing arrangements, Japan is a unitary, not a federalist state. In this regard, it more closely resembles the continental rather than the Anglo-American idea of government. In the last century, centralized solutions to the threat from encroaching imperialism were the preferred means to save Japan, which has, as Williams notes, "a political system that admits few of the federalist or decentralizing or devolving impulses that have so influenced the nature of the American, British, German or Canadian polities. The Japanese state admits no constitutional dilutions of its authority." Japan's central authorities instinctively retreat – undoubtedly encouraged by the bureaucracies – from polycentrism rather than viewing themselves as sharing political legitimacy with other, more local centers. "As a capital, modern Tokyo is the twentieth-century answer to nineteenth-century Paris. It rules" (1994: 22). As a ritualizing and rationalizing center, Tokyo is home to the ordained institutions where state policies are forged, approval for commercial and public endeavors petitioned, violators of the civic order sanctioned, procedures for numerous activities designed, and national goals implemented. It decrees, directs, and dictates the practices of the peripheral areas.

The history of local government

The modern history of local government in Japan is one of alternating concentration and deconcentration of power, and it demonstrates how the center has attempted to rationalize control over the periphery. The peripheries have experienced centralization (Meiji Restoration to 1945), decentralization (postwar reforms), recentralization (the "reverse course" after the Occupation), and to some degree, decentralization (mid-1960s to present). Currently, an uneasy balance between the center and the peripheries exists, with local governments demanding more leeway, while some central authorities still feel that centralized decision making is in the nation's best interest.[44] Though arguably such a state of affairs exists everywhere, in the case of Japan this tug-of-war between the center and peripheries seems to be exacerbated by a lack of a mediating civil space rooted in common concerns that transcends both centralized state and highly localized, particularistic interests.

The leaders of the Meiji Restoration, in their endeavor to strengthen Japan, saw the need to centralize and rationalize local governments (though they saw no need to mention local government in the Meiji Constitution). In 1869, the central government decreed that *daimyō* (feudal lords) would be domainal governors, and that they would henceforth be officials authorized by imperial appointment, rather than lords of hereditary fiefs. Also, to symbolize that local governments would now be under the imperial rule, the land and people registers were returned to the emperor (*behanseki hōkan*). In 1871, the domains were abolished and prefectures were established (*haihan chiken*). The central authorities appointed chief prefectural executive (*kenrei*, later *chiji*) from different parts of Japan. Eventually, the 302 prefectures would be reduced to seventy-two and three major urban areas. Due to the requirements of the Family Registration Law of 1871, nine census districts below the prefectural level were set up for censuses (*daiku shōku*). In 1873, the Home Ministry (*Naimushō*) was established to administer local affairs. In 1888, the central government drafted codes for city, town, and village organization, and two years later, did the same for prefectures (*ken*) and districts (or counties, *gun*). These codes constituted what was referred to as the Local Autonomy System (*Chihō jichi seido*). However, though some local bodies did have assemblies, local government was not in fact autonomous.

The Three New Laws System (*San shimpō*) of 1878–88, advocated by Home Minister Ōkubo Toshimichi, consisted of three programs. The first was the creation of *ku* (wards) in cities which occupied the same level as districts (*gun*). Within districts were cities (*machi* or *chō*) and villages (*mura* or *son*), whose leaders were appointed by prefectural governors in 1884. Towns and villages possessed a "dual nature": they were simultaneously units of national administration and units of local citizens' self-government. The Law on Ward, Town, and Village Assemblies (*Ku-chō-son kai hō*) of 1889 attempted to broaden citizen participation by setting up local assemblies. In 1884, town and village heads were made appointive positions, as were the presidents of assemblies. During this period, the amalgamation of towns and villages proceeded at a rapid rate.

The second program was the establishment of assemblies in all prefectures. Only the prefectural governor could draft legislation and prorogue the assemblies. Though only 5 percent could vote and even fewer could be elected, this was an important step. The third program, made official by the Local Tax Regulations (*Chihōzei kisoku*), was the uniform collection of taxes at the prefectural and subprefectural levels. Though there was local opposition in the early 1880s to taxes, this was suppressed by 1885.

The Three New Laws System was soon superseded by the Meiji Local Autonomy System. Home Minister Yamagata Aritomo believed that a codified system of local rule would make Japan stronger. He was attracted to the Prussian institutions and put a Berlin jurist, Albert Mose, on an investigatory committee on local government law. Mose's influence was seen in the Municipal Code (*Shisei*) and Town and Village Code (*Chōsonsei*) of 1888. These codes set up city assemblies (*shikai*) and stipulated that mayors of cities were to be chosen by the Home Ministry from three candidates. The selection of town and village chiefs required the permission of prefectural governors, but not that of the Home Minister. City councils (*shisanjikai*) consisted of a mayor, assistants, and six to twelve honorary councilors. Though the council executed the assembly's orders, it had ultimate power over the assembly. Towns and villages lacked councils.

The Prefectural Code (*Fukensei*) and District Code (*Gunsei*), both issued in 1890, did not take full effect until 1899. The former established prefectural councils (*ken sanjikai*) and prefectural assemblies. Districts, which were modeled on the Prussian *Kreis*, controlled towns and villages. District executives (*gunchō*), under which were district councils, were appointees of the prefectural governor. A new organ under the Meiji system were district assemblies (*gunkai*). The Meiji system distinguished *jūmin* (residents; all who lived in a locality) from *kōmin* (male residents who met the criteria of age, financial and familial conditions, and tax-paying status). Under the Meiji system there were forty-six prefectures, forty-three of which were *ken*; three *fu* (major urban areas); and one administrative province (*dō*: Hokkaidō).

In the following years, there were some changes in the Meiji system: in 1899 the Prefectural and County Codes were reformed; in 1911, the New Municipal Code and New Town and Village Code were enacted; and in 1921, districts were stripped of their local self-governing functions and became administrative units of state. However, the basic structures of the Meiji Local Autonomy System endured until 1940. During the period of "Taishō Democracy" (1920s), the central authorities loosened their controls over the local areas. Significantly, the Home Ministry's power to intervene in local budget making was weakened, thereby strengthening the prerogatives of prefectural assemblies at the expense of centrally appointed governors. Also, large cities gained in decision-making power.

Any gains made by local governments were lost during the war years. In order to tighten its grip at the local level, the Home Ministry created *chōnaikai* (community associations) in cities, towns, and villages, and *tonarigumi* (groupings of around ten households) through which police, welfare work, food rationing, and the encouragement of "war spirit" were administered. In 1943, the governors' powers were strengthened at the expense of the prefectural and municipal assemblies, and Japan was divided into nine regional administrative councils (*chihō gyōsei kyōgikai*) to enhance central control.

After the war, the Occupation authorities attempted to dismantle an extremely centralized local government system in which prefectural governments were considered an extension of the central authorities. The Occupation authorities initiated local government reforms, which basically consisted of: "(1) decentralization or abolition of authoritarian structures that had limited basic liberties in the prewar years; (2) expansion of citizens' participation in and control of local government; and (3) deconcentration and restraint of executive authority by local assemblies" (MacDougall 1989: 145). In order to effect these reforms, the Home Ministry was disbanded on 27 December 1947. The fundamental principles of local government were set forth in the Constitution of 1947 (Chapter 8, Articles 92–95) and legislation defined and enhanced local powers: the 1947 Local Autonomy Law (*Chihō jichi hō*) (which has been revised yearly as local powers expanded); the Local Finance Law (*Chihō zaiseihō*) (1948); the Local Tax Law (*Chihōzei hō*) (1950); the Public Office Election Law (*Kōshoku senkyo hō*) (1950); the

Local Public Service Law (*Chihō kōmuin hō*) (1959); and the Local Public Enterprise Law (*Chihō kōei kigyō hō*) (1952). Though postwar reforms decentralized the police and education system, these were gradually recentralized during the 1950s. The Home Ministry (*Jichishō*: literally, Self-government or Autonomy Ministry) was established in 1960.

MacDougall divides the history of postwar local government into four overlapping phases: (1) administrative recentralization (first postwar decade); (2) rapid economic development (mid-1950s to mid-1960s); (3) local initiative and reactions to social problems (e.g. pollution) (late 1960s to early 1970s); and (4) "The Age of Localism," when local bodies became more assertive and attempted to solve their own problems. This is called "localism" (*jimoto-shugi*) (mid-1970s to present) (*ibid.*: 148–155). Currently, there are forty-seven prefectures. Prefectural administration is quite similar to that of the national government, with a prefectural official ranking one step below a national official with the same title. As of April 1993, there were 3.27 million local government employees. At the subprefectural level are about 3,300 (towns and villages), each with its own bureaucracy. Though local governments have expanded their powers (often led by opposition parties) since the 1970s, they still face resistance from the central authorities, which attempt to circumscribe their powers. The center's "tutelage" of the peripheries is effected through five types of relation: (1) personnel (*shukkō*; see below); (2) administrative guidance (discussed above); (3) delegated functions (see below); (4) approval and permission; and (5) finance (see below) (Samuels 1983: 39–48).

Even today, prefectural governors have a "dual role": as popularly elected chief executives, they enforce prefectural laws, coordinate administration, present legislation to the prefectural assembly, and appoint and supervise local officials (the lieutenant governor and chief treasurer are appointed by the governor with the consent of the prefectural assembly). However, under the system of "agency delegation" (*kikan inin jimu*), governors, mayors, and administrative committees must enforce national laws and are subject to the national ministries, and a prime minister can legally remove any governor that fails to do so. Governors who want to create a new organization must first consult with the Ministry of Home Affairs (Shindo 1984: 115).[45] This is why "the relationship between national government and local government under the prewar system can still be observed in present-day Japan" (*ibid.*: 119). Also, it should be mentioned that governors and mayors are often local ex-bureaucrats, who may have been posted in an area by the central government. This sometimes means that local government is bureaucratized and depoliticized (in the sense of tying Tokyo closer to local areas). Another threat to local autonomy is the eight to ten regional areas into which the central government has divided Japan in order to go over the boundaries of prefectures to implement its policies.

One way in which the center controls the peripheries is through the *shukkō* (transfer) system, in which national officials are dispatched from the center (often from the Ministry of Home Affairs) to the local areas for one or more years. The ministries (particularly Home Affairs, Education, and Agriculture, Forestry and Fisheries) are always eager to expand their influence and jurisdiction in the peripheral areas and to observe how the local governments spend national funds. Ministries have *desaki kikan* (branch offices) through which central bureaucratic decrees are implemented at the local level. From the local perspective, such bureaucratic oversight is not always unwelcome, since local officials receive talented workers and may be able to form connections which are valuable for obtaining money.

Financially, the situation of postwar local government is similar to that of the prewar period: the budgets of local governments are tied to those of the central authorities, 70 percent of taxes collected by the national government remain in central coffers, while local government retains only 30 percent (thus the saying "30 percent local autonomy"), granting the central authorities effective control over local expenditure. Also, bureaucratic red tape makes central government funding difficult. As reported by Kim, financial support for the construction of a rural road may require approval from the Ministries of Finance, Transport, Construction, and Agriculture, Forestry and Fisheries, and the National Land Agency. This is why a prefectural governor may spend about one week in four in Tokyo, and department heads, on the average, five to seven days there every two months (1988: 70).

Recently, calls for administrative reform have been heard for local government. The most commonly heard complaint is that the central authorities should grant more power to the local government.[46] Declining tax revenues and an aging society have forced local governments to grapple with reform. The Ministry of Home Affairs, concerned about inflated local government, has compiled an administrative guideline ("Bloated local governments must shed fat too," DY 22 November 1994: 7).

Another difficulty confronting local authorities is "vertical administration" or "vertical compartmentalization" (*tatewari gyōsei*), a tenacious problem whose appearance should not be surprising in a highly bureaucratized political environment. MacDougall refers to *tatewari gyōsei* as "an inability to coordinate horizontally the public policy involvement of national authorities at the local level" (1989: 162). Vertical administration (or in Campbell's words, "slivered administration," 1989: 122–3) hinders the effective implementation of programs and leads to waste. The lack of a strong sense of common civility only enhances the divisiveness of vertical administration.

Local government and rationalization

Reed argues that Japan is not as centralized as it may appear at first glance; rather, it is "highly nationalized." Japan is dominated by a "myth of centralization," which "conditions people to look toward the central government for conflict resolution." Moreover, this myth "prods the ministries to take responsibility for everything" (1982: 159). The myth of centralization is an aspect, I would argue, of the bureaucratic ethos that dominates Japanese sociopolitical life. "Because of the myth of centralization, all actors tend to assume that uniformity is the norm" (*ibid.*: 163). Local policy, in fact, was sometimes regarded as "irrational" (*fugōri*), meaning that "there is no particular reason for local policy to deviate from national policy. Both central and local officials operate on the assumption that uniformity should prevail unless some particular reason to allow local variation can be given." After all, "In Japan it is diversity that needs justification" (*ibid.*: 160). And, though this is probably not as obvious, this same myth resonates with the idea that "being Japanese" means being uniform.[47]

Local autonomy and civil society

Some Japanese say that in reality Japan lacks local government, but perhaps, from another angle, it may be said that the lack of strong local government is one aspect of Japan's lack of a clearly defined civil society. Maruyama wrote that because postwar political parties focused on national-level power politics, they abandoned their functions of linking government and interest groups and encouraging healthy popular participation. Therefore, at the local level, fragmented, stop-gap, and emergency groups took over the role of interest groups (1964: 531). Local government may be considered one more layer between the central state structures and the individual, but in order for it to function effectively, it requires the type of justification that a neutral arena (public) may provide. In the same way that civil society may buffer the individual from too direct state intervention, prefectural and municipal autonomy affords the local citizen protection and a sense that central officialdom is only one type of authority among several. In any case, local governments are a much needed balance *vis-à-vis* the center. "This is particularly the case because of the failure of Japanese political parties and interest groups to adequately convey grass-roots opinion and influence to political leaders and because of the strong sense of localism that continues to pervade Japan" (MacDougall 1989: 164–5). Also, if central authorities cannot – or perhaps more to the point, will not – solve certain problems, then local levels are forced to tackle them. This may not necessarily be a bad thing, of course.

CONCLUSION

Both the critics and detractors of the ministries agree that the imperatives of "technical effectiveness" have predominated over "democratic responsiveness" in postwar Japan (Campbell 1989: 114). This pursuit of technical effectiveness has all too readily led to government by administrative calculation. Though some may say that every society gets the government it deserves, it is perhaps more true that every government reflects the society it serves. Japanese have a taste for a bureaucratic ethos because it shuns (though it does not preclude) conflict and struggle. Rationality and rituality do not openly display messy and face-threatening maneuvers. Bureaucratized social practices provide an automaticity of hierarchy and classification, fixing positions and roles. And if decisions can be reached without messy democratic debate and face-threatening maneuvers (resulting in "bureaucratic informalism"), then the demons of power can be tamed for the collective good:

> When combined with a constant rhetoric of consensus and harmony, informality also masks the decision-making process and even the existence of decisions at all. Without a formal and open policymaking process, government policies can appear as the inevitable and natural results of custom and consensus rather than as the conscious political choices among mutually antagonistic interests that they actually are. Because they appear natural and inevitable, policy decisions are considered socially legitimate and are virtually immune to legal and political attack.
>
> (Upham 1987: 208)[48]

5 Rationality, bureaucracy, and belief in the state[1]

INTRODUCTION: RATIONALITY AND STATISM AS RELIGION

In the last chapter I described the state structures of Japan. But these visible institutions must be supported by invisible institutions. Stated differently, official structures require ideological justification, so that there must be a conviction, even if minimal, in the "secular theodicy" (Herzfeld 1992) of these structures. As in any religion, faith and its legitimacy and authority are central concerns (cf. Schaar 1969). In Japan, political legitimacy is officially located in the constitution, Diet, and other government organs. Elections, parties, and abstract ideologies such as national solidarity and democracy also legitimize Japan's political life. However, these are just the more obvious institutions that sanction political authority in Japan. Resolute legitimacy and authorization are far more subtle and require more than the official structures usually examined. The invisible institutions of a society and its state, and how they are put into place, also deserve analytical attention, and in the next two chapters I examine how the state attempts to place its values in the self, but for now I point out only the nature of the problem.[2]

The relation between state, society, and self is often conceived as hierarchical, so that the self is placed beneath either society or state. The self is regarded as subordinate to, or a smaller part of, a larger collectivity. But I want to suggest another conceptual diagram, which illustrates the inherent inseparability and linkages between self, society, and state. Imagine three prisms, each representing self, society, and state, which are aligned in such a way that light refracted by one passes through the other two. The light represents bureaucratizing/ rationalizing tendencies (hierarchical, taxonomic, and formalizing schemata), so that state ideology is refracted through society and then through the self. The crucial point is that the self, through everyday practices[3] and special activities (voting, paying taxes, participation in national rituals, etc.), refracts this ideology back to the state.[4] There is a danger, of course, in treating the state as a unitary and monolithic actor (*cf.* Migdal *et al.* 1994: 7–34),[5] but it must be pointed out that, from the point of view of the social actor, the state is more often than not *perceived* as a single agent.

As in many other places, faith in the Japanese state entails some basic bureaucratic classificatory operations (i.e. how the nation is bureaucratized), such as nationality (Japanese/non-Japanese) and gender. The former categorization, as I examine below, is intimately linked to and bolstered by visions of being an "average Japanese" and the sociopolitical uses of language. It is also a type of "common sense" (i.e. being born in Japan makes one both racially and nationally Japanese). I also examine the role of the emperor in legitimizing belief in the nation-state. An appreciation of belief in the Japanese state requires an understanding of how state-directed rationalization policies and practices, driven by nationally strategic economic interests, have defined the meaning of public and private in Japan and other mythologies of state. This is the purpose of the section "Japan's strategic economy: the rationality of state goals" (p. 117), in which I examine how economic interests and state guidance strongly encourage faith in rationalization.

"THEOLOGIANS OF THE STATE" AND THE BUREAUCRATIC VISION

If nationalism can be viewed as religion, "bureaucratic actions are its most commonplace rituals" (Herzfeld 1992: 37). How does nationalism relate to bureaucracy in Japan? Though speaking of another place and time, Marx's quips that "The bureaucrats are the Jesuits and theologians of the state" and "The bureaucracy is *la république prêtre*" apply well to Japan's mandarinate (in Tucker 1978: 23). Though modern bureaucracy did not emerge in Japan until after the Meiji Restoration and its breakneck race toward nation building,[6] before that time Japan had had a centuries-long tradition of governance through bureaucracy. Many intellectuals of the Tokugawa period theorized about the need for human-created political institutions that could respond readily to social needs. They emphasized the rational, instrumental, and practical aspects of governing bodies, expressed in the dictum "pragmatic content over form" (*na yori mo jitsu*) (Najita 1974: 41).[7] Indeed, some of the ideas of pre-Meiji thinkers have a distinctly modern ring, and their advice on the art of governing resonates with much of Japan's policies in the late nineteenth and twentieth centuries. For instance, the ideas of Satō Nobuhiro (1769–1850) are "less and less reminiscent of the benevolent feudal prince, and increasingly suggestive of the centralized, development-oriented nation state." In *Suitō hiroku* (Confidential Memorandum of Government), Satō wrote how the ideal society would have a state-controlled economy and be governed by ministries (*fu*), and he emphasized development through "education, training, and the introduction of new technologies" (Morris-Suzuki 1989: 35–6). Discussing the Tokugawa period, Arnason writes that "While there is no denying its extremely repressive – in some ways even proto-totalitarian – character, it was certainly a much more complex, rationalized and dynamic social order than the idea of an artificially prolonged feudalism would indicate." He continues:

> The Meiji Restoration and the profound changes which followed it were thus not the result of a "fortuitous conjunction" of the "two forces of internal decay and external pressure." Rather, a modernizing process that had been initiated in Japan long before and blocked in some respects but continued in others – for example with regard to urbanization and education – during the Tokugawa era was both accelerated and radicalized by the challenge from the West.
> (1989: 238)

Though there have been counter-traditions in Japanese political philosophy to "bureaucratism" and its excesses (captured in sayings such as *kanson minpi*: "exalt the bureaucrats, despise the people"), government administered through bureaux continues to be attractive to the Japanese.[8]

Since the Meiji period, the state was ideally conceived not as an array of institutions to resolve conflict but as an inherently organic collectivity that was ideally apolitical and tension-free. Though the notion of *kokutai* (national polity or the essence of the nation; literally, "the body of the nation") has pre-Meiji roots, it became a key term in the idiom of national identity during the late Meiji. "*Kokutai* provided a past that was ageless, continuous, and secure in its ancestral tradition. Amuletic and ambiguous, eventually *kokutai* served to identify the nation and separate 'them' from 'us'" (Gluck 1985: 145). The key word here is "ambiguous," pointing to a conflation of and confusion between past "tradition" and present realities, state and ethnic group, and as I have discussed in Chapter 2, public and private spheres, evident in prewar slogans such as "sacrifice self in service to the public" (*messhi hōkō*).

In March 1899, Yamagata Aritomo, a major architect of the Meiji bureaucracy, used new ordinances concerning the status and disciplining of ministry officials to prevent political parties from gaining power in the bureaucracy, thereby helping to give birth to a powerful bureaucratic elite. Democracy was "seen less as a means for resolving conflict and disagreement and more as a technique for avoiding it. The result is that in Japan a 'democratic' decision is defined in principle not simply as majoritarian but as unanimous" (Abe *et al.* 1994: 204–5).[9] In Japan, democracy was a means to an end, not an end in itself. This is related to the lack of the Euro-American style of a public in which popular interests are collectively presented to the governing elite. Consequently, "the concerns of daily life have never completely fused, or overlapped, with those of politics in the minds of citizens" (Matsumoto 1978: 37).

SACRALIZING THE SECULAR

The Japanese state's prewar use of religion is well-known. Much has been written about the grounding of state legitimacy in sacred traditions, the Japanese as a chosen race to rule Asia, the invention of state Shinto (Hardacre 1989), and the emperor-as-god. Here I want to treat the more everyday assumptions that legitimate the state which, though not overtly religious, nevertheless are analogous to sacralizing activities. It is useful to remember that the state is a construction in progress, built daily through mundane practices. These practices are not just the obvious ones, the usual focus of conventional political science (i.e. policy making, debating, voting, elections, etc.), but also the less apparent, more quotidian activities. "Every bureaucratic form is the icon of some edict, every rubber stamp the icon of a state seal. This pervasive reproducibility gives each bureaucrat a rhetoric of *common sense*, backed by the authority of law, that challenges and deflects close inspection" (Herzfeld 1992: 76, italics mine). As pointed out in Chapter 2, the rhetoric of "common sense" – and its conceptual cousin, rationality – is an extremely powerful legitimizing ideology. Herzfeld's observations on the modern belief in bureaucracy and rationality are relevant here:

> One of the most commonly held assumptions of modernity is that the bureaucratically regulated state societies of "the West" [and Japan as well as other "developing" nations] are more rational – or less "symbolic" than those of the rest of the world. This division is based on a circular argument, which provides the definitions of

rationality and then finds it at home. It treats rationality as distinct from belief, yet demands an unquestioning faith not radically different from that exacted by some religions. Even critics of the state bureaucracy implicitly accept its idealized self-presentation. The nation-state represents perfect order; only the human actors are flawed. This has all the marks of a religious doctrine.

(*ibid.*: 17)

Consider how simple and commonsensical forms seem. These are tools, technical devices used by various levels of government. The most basic form records one's name, place of residence, age, date of transaction, affiliations, and the business at hand. More involved forms demand other data, such as additional details and specifics about people, places, and other dates. They temporally and spatially fix one within a complex web of duties, demands, and responsibilities. If knowledge is power, then forms are the information-gathering devices used to drive government action. But regardless of their commonsensical appearance and their obvious uses, forms are also often regarded as fetishes. More times than I care to remember, people behind the desk would not accept forms that had obviously been corrected. Cross-outs and white-outs, no matter how neatly done, would invalidate forms. I was once told to take a three-hour bus ride to a university foreign students' office to redo a form on which I had made a minor change. Such concerns, of course, are usually rooted in the fear that subordinates have in submitting marred forms that even hint at improbity, or perhaps, some sacrilege.

Desecration of and challenges to the order must be dealt with. This is why the "most trivial arguments about driver's licenses or parking privileges reproduce the same debate – a debate, in effect, between semantic fundamentalism and authoritative interpretation – in much the same way as a theological dispute may reproduce and reaffirm the common grounds of doctrine and the authority of the Word" (Herzfeld 1992: 110). Consider the role that apologies play in Japan. These are written out and used in many situations, from schools, business offices, and police stations to the judicial system. The reintegrating role of repentance (into a hierarchy and its classificatory system) is religious in nature. Like guardians of a sacred order, "bureaucrats exact their own array of self-exonerating, supplicatory, and punitive practices" (*ibid.*: 37).

Portrayals of Japanese attitudes toward the powers-that-be are commonly characterized by a submissiveness to authority, resignation, and paternalism rooted in history. The "no-use-in-complaining" mentality, of course, is not unique to Japan, though some might argue that it is more conspicuous there, commonly heard in expressions such as *shō ga nai* or *shikata ga nai*, both meaning "it can't be helped." Maxims such as "one is as powerless before the manor lord as with a bawling child" (*nakuko to jitō ni wa kanawanu*), "revere the powerful" (*jidaishugi*), and "take the side of power" (*nagai mono ni makarero*) are said to reflect such thinking. Such attitudes have resulted in a "givenness of authority" that has historically been rarely questioned (*cf.* Koschmann 1978). Not surprisingly, Matsumoto notes, there is a Japanese tradition of conceptualizing the state as "a prior and self-justifying entity, sufficient in itself" (1978: 38). Indeed, "the question of why the state exists would never assume the proportions of a compelling intellectual issue," and in Japan "contemporary government rests on the same shaky philosophical foundations that supported the Japanese state during its modernization" (*ibid.*: 44). These views are often reported to illustrate the premodern, feudalistic features of Japanese thinking about power relations.

Whatever the relevance of these views for modern Japan, the "no-use-in-complaining" attitude supports a cosmology of officialdom that is related to questions of political legitimacy and accountability. This, of course, is true everywhere (North Americans have their "you-can't-fight-city-hall" conviction). Unsuccessful dealings with officialdom are just as important for supporting the state, since these are often spoken of as matters of fate, which then becomes "a fitting object for blame, especially as its very immunity from resistance allows the individual to lose any number of battles without losing self-respect" (Herzfeld 1992: 139). Furthermore, "Whenever citizens blame the bureaucracy for some embarrassing humiliation, they reaffirm the teleology of the state itself" (*ibid.*: 37). We should pay close attention to the way people passively support state structures, because such assistance also lends strength to official hierarchies, categorizations, and significantly, nationalism.[10]

CLASSIFICATIONS THAT ARRANGE SOCIOPOLITICAL REALITY

Much of bureaucratic practice consists in the "management of taxonomies" (Herzfeld 1992: 39; *cf.* Douglas 1986; Handelman 1976, 1978, 1981, 1983). The history of government may be viewed as the increasing improvement of technologies for labeling, division, indexing, codifying, and classifying populations. All these practices of control can be quite complex, to the point that in Japan, a "federation of ministries" governs the individual's everyday life:

In a functional sense, all aspects of the lives of the people are divided and governed by ministries that are more or less independent. Another way of putting it would be that a functionally organized federation of ministries regulates the people's lives. Just as the states are sovereign in federal systems, in federations of ministries, each ministry is more or less sovereign and tries to guard its own turf and go its own way.

(Kyogoku 1993: 223)

Studies of classification have been central to anthropological theorizing, from Durkheim (particularly his sacred/profane distinction) and the early French sociologists, to ethnoscience and the more recent sophisticated versions of cognitive anthropology.[11] However, Herzfeld notes that "Symbolic classification belongs to the domain of the exotic, bureaucracy to that of the modern and mundane." Such thinking "has left the symbolic analysis of bureaucracy relatively marginal within the discipline" and that "The anthropological study of modern political forms runs the risk of reproducing the ideology of modernity itself" (1992: 39). And the fact that government agencies everywhere manage identities that are so naturalized and essentialized (gender, racial, national) only serves to obfuscate the bureaucratically built nature of reality and encourages cults of procedure and precedent. As in many places, the very organization of each of Japan's ministry represents and establishes the taxonomic templates that are imposed on society.

Bureaucratically building gender and generational distinctions

A central theme of feminist anthropology has been how female/male gender definitions correspond to private/public social spheres. Women, as producers of children, have been considered closer to nature, while men have been closer to culture (Ortner 1974; Rosaldo and Lamphere 1974; Rosaldo 1974). Thus, women's domain is the family, kin, and self-interest (private), while the domain for men is that of strangers, politics, and the social good (public). These distinctions, while certainly possessing much cross-cultural relevance, have been shown to have limited application, or at least require subtle reinterpretation, since many cultures lack sharp divisions between private/public, domestic/work, and other spheres that researchers may take for granted (Bourguignon 1980; Rogers 1978; Tiffany 1979; Tuchman 1980; Yeatman 1984). In any case, like other industrialized societies, the sexual division of labor has become accepted as a natural feature of the socio-economic landscape in Japan, with women relegated to society's inner, domestic, and hidden sphere, while men are placed in society's outer, occupational, and exposed areas. These gender definitions are associated with other dichotomies, such as emotion/intellect, passive/active, and quiescent/creative. Significantly, these gender meanings are legitimated by the bureaucratic taxonomic system, so that the state and gender are linked via a project to make "good Japanese women." The Ministry of Education has its Women's Education Division in the Lifelong Learning Bureau. The Ministry of Labor has an entire bureau devoted to women, consisting of the Women's Policy Division, Women's Labor Division, and the Women's Welfare Division. In the Ministry of Agriculture's Agricultural Bureau there is the Women and Life Division. The Ministry of Health and Welfare's Children and Family Bureau contains the Mother and Children Welfare Division and the Mother and Children Health Division. There are no corresponding agencies or offices for men.[12] In other words, as people who are somehow more private (presumably because they are "closer to nature"), women require special attention from the state.[13] Generational differences are also established. The Ministry of Education has many divisions that differentiate school grades and educational levels, and it also has a Lifelong Learning Bureau, with a Youth Education Division. The Ministry of Health and Welfare's Senior Citizen Insurance and Welfare Bureau has the Senior Citizen Welfare Planning Division, the Senior Citizen Welfare Promotion Division, and the Senior Citizen Insurance Division.

CONSTRUCTING JAPANESENESS: HOW NATIONALITY IS BUREAUCRATIZED

The most central categorization in any modern state is nationality. The Japanese/non-Japanese distinction is organizationally embedded into a number of ministries, usually indicated by use of the word "international" (i.e. non-Japanese). The Ministry of Education's Science and International Affairs Bureau has the Foreign Student Exchange Division, the International Affairs Division, and the International Scientific Affairs Division. The Ministry of Agriculture has an International Department composed of the International Planning Division, the International Economics Division, and the International Cooperation Division. The Trade Policy Bureau at the Ministry of International Trade and Industry has divisions corresponding to geographical areas and includes the International Economic Department and the Economic Cooperation Department. The Transportation Policy Bureau at the Ministry of Transportation has several divisions prefixed with "international." The Ministry of Post and Telecommunications has an International Department. The Ministry of Labor's Secretariat has an International Labor Division and the same ministry's Occupational Safety Bureau has a division for policy for foreign employers. The Ministry of Finance has a number of divisions dealing with matters international. *Vis-à-vis* the outside world, the bureaux at the Ministry of Foreign Affairs impose a template that partitions the world into Asia, North America, Europe, Central–South America, and Middle East–Africa.

Japanese students overseas – who are, after all, out of place – have the Overseas Japanese Children Education Division at the Ministry of Education's Local Education Support Bureau. "Returnee" students – often discussed in the media as if returning from another planet – present Japan with the problem of how to reintegrate them into an educational system shaped by a rigid ladder of examinations. Being outside the system (i.e. receiving a "foreign" education), even for a short time, may seriously hurt a student's chances of climbing up the ladder (Goodman 1993). And anyone who has worked outside Japan as an adult for an extended length of time may have difficulty being accepted back into Japanese society (White 1992).

The classificatory operation of the bureaucracy in ensuring the Japanese/non-Japanese distinction is apparent in many ways. One way is the gatekeeping practices of the Immigration Bureau and its Registration Division at the Ministry of Justice, which keep unwanted non-Japanese out. Local governments do their part by keeping track of non-Japanese residents using a foreigner registration card system. This card, with a photograph and fingerprint of its carrier, is a source of much contention among many Chinese and Koreans who have lived in Japan for generations but have not applied for Japanese citizenship.

The category of "Japanese," besides being managed by bureaucracy, is also grounded at the popular level in nature ("racially"; i.e. physical appearance), language, folk crafts, food, manners, and dress. For many, being Japanese (racially, ethnically, linguistically) and nationalism (both its rabid and less offensive species) are often linked in an almost religious sense. Indeed, nationalism resembles religion in that both claim an immanent status. Nationalism claims to "transcend individual and local differences, uniting all citizens in a single, unitary identity. Furthermore, the forms of most European (and many other) national-isms transcend even their own national concerns, in that the principle of national identity is considered to underlie and infuse the particulars of nation and country" (Herzfeld 1992: 6). Though technically the criteria to become a naturalized Japanese are not insurmountable (though some who have tried would disagree with this assessment), the myth still persists among many (Japanese and non-Japanese) that it is close to impossible. In a nation that prides itself on "racial homogeneity" and often conflates race with nationality, it is not surprising that the authorities do not seem terribly interested in dispelling this myth.[14]

As I learned from my own teaching experiences with Japanese students, in societies where physical appearance, language, and nationality are unquestionably linked, appreciating and deconstructing the fictive nature of social identity can be a difficult task indeed. Some students, no matter how carefully I would dismantle the myths of being Japanese in class, would fill their reports and examinations with tenets about "the purity of the Japanese race," "the uniqueness of Japanese culture," "the homogeneity of the Japanese," "the Japanese are harmonious," and "Japanese are like *x* because our country was closed during Tokugawa" or "because Japan is an island country." For many, there is an essential "Japaneseness" beyond the constituting factors of language, citizenship, physical appearance, culture, and place of residence (i.e. "being in Japan") that cannot be dissected.[15] In other words, "being Japanese" is a type of religion, apparent in the formulaic, catechism-like feel of some my students' writings. There is an essentialist or unassailable natural "Japaneseness" that cannot be questioned, any more than true believers could deconstruct their sacred text as if its contents were fictional.

Language and national identity

Nationalism is intimately tied to language, and its use (or abuse, as the case may be) leads to and reflects intranational cleavages and disputes. Thus, "the idea of national language works to represent each individual's speech as an icon of the whole, a refraction of the immanent national essence; indexical relationships between speakers (the marks of differences in class or regional origin) are discounted" (Herzfeld 1992: 111). For the modern nation-state, language reform is also indispensable for purposes of rationalization, consolidation, and control.[16]

The Japanese/non-Japanese distinction is part of the "modern myth of *Nihongo* (Japanese language)." This "is not simply a set of approaches to the Japanese language, not merely a system for viewing and thinking about the Japanese language," but a myth that "has extended its tentacles until they reach deeply into every nook and cranny of Japanese social behavior." And it is a myth that "leaps to the fore whenever the society with which it is thus elaborately entwined begins to display unusual stress or difficulty [i.e. when confronted with "foreign-ness" from the outside]" (Miller 1982: 222).[17]

Language and language use are the *sine qua non* of marking and building identity. The daily use, ubiquitous nature, and body-mediated aspect of language make it a powerful and effective tool in forging identity. In Japan, the Japanese language is regarded as the essential element in making the Japanese Japanese. Furthermore, its socio-linguistic rules are also considered indispensable by many Japanese for symbolizing and maintaining social status, and hierarchical and gender distinctions. This is why proper language use is part of moral education in many schools. Companies often train new employees how to speak properly and use polite language. A well-bred Japanese is expected to know how to use *aisatsu*, a term that is usually translated as "greetings" but whose range of meanings is actually quite wide, indicating anything from a simple nod of the head to a formalized greeting to a lengthy speech. The reform and rationalization of Japanese has also been thought a necessary tool in building an economically powerful nation-state, and *kokugo* (Japanese language; literally, national language) is one of the core subjects of the Ministry of Education-ordained curriculum that students must master for examinations.[18]

Within the Agency for Cultural Affairs, the Japanese Language Division (*Kokugo-ka*) of the Cultural Affairs Department (*Bunka-bu*) is responsible for administering the nation's linguistic matters. (Our Country's Education Policy) *Waga kuni no bunkyō shisaku* devotes a chapter to the Japanese language (1988: 175–206). The history of language reform is outlined and the conclusions of the various councils that have met to deal with the Japanese language are explained. Also, problem areas such as language "corruption" (*midare*), changes in verbal conjugations, honorific expressions, and how information technology affects language are identified (*ibid.*: 196–98). The Kokuritsu Kokugo Kenkyūjo (National Language Research Institute), which is attached to the Agency for Cultural Affairs, publishes a wide range of books about the Japanese language.[19]

A Japanese version of equality

We are used to hearing about Japan as a "vertical" and "hierarchical" society, so it may seem odd to discuss egalitarianism in Japan. But all societies possess horizontal as well as vertical relations, though one characterization may appear predominant or at least dominate the discourse about that society. Whether horizontal relations necessarily constitute egalitarianism is, of course, debatable, but in Japan there is a strong sense of "sameness" among people that counterbalances the many hierarchies that rank individuals. This sameness is noticeable in how many Japanese will preface a description about themselves with *"ware ware nihonjin* [we Japanese] are *x."* It is also apparent in how, as often reported in the media, 90 percent of Japanese believe they are middle class, though economic statistics would indicate otherwise. Believing that one is part of a large, homogeneous, and relatively egalitarian collectivity goes a long way to bolster the powers that be, and such a belief is useful for convincing individuals that are in the same economic class, though in fact they merely belong to the same mass (*cf.* Murakami's *Shin chūkan taishū no jidai* (The Era of the New Middle Masses) (1984). Here mention should be made of the use of the term *seken* ("observing others") introduced in Chapter 3. One should conform to the *seken-nami* (average, ordinary standard of *seken*), and avoid being *seken-banare* (different from *seken*, eccentric, strange) or *seken-shirazu* (unaware of *seken* rules, naive).

As the moral guardians of the state, Japan's bureaucrats have historically recognized and feared a sentiment that many moderns, accustomed to a prosperity spread far and thick and all too often taken for granted, have forgotten: envy.[20] This passion of the masses had to be kept in check. Thus, equality, welfare, a simple lifestyle, and regulation became the preferred terms of the bureaucrats. Words they disliked were disparity, competition, luxury, and freedom. "Salvation of the poor went hand-in-hand with clamping down on the rich" (Ueda 1994: 133). This philosophy is apparent in postwar bureaucratic thinking. A former ministry official reports that he was told: "Don't be concerned about poverty, but about inequality" (*ibid.*: 128).

> What is most distinctive about Japanese political democracy is the focus on equality in human welfare. This is not to say that Japan is a more advanced "welfare state" than those in the West; it is not. Rather, it is to note that to an extraordinary degree political democracy in contemporary Japan emphasizes that all Japanese, no matter where they live and what their station in life and work, should be treated equally by the state, which shares with them a responsibility for their welfare. . . . This emphasis on equality in human welfare exists despite a fine sense of hierarchy and significant inequalities in status within Japanese society. These views, however, are not necessarily contradictory when one realizes that it is in the public domain that equality is demanded, while inequal-

ities in private life are accepted as a natural, and even desirable, principle of social organization.

(MacDougall 1989: 166)

JAPANESENESS AND NATIONALISM

Though belief in egalitarianism may lead to group solidarity and cooperation, it may just as easily support a naturalist, essentialist view of Japaneseness and a certain type of nationalism: "since we are all the same, there's no need to take differences seriously."[21] Such thinking has implications for civil society, because nationalism – whether ultra or faint – may weaken reflexivity and the ability to view the social world as "a product of social relationships and social processes" (Tester 1992: 11), where diversity is seen as enriching, not threatening, the socio-political order. Abe *et al.* note that

> To the extent that national identity is seen as necessary by the Japanese, the sole appropriate way of achieving it is through popu-lar solidarity, then what is needed at present is a civil society on a plane quite apart from that of the state. In the past, the Japanese experienced the parochial fusion of family, village, and state, but they have never experienced universalistic social solidarity. One of the most glaring gaps in contemporary Japanese education is the absence of any effort to instill the meaning of civic solidarity in young people. What is essential is the creation of national solidarity *independent of the state*.
>
> (1994: 233, italics mine)

The transformation of Japan (much of which, to be sure, was state-orchestrated) from a militarized, imperialist power mobilized for total war to a pacifist nation-state dedicated to world peace with a "peace constitution" draws attention away from a national amnesia about Japan's wartime atrocities (in spite of the sincerity of many Japanese). For instance, the annual rituals of "Japan as victim of the Pacific War" seen in Hiroshima and Nagasaki have helped to construct an interesting type of Japaneseness intimately bound up with a type of nationalism centering on the Japanese as inherently peaceful, harmonious, and vic-tims of the Pacific War.[22] As one student proudly explained to me, "being in a country that has experienced the atomic bombing is what it means to be Japanese." Another example of this postwar nationalism is the denial of Japan's armed forces. One of my best Japanese students insisted that the 250,000 or so well-equipped personnel of the Self-Defense Forces is not a military force.[23] Such national sentiments – disparagingly called "peace stupor" and "one-nation pacifism," have engendered dangerously naive views that Japan has no potential enemies and can isolate itself from any international turbulence.

There are countless rites, practices, and objects that construct nationality in Japan. Some of the more mundane ones have already been mentioned (food, clothing, language, etc.), but what these lack in explicitness they make up for in sheer ubiquitous and repetitiveness. There are much more obvious nationalizing rituals and components of the symbolic machinery of the Japanese nation-state, such as the "unofficial" national anthem (Kimigayo) and flag (Hinomaru), which the Ministry of Education has "advised" schools to use in school functions in recent years.[24]

Space is pressed into ideological service in Japan's national cosmology. Japan itself is often described as special because of its natural beauty (and the only place with four seasons). The most obvious and controversial examples of sacralizing space is Yasukuni Shrine, where the spirits of Japan's war dead and heroes are "worshipped." One of the buildings within the Yasukuni Shrine is the Yūshūkan, which may be described as essentially "a museum of the Pacific War" (Crump 1989: 194). Certain government officials have attempted to rehabilitate Yasukuni Shrine. This started in 1975, when Prime Minister Miki Takeo paid a private visit on 15 August, the day on which Japan commemorates the war's end. Two other prime ministers, Fukuda Takeo and Suzuki Zenko, did the same. But it was Prime Minister Nakasone Yasuhiro, accompanied by 200 LDP members and most of his cabinet, who sacralized Yasukuni Shrine by offering flowers paid for with government funds.

Time is also pressed into political service. Years are designated by *gengō*, or era names (though already in actual use, *gengō* was made law in 1979), and in 1966, 11 February was designated an official holiday, National Founding Day (*Kenkoku kinenbi*), in spite of controversy because it is on the same day as the prewar Empire Day (*Kigensetsu*). In the next section I examine the emperor, the most important symbol of Japanese nationalism.

THE EMPEROR: THE SYMBOLISM OF SYMBOLISM

Article 1 of the Japanese constitution refers to the emperor as the "symbol" (*shōchō*) of the state . This is usually interpreted to mean that he is not a living god, mystically bound up with Japan's sacred destiny. Rather, the emperor merely "represents" Japan. The emperor's acts may be divided into three types: (1) private acts; (2) acts in matters of state; and (3) public acts which are not acts in matters of state, but whose constitutionality is unclear. The term "symbol," of course, also has an anthropological definition, and the emperor, regardless of the often-heard statement that the majority of today's Japanese do not take the imperial family seriously, fulfills a key function, if not in explicitly sup-porting, then at least in defining, Japaneseness. The very act itself of referring to the emperor as a "symbol" (here meaning representation) is a type of symbolism (in the anthropological sense), since regarding the emperor as a mere sign guards against a deeper appreciation of just how powerful the political significance of the emperor may actually be (or become).[25]

The emperor defines Japaneseness by being positioned at the apex of the hierarchy of "being Japanese" and in the ultimate *uchi* ("inside"; see Chapter 3) of Japan (*cf.* Crump 1989: 36–54, 94). The emperor actually performs a dual symbolic function. He is more than just the symbol of Japan the state. He is also the symbol of an ethnic group, the Japanese people. In one person, two separate entities are merged, state and nation.[26] This dual operation, no small ideological feat, sacralizes the state while making "being Japanese" natural and essential. Japan's "unique" culture, "homogeneous race," and other myths are all associ-ated with and sanctioned at some level of subjectivity by the emperor.

Traditionally, the emperor has been "more of a pope than a king. The office he held conferred upon him certain powers, which were religious more than political" (*ibid.*: 2). Historically, the emperor has been used for different political purposes. Indeed, in prewar times, he was called a "tool" (*dōgu*) (*ibid.*: 88–9). Titus (1974) notes how the emperor was used to "privatize" rather than "socialize" conflict in the prewar period. Emperors are used to represent entire periods. The Meiji Emperor (1889–1912) and the postwar reign of the Shōwa Emperor (who died in 1989) were similar: "In both cases, the emperor was allowed to take credit for a period of enormously successful expansion, when in fact he had done very little to bring it about" (*ibid.*: 189).

A symbolic thicket surrounds the emperor and imperial family. When discussing the imperial family, the media uses special words reserved just for that purpose; the imperial family is not accessible to the general public;[27] and the likeness of an emperor, live or dead, "may never be impressed upon a note, coin or stamp" (*ibid.*: 8–9). After the Shōwa Emperor died on 7 January 1989, much of Japan went into a state of "self-imposed control" (*jishuku*), here meaning voluntary abstinence from festivity and entertainment. In postwar Japan, right-wing activists have shot, bombed, and generally intimidated those who, in their opinion, have disrespected the imperial family. The Shōwa Emperor has been labeled a war criminal on a par with Hitler and a pacifist that helped to end the war and inspired hope during the reconstruction period. The debates and wildly disparate opinions about the Shōwa Emperor reflect the still unresolved feelings about Japan's role in the Pacific War. He has, along with the entire imperial system, become a lightning rod for powerful ideological forces.

In spite of official declarations about the emperor, his role is ambiguous. He represents a modern secular state, and is public (*soto*), open to the outside world (*omote*). But he is also sacred, and in a sense is ultimately private (*uchi*), charged with the traditional, inner essence (*ura*) of Japan. Lebra notes how for the Shōwa's Emperor's funeral, "a double, sequentially staged ceremony was mandated, the first part being Shinto-loaded and thus 'private,' the latter more secular and public. It was a clumsy but characteristically Japanese solution to the dilemma" (1993: 356–7). However, the succession ceremonies of November 1990 were more problematic, particularly the heavily Shinto *Daijōsai* (the grand rice-offering ceremony). Though the actual accession ceremony was a "state affair" (*kokuji*), the *Daijōsai*, "with its strong religious component, could not be a state event, nor should it be reduced to a totally private one. It was therefore designated a 'public affair of the imperial house' (*kōteki kō-shitsu gyōji*), to be funded from the court treasury." Therefore, "The government's naming of the *daijōsai* as a public affair of the imperial house" is "a barely disguised attempt to link the two 'bodies' of the emperor, public and private" (Lebra 1993: 357). In other words, it was an attempt to sacralize the state as being essentially Japanese.

In Japan's postwar political cosmology, the emperor spatially and temporally occupies a central place. His residence, the Imperial Palace, is in the heart of Tokyo, which is Japan's capital and largest urban area. Besides being ringed by a moat, it is surrounded by markers symbolizing Japan's prefectures. As for time, the emperor's lineage stretches back to Japan's ancient past. Furthermore,

> Order is best acted out through cycles of "fixed" rituals performed
> both inside and outside the palace by the emperor, his surrogates,
> ritualists, and support groups. These rituals dramatize the imperial
> house as a storehouse of ancient tradition, and give the reassuring
> impression that "nothing has changed for two thousand years," as

a palace ritualist put it. The permanence, uniformity, and orderliness highlighted by such rituals may indeed work as a symbolic compensation for the present "reality" of Japan, where the people seem to share an equally exaggerated sense of impermanence, diversity, and chaos.

(*ibid.*: 361)

Many young Japanese say they have no interest in the imperial family. In one sense, this is true. But the public is hungry for news about the imperial family, and one image I have from the Shōwa Emperor's funeral is of a lone junior high school girl in her sailor uniform, frozen in a respectful bow facing the Imperial Palace. We do not have to assume that Japanese are closet fascists or that they really believe that the emperor is a god (as many non-Japanese seem prone to ask) merely because they respect the symbol of their country. Like many icons of the nation-state, the emperor symbolically operates on individual subjectivities in complex ways, tying together a host of symbols about being Japanese.

JAPAN'S STRATEGIC ECONOMY: THE RATIONALITY OF STATE GOALS

Japan's present economic system is often described as "managed capitalism" or "successful communism," or as having achieved a "balance between socialism and capitalism." Whatever the weaknesses or strengths of these descriptions, it is difficult not to see that in Japan, economics is primarily for production, not consumption; market control, not profit; and defensive, not commercial, in aim. Thus, capitalism is "by the government, of the government, and for the government (state)":

It is rather difficult to explain much of Japan's economic conduct without reference to some intention to establish political influence over other nations. Why does Japan limit consumption to a fraction of production? Why does it restrict inflow of scarce and widely desired foodstuffs? Why does it sell products and lend funds abroad at rates less than the market rates at home?

(Huber 1994: 114)

I have already mentioned that since the Meiji period, Japan's elite have set out to develop economic power as a means of national self-defense and pacifying the country. The historical relation between the state and economics is complex, but here it should be pointed out that there has been a government-centered, activist streak to economic thinking in Japan. And importantly, economics has been viewed as a fundamentally moralistic endeavor. Significantly, the word for "economics" in Japanese is *keizai*, which is an abbreviation of the classical term *keikoku saimin* (or *keisei saimin*), meaning "administering the nation and relieving the suffering of the people" (Morris-Suzuki 1989: 13).

With this in the background, it is not surprising that when the Meiji modernizers looked for models of nation building, they were attracted to the Prussian model, and "the profound German mediation on the practical problems of turning the state into a war machine, on how to achieve bureaucratic rationality and efficiency, on the principles of national identity in an era of ethnic conflicts, on the economics of national competition, and on revolution 'from above' to achieve such policy ends" (Williams 1994: 122–3).[28] Friedrich List's (1789–1846) "economic nationalism" (*cf.* his *National System of Political Economy*, 1922 [1844]), the German Historical School, and neomercantilism were to have a profound influence on Japanese economics that would span the Meiji and postwar periods. Even more so than List, Gustav von Schmoller (1838–1917) emphasized the collection of factual economic data rather than the analysis of abstract theories. For him, economics was not a neutral science, but an endeavor with profound ethical implications for a nation's society. The government, rather than playing a morally neutral role, had a definite responsibility toward its citizens that should be expressed in concrete measures. Von Schmoller and his followers established the "Association for Social Policy" (*Verein für Sozialpolitik*) in 1871, which was to act as a model for the Association for the Study of Social Policy (*Shakai seisaku gakkai*). This group, established in 1896, spread the ideas of the German Historical School, greatly influencing Japanese economic thinking at the turn of the century (Morris-Suzuki 1989: 62–4).

In this section, I examine how Japan's "economic nationalism," as a general policy, is transformed into particular practices via state bureaucratization. As already discussed in Chapter 2, "common sense" – whether glossed as everyday reasonableness or "practical" economic activity – is a cultural construction. Its power to persuade people of the intrinsic rationality of a course of action is rooted in politico-economic structures. In this section, I attempt to show how the state (politico-economic interests and goals) equals rationality (socio-economic practices) equals common sense (inherent reasonableness), thereby building legitimacy. Also, the rationalizing tendencies of state machinery result in the merging – or at least the blurring – of state and society, thereby obviating a civil society free from state intervention and tying official ideology to individual intention.

Japan's strategic economy

In order to account for Japan's remarkable economic growth, Huber argues that, like a military organization, Japan's leaders have set strategic goals at the highest levels of state power and then expected the lower levels of economic production to execute the tactical means of accomplishing the strategic goals. Thus, like a military high command (such as America's Pentagon), the officials in the Ministry of International Trade and Industry (MITI), the Ministry of Finance, and the other economic bureaucracies, devise plans, announce their goals, and then expect industries to develop their own tactical plans, "much as subordinate military staffs orient their plans to those of higher headquarters" (Huber 1994: 19). "To succeed, the plans must precisely synchronize the increased availability of every production factor: capital, skilled technicians, raw materials, construction assets, product and process technology, producers' durables, transport for materials and products, and markets for the product" (*ibid.*: 6). There are about 200 "strategic corporations," each of which has from eleven to 200 affiliated companies. In total, then, there are about 10,000 firms that constitute the strategic part of Japan's economy. MITI and other ministries mobilize and orchestrate financing and material allocation for the sectors that are regarded as having strategic value.

Many neoclassical economists bristle at the argument that Japan's economic success can be attributed to state planning. But to give credit to Japan's economic bureaucrats misses the point because, though in some aspects the Japanese economy can be said to be planned, the ministries are very flexible and harness the power of market forces to achieve their strategic ends: "Competition is not in spite of the planning; it is the purpose of the planning" (*ibid.*: 14). Like regular military units, Japan's strategic corporations "compete at engaging the mission [economic growth], not each other" (*ibid.*: 43). It is not a question of whether Japan has a planned or a market economy.[29] What is more significant is the Japanese genius and ability to balance state intervention and market forces. I am not arguing that the state is necessarily the main or most important variable in explaining Japan's economic prowess, but the state's role must certainly be factored into any serious account of Japanese economic strength. Like "democracy" and other ideologies, Japan's elites have deployed and "planned" capitalism and

"governed" the market (*cf.* Wade 1991) for their own strategic purposes.[30] Johnson points out that even the transition from a producer-
oriented, high-growth economy to a consumer-oriented economy
and headquarters for all of East Asia appears to have been planned
(1995: 8).

Huber notes that what makes Japan's strategic economic planning on
such a massive scale possible is the same organizational device that
makes the coordinated movement of modern armies possible: "mediating levels of strategic coordination" (in modern armies, usually at the
divisional level). Connecting the grand goals of the high command with
the specific operations of tactical units has been a perennial military
problem, but once it had been recognized that an intermediate level,
standing between strategy and tactics, could execute orders that (while
general in scope, were not too specific to be inappropriate for local
circumstances) a type of organizational freedom was devised that
afforded flexibility, granting the lowest ranks relatively unrestricted
operational effectiveness.

Thus, three main levels in Japan's politico-economic system are evident. The first has already been mentioned (the goal-setting organs,
such as MITI's Bureau of Industrial Policy and other key organizational units empowered to formulate grand strategy). This is the level of
overall planning, where grand strategies are contemplated and outlined.
The next level, whose role has not been adequately appreciated, consists
of "mediating levels of implementation," such as the less powerful ministerial bureaux and their divisions, which carry out more concrete policies. The second level is vitally important to the realization of the
planners' grand designs, since it communicates and connects their strategy to the lower-level subordinates who execute the concrete practices
and activities required for success. This level, in military fashion,
receives "strategic instructions" (or as discussed in Chapter 4, "administrative guidance") from the ministries. Included at this level are the
critically important *keiretsu*, the "industrial groups" or "developmental
conglomerates" that connect companies vertically and horizontally.[31]
Keiretsu are the institutional reincarnations of the prewar *zaibatsu*,
which were companies connected by cross-shareholdings, loyalties, and
informal but regular meetings of senior executives (Huber refers to the
postwar *keiretsu*, apparently to emphasize continuity with prewar times,
as *neo-zaibatsu*).[32] Also included in this intermediate level are the several important industrial associations (the most important being the
Federation of Economic Organizations, *Keidanren*) that can shape strategic planning themselves and set the tone for their member companies.
Other important mediating-level organizations are cartels, which are

analogous to military task forces and are charged with specific economic goals. The third level is the individual companies and businesses that constitute the economic fabric and perform the tactical, practical activities that drive Japan's economic system and employs its workers. This level may be described as tactical, where the specifics of strategy are accomplished.

In addition to the 10,000 or so strategic corporations, there are another 1.7 million corporations and eleven million small businesses, which are not are considered vital to Japan's economic might. These companies, less prestigious and more vulnerable to economic downturns, receive less bureaucratic attention, resulting in a "dual economy" of vital, strategic corporations and non-strategic companies. However, whether regarded as strategic or not, these smaller companies must still dance to the rationalized tune composed by the central economic bureaucrats.

What does society look like if the economic landscape is shaped by strategic state interests? If the government, through administrative guidance and other forms of intervention, becomes so closely tied to private economic activity, is there any room left for a collective neutral space that is not under state auspices? There are many things that could be said here, but it is worth quoting Huber: "The strategic corporation viewed functionally is not exactly what we think of as a private enterprise. It may be more useful to think of it as a sophisticated, modern public institution" (1994: 87). In fact, Japanese officials appear "to view strategic corporations as actually being agencies of the public interest, not of the private interest, and thus regard cooperation among them for approved goals as very much representing the public interest" (*ibid.*: 40). Perhaps the word "public" might be replaced with "state," or at least "para-state." Scholars who argue about whether the Japanese state is strong or weak *vis-à-vis* the private sector miss an important point: as far as officialdom is concerned, the relation between the state and corporations is not a zero-sum game. A vigorous private sector does not necessarily mean a weak state, since the latter wants robust business organizations for reasons of economic nationalism. In other words, Japan's state elites do not necessarily make a sharp distinction between political structures and economic activities, since both can contribute to a strong Japan in their own way.

How do workers and their concerns fit into Japan's strategic economy?

> Labor relations in the strategic corporation are vestigial and stylized. They are like a morality play where the players know their

parts – the community also knows the players' parts – and the happy ending is known in advance to everyone. The scenario is that each March, company management offers a modest pay increase; union leaders reject this proposal as inadequate and schedule a strike of one or two days duration, always timed to coincide with good April weather. Management, faced with this overwhelming gesture, offers a little more, which the union leaders now accept, followed by general self-congratulation all around. This same pattern of conduct, the same gestures with the same results, has been almost universal among strategic corporations since the first "spring struggle" was organized by the Sohyo federation of unions in 1955.

(*ibid.*: 81)

In short, "Strategic unions reduce the costs of labor conflict in large part by formalizing it, that is ritualizing it" (*ibid.*: 80).

Related to the question of labor is "corporatism," in which giant interest groups in business, agriculture, labor, and other sectors speak for all the groups in one sector and are officially recognized. This term is often used by the Japanese themselves to describe socio-economic relations in Japan. Unlike pluralism, in which many interest groups seek benefits with the central government playing the role of referee, corporatism reaches policy through agreement made between several giant, inclusion-oriented groups. But an argument can be made that corporatism, whatever its advantages, results from an increase in rationalization encouraged by the central government and economic elites. If groups can be dealt with in the aggregate, all their members may become easier to control, if not directly by the state, then as least by the groups' leaders. If pluralism describes a situation in which various organized interests all compete freely in an officially endorsed arena, a public market place of ideas, then perhaps it can be said that corporatism encourages co-optation into larger and larger structures that move closer to officialdom, thereby precluding the need for a strong civil society detached from state authority (*cf.* Abe *et al.* 1994: 50–1).

I conclude this section by suggesting that Huber's argument for a three-tiered structure of Japan's economic bureaucracies and system actually applies to other state agencies and social organizations in Japan. Strategic, intermediate, and tactical institutions construct kinship units (nuclear family), gender definitions, generational distinctions, and forms of knowledge, tying together various social, economic, and political systems into a tightly woven web of rationality.[33] It is the existence of the intermediate institutions that seems to leave little room for a citizen-initiated public sphere. In the next chapter, I analyse the Ministry of Education by focusing on its goal-setting, mediating, and tactical institutions, demonstrating how general strategic goals are transmuted into particular rationalized practices at the local level and within individual subjectivities.

6 Japan's Ministry of Education

Rationalized schooling and the state

INTRODUCTION: JAPAN'S STRATEGIC SCHOOLING

In *MITI and the Japanese Miracle*, Johnson highlights Japan's political economic philosophy by comparing it with the American model of *regulatory orientation*, in which the state's laissez-faire approach to the market is ideally impartial and concerned with procedural matters. The Japanese model of *developmental orientation*, however, views the state as more involved in the market, concerning itself with plans, goals, and specific outcomes (1982: 18–19). "Industrial policy" and "administrative guidance" (*gyōsei shidō*) are the conceptual footmen of what has come to be known as the capitalist developmental state, a view that dovetails with the "strategic economy." Huber (1994) sees the state, in league with elite economic interests, integrating, building hierarchies, and in general ordering the relations between different government organs and commercial enterprises (discussed in Chapter 5). These rationalizing tendencies are visible in other state–society relations, such as Japan's educational bureaucracy, the ideological instilling institution that is charged with reproducing the beliefs necessary to run Japan's economy. In the pedagogic sphere, the counterpart of the developmental orientation may be called an *education of cultivation*. This is an academics of inducement, designed to motivate and exhort students to learn. The teacher's role is to bring about learning by supplying knowledge. Because the state's role is activist, it assumes that it has a stake in the "what" of learning. In other words, the state is granted the right and responsibility to furnish the necessary knowledge, morals, and civility for a modern, highly rationalized, and industrialized nation-state.[1] Of course, it can be argued that all sociopolities have an education of cultivation, but it is a matter of degree; i.e. relatively speaking, in Japan, the "what" takes precedence over the "how" of learning, so that there is an emphasis on training over teaching, socializing over studying.

In this chapter I analyze the organization of the Ministry of Education, and how its structure, educating, training, and socializing mission reflects the rationalizing operations of Japan's politico-economic elite.[2] I do this by viewing the Ministry of Education (Monbushō) as forming the apex of a nationwide organization with three levels corresponding to Huber's analysis of the economic bureaucracies (as described in Chapter 5). This chapter is divided into three main parts, corresponding to the three levels, and the problem that it addresses is how the nation-state connects its goals with the school life of the individual student. Stated differently, how do the ambitions, philosophy, opinions, and ideological leanings of a powerful elite influence, indeed, construct, knowledge and individual subjectivities among millions? This is certainly not a novel question, and any attempt at an answer can only be partial, but in this chapter I want to at least delineate the major structures involved.

The first, or strategic, level, is composed of the Monbushō's Secretariat and advisory councils, especially the Central Council of Education.[3] The policies of these organs are, in the most general terms, shaped by economic nationalism, but more specifically, particular business interests and ideological pressures emanating from the Diet. The second level, or the mediating levels of implementation, are composed of ministerial bureaux, their divisions, prefectural and municipal boards of education, special corporations, and authorized juridical persons. This level receives "guidance, advice, and assistance" from the Monbushō. These three terms appear in official publications about the Monbushō so constantly that they form a sort of bureaucratic litany and are the most commonly encountered terms. What is notable about the way these words are used is that they inevitably describe administrative processes moving top-down, never from the bottom up (from the "people"). The strategic instructions passing through the second level are then transmitted to the third, or tactical, level, which is composed of the thousands of schools, education personnel administered, students, and other sites monitored by the Monbushō (Figure 6.1).

Before proceeding, a few words about the meaning of "strategic," which is usually used to mean the overall planning and conduct of large-scale military operations. This is not how I employ the word here. Rather, I mean a plan of action, decided and designed by an elite with definite goals in mind that determines more task-specific tactics.[4] Any organization, of course, is "strategic" to some degree, but some are better organized and more strategic than others. My justification for calling Japan's educational bureaucracy "strategic" is its highly structured, goal-oriented nature. These aspects of Japan's educational

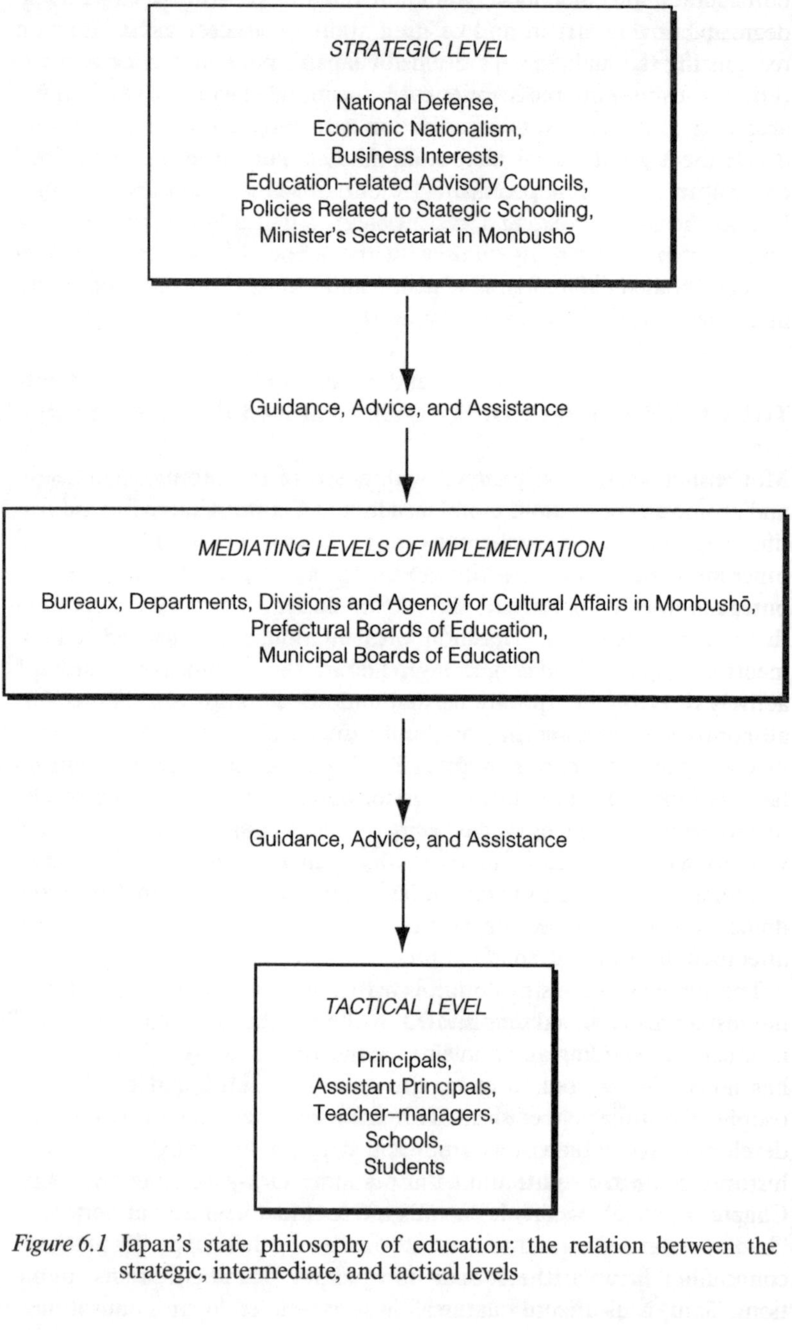

```
┌─────────────────────────────────────┐
│            STRATEGIC LEVEL            │
│                                       │
│            National Defense,          │
│          Economic Nationalism,        │
│            Business Interests,        │
│    Education–related Advisory Councils,│
│   Policies Related to Stategic Schooling,│
│     Minister's Secretariat in Monbushō │
└─────────────────────────────────────┘

          Guidance, Advice, and Assistance

┌─────────────────────────────────────────────────┐
│        MEDIATING LEVELS OF IMPLEMENTATION         │
│                                                   │
│ Bureaux, Departments, Divisions and Agency for Cultural Affairs in Monbushō,│
│            Prefectural Boards of Education,        │
│             Municipal Boards of Education          │
└─────────────────────────────────────────────────┘

          Guidance, Advice, and Assistance

┌─────────────────────────────┐
│        TACTICAL LEVEL         │
│                               │
│          Principals,          │
│     Assistant Principals,     │
│      Teacher–managers,        │
│           Schools,            │
│           Students            │
└─────────────────────────────┘
```

Figure 6.1 Japan's state philosophy of education: the relation between the strategic, intermediate, and tactical levels

bureaucracy are, of course, found in other nation-states to varying degrees, but this fact in and of itself should not steer us away from recognizing the Monbushō's decidedly strategic nature. To claim that other educational bureaucracies everywhere display centralizing, hierarchizing, and classifying processes is to run the risk of ignoring to *what degree* the Monbushō has institutionalized its operations of command, control, and communication, and what this means for Japanese society.[5] Education, with the strong approval of the political elite intent on economic defense, has became interwoven with business demands, so that the development of human resources has come to shape an "education investment theory" (*kyōiku tōshi-ron*).

THE STATE'S PHILOSOPHY OF EDUCATION

Monbushō officials are charged with the task of guiding, managing, and promoting education, moral development, cultural activities, scientific progress, and even religious matters. Their mission, like those of other ministries of Japan, is activist and goal-oriented. Attention to the bureaucratese of Monbushō officials furnishes a sense of how they view their calling. The most common word encountered in official documents is "guidance" (*shidō*), though it often denotes more of a sense of actively directing or strongly persuading others.[6] This word is used by all ministries (discussed in Chapter 4, "administrative guidance") and its use suggests a blurring of the lines between society and state. Other favorite words of the Monbushō (and other ministries) are *shinkō suru*, to promote, encourage; *suishin suru*, to drive forward, promote; *kanri suru*, to manage, control; *kantoku suru*, to direct; *sōgō*, comprehensive, integrated; *tōitsu suru*, to standardize, make uniform; and *ichigenteki*, unified, centralized. The constant use of these terms suggests the state's attempt at heavy involvement in society.

The Japanese state's profound involvement in educational affairs is not just an institutional remnant from Japan's nationalistic and militaristic period. The bureaucratic elite's concern for "guiding" education has much deeper roots and is part of a fundamental political philosophy about the role of the state in individual intellectual and moral development that is visible from the beginning of modern Japan's history as a nation-state until the present. As already mentioned in Chapter 2, efforts to divide Japan's modern history into "abnormal," "bad" prewar Japan and "normal," "good" postwar Japan ignore the continuities between the prewar and postwar ideologies and institutions. Thus, while describing the Monbushō's internal structures, I will also point out the educational bureaucracy's institutional incarnations since the Meiji period in order to demonstrate the institutional memory, organizational weight, and ideological lineage that have shaped the present Monbushō. Pointing out these continuities affords a sense of the state-centered philosophy of education and the Monbushō's historical development.[7] Below I outline this state-centered philosophy.

1   In order to achieve its goals and maintain national defense via economic power, the state regards a well-educated, socialized, and trained citizenry as indispensable. For this reason, education is subservient to national defense. Indeed, until 1932, Japan's education budget was larger than its military budget (Stephens 1991: 79). Postwar education has had two intimately linked aims, nationalism ("Japaneseness") and utilitarianism (rationalism) (Kobayashi 1978: 163), and has continued the prewar tradition of "catch-up education."

2   Thus, the state has the prerogative to set standards, control curriculum, and oversee the administration of educational matters. Furthermore, the state's interest in education, being basically a mobilization of minds, is comprehensive and elastic, and subsumes morality, health, physical education, religion, culture, and other matters regarded as ideological. Consider the extent of the Monbushō's pre-1945 institutional attempts at monitoring, controlling, and coordinating ideology, educational and non-educational. The Student Affairs Department (*Gakusei-bu*) was established in July 1930, and five years later, was upgraded and called the Ideological Control Bureau (*Shisō-kyoku*). This bureau, which supervised student "guidance" and investigated teachers, schools, and social education groups, became the Nationalism Instruction Bureau (literally, Educational Affairs Bureau: *Kyōgaku-kyoku*) in July 1937, and was organizationally external to the Monbushō. This bureau focused on preserving the "national essence" (*kokutai*), and in order to accomplish these goals, dispatched "nationalism instructors" (*kyōgaku-kan*) and "deputy nationalism instructors," who organized "nationalism research groups" and other activities throughout the country. In November 1942, the Nationalism Instruction Bureau, working closely with the Special Police and bureaux, published and distributed various propaganda materials,[8] absorbed the Indoctrination Bureau (*Kyōka-kyoku*) and was given control over social education and religious affairs. The Monbushō, in order to cooperate with these directives, used neighborhood associations to organize and inform citizens. The infamous Minis-

try of Home Affairs (*Naimushō*) controlled local education offices, and to some degree, the Monbushō itself. On 11 July 1945, the General Affairs and Physical Education Bureaux were combined to form the Student Mobilization Bureau (*Gakuto dōin-kyoku*).[9]

3 Whether by prewar "imperial decree" or postwar "democratic processes," the state has ensured that some type of legitimacy has accompanied the development of its educational structures. The state, in order to legitimate its educational plans, practices, and procedures, has sanctioned its policies using imperial orders (*chokurei*), cabinet orders (*seirei*), notifications (*futatsu, tsūchi*), regulations (*rei*), instructions (*kunrei*), announcements (*kokuji*), tentative plans (*shian*), and laws (*hōritsu*) enacted by the Diet. Advisory councils – which were also legitimizing devices in prewar times – are also used to furnish the semblance of popular involvement and input. Once officially sanctioned, the state standardizes and codifies its educational policies and regulations in detailed legal form.

4 The educational experience has two primary focuses. First, it provides knowledge that meets the demands of economic rationalization (i.e. mathematics, natural sciences, and Japanese for reading and writing). Other subjects, such as history, foreign languages, and social studies, are of secondary importance. Second, the educational experience instills the proper social values and attitudes necessary for an obedient, gendered, and relatively apolitical workforce. Socializing students to believe in Japan's cultural uniqueness, exceptionalism, or subtle racialist theories is often an effective way to explain, excuse, and legitimate any distressing sociopolitical conditions, thereby diverting critical attention away from the political decisions that produce these conditions.

5 Practical and scientific knowledge is to be gathered from abroad. This can be done in two ways: by sending students to other countries, or by inviting foreigners to teach in Japan.

I: STRATEGIC LEVEL

With Japan's state-centered educational philosophy in the background, the institutional arrangements of this philosophy can be delineated more specifically. The LDP, since it was formed in 1955, has played a significant role in shaping educational policy. Its "education clique" (*bunkyō zoku*), the unofficial group of LDP Diet members interested in educational policy, has pushed a nationalist agenda, arguing that some Occupation educational reforms need to be undone because they hinder the acquisition of "Japaneseness" by students. These same Diet politicians have also ensured that economic interests have shaped educational policy. More official than the "education clique" are the LDP's two education committees: the Education System Research Council (*Bunkyō seido chōsakai*), dominated by more senior education experts (including former Monbushō ministers), has examined education-related issues from a long-range perspective since 1955; and the Education Division (*Bunkyō bukai*), has dealt with all legislation originating in the Monbushō and going to the Diet Education Committee. The fact that educational policy emanates from within the Monbushō (bureaucracy) indicates its powerful role *vis-à-vis* the Diet (legislature).

The role of leading business organizations has been critical in ensuring that educational policy follows economic interests (*cf.* Kakinuma 1992). The most prominent examples are the Federation of Economic Organizations (Keidanren), the Japanese Federation of Employers' Associations (Nikkeiren), the Japanese Committee for Economic Development (Keizai Dōyūkai), and the Japan Chamber of Commerce and Industry (Nisshō). Members of these prestigious organizations sit on educational advisory councils (discussed below), as do other individuals from other sectors of the *zaikai* (financial world).[10]

As discussed in Chapter 4, advisory councils are attached to ministries and are often used by elites to add legitimacy to official policies. In the case of the Monbushō, the Central Council on Education (*Chūō kyōiku shingikai* or *Chūkyōshin*), a permanent advisory council established by law in 1952 to advise the minister of education, is the most important. Other important councils include Lifelong Learning, University (both established by law), Curriculum, and Education Personnel Training (the latter two were set up by ministerial and cabinet ordinances). The other seven Monbushō councils are: (1) Science Education and Vocational Education; (2) Textbook Authorization and Research; (3) Science; (4) Geodesy; (5) Health and Physical Education; (6) Selection of Persons of Cultural Merits; and (7) University Chartering and School Juridical Person. There are also four councils under the Agency for Cultural Affairs, an external organ of the Monbushō: (1) Japanese Language; (2) Copyright; (3) Religious Juridical Persons; and (4) Protection of Cultural Properties.

There are other organizations that influence grand policy making, such as various associations that have official recognition. Many of these groups fall into the conservative camp. Unlike these "incorporated interests," which are closer to the policy-forming center, opposition groups are excluded from policy making, the most famous case being the Japan Teachers Union (*Nihon kyōshokuin kumiai*; or *Nikkyōso*). In fact, as Schoppa points out, some groups "work closely with the government to a degree which makes them almost a part of the formal governmental structure" (1991: 120–1). This is an example of the bureaucratic blurring of state/society distinctions.

The organization of the Monbushō

The Monbushō was originally the Department of Education, founded on 2 September 1871. It was one of the government departments headed by a secretary (*kyō*), who served on the Grand Council, which had been established three years earlier. In order to get a sense of institutional continuity, it is useful to look at the Monbushō's earliest organization. The department was built upon units of what was then called the Eastern College of the University and Southern College of the University. These schools were abolished on 28 September 1871, and parts of them were absorbed into the new department. Also absorbed into the Department of Education were the Archives Division (*Kiroku-ka*) and Applications Division (*Uketsu-ka*). Together, these latter two divisions became part of a new government organization comprised of Teachers (*Kyōshi-ka*), Accounting (*Kaikei-ka*), Personnel (*Shokuin-ka*), and Publications Divisions (*Shoseki-ka*). On 22 December 1885, the Grand Council was replaced by the cabinet system, and departments became ministries, and secretaries became ministers, so that the latter became cabinet members and participated in planning the affairs of state in addition to their administrative work. Thus, the secretary of education (*monbu-kyō*) became the minister of education (*monbu daijin*). On 26 February 1886, the Ministries Organization Order (*Kukushō kansei*), which included the Ministry of Education Organization Order (*Monbushō kansei*), was put into effect.

Like other ministries, the present-day Monbushō consists of a central organization (*honshō*) and numerous advisory councils (*shingikai*; discussed above), which research and deliberate on specific matters under the ministry's purview. The Monbushō has one external agency (*gaikyoku*), the Agency for Cultural Affairs (*Bunkachō*; discussed below). Principal subdivisions within the Monbushō include a secretariat and six bureaux (headed by *kyokuchō*), two of which have departments (headed by a *buchō*). Bureaux and departments are subdivided into divisions (headed by *kachō*), and these are further divided into offices (headed by *kakarichō* or *shitsuchō*). In 1994, the Monbushō had 137,765 employees (most personnel are teachers), making it the second largest of the twelve main ministries (*shō*) in terms of personnel.

The highest positions in the Monbushō are the politically appointed minister of education and the Monbushō parliamentary vice-minister (*monbu seimu jikan*). Next in line is the Monbushō permanent vice-minister (*monbu jimu jikan*), who is a career civil servant and occupies the top post in terms of actual power. Assisting the minister is the Monbushō secretary to the minister (*monbu daijin hishokan*).

Minister's Secretariat

The Minister's Secretariat (*Daijin kanbō*) employs 555 personnel and is headed by a director-general (*kanbōchō*) under whom is the director-general (or councilor) for policy coordination (*sōmu shingikan*). Under the latter are seven deputy directors-general (*shingikan*) and planning directors. The secretariat has six divisions: the Personnel Division (*Jinji-ka*); the General Affairs Division (*Sōmu-ka*), which contains the Legal Affairs Office, Parliamentary Relations Office, Administrative Management Office, and Press and Information Office; the Budget and Accounts Division (*Kaikei-ka*); the Policy Planning and Coordination Division (*Seisaku-ka*), which contains the Computing and Information Office; the Research and Statistics Planning Division (*Chōsa tōkei kikaku-ka*); and the Education Personnel Benefits Division (*Fukuri-ka*).

The secretariat was established in December 1885. In June 1890, the Editing Bureau was absorbed into the secretariat, as were the General Affairs and Accounting Bureaux in July 1891. In April 1959, the director for the Minister's Secretariat was established. In May 1966, the Research Bureau (which was not a part of the secretariat) was eliminated, and its functions – research, statistics, and planning services – were concentrated in the secretariat, making it stronger.

Under the secretariat's control is the Department of Facilities Planning and Administration (*Bunkyō shisetsu-bu*), which is comprised of 158 personnel and is headed by a director-general (*buchō*) and a deputy director-general (*gijutsu sanjikan*). Three divisions make up this department: the Facilities Planning Division (*Shidō-ka*), which contains the Office of Contract and Supervision; the National Facilities Division (*Keikaku-ka*), which contains the Facilities Planning Office; and the Technical Affairs Division (*Gijutsu-ka*). This department also contains the Regional Facilities Administration Offices.

The Department of Facilities Planning and Administration is rooted in the Educational Facilities Bureau (*Kyōiku shisetsu-kyoku*), which was set up in June 1947. In May 1949, the Management Bureau (*Kanri-kyoku*), which contained the Educational Facilities Department (*Kyōiku shisetsu-bu*), was established. In June 1984, the Management

Bureau became the Department of Facilities Planning and Administration within the secretariat (some elements of the Management Bureau were placed within the Local Education Support Bureau and the Higher Education Bureau's Department of Private Education Institution).

II: THE INTERMEDIATE INSTITUTIONS

The mediating levels of implementation are what make the fairly uniform and nationwide educating, socializing, and training of students possible. The main function of these intermediate institutions is to transmit strategic instructions to the lower tactical units. In the following sections, I examine the internal organization of the Monbushō, paying particular attention to the Lifelong Learning Bureau and the Elementary and Secondary Education Bureau (which form the two main institutional axes on which Japan's educational bureaucracy turns), the Agency for Cultural Affairs (which manages a state-defined notion of "culture" and Japaneseness), the boards of education (which are vital for linking strategic with tactical levels), and special corporations concerned with education.[11]

LIFELONG LEARNING BUREAU

The Lifelong Learning Bureau (*Shōgai gakushū-kyoku*) is headed by a director-general (*kyokuchō*) and a social education supervisor. It employs seventy-five personnel and has five divisions: the Lifelong Learning Promotion Division (*Shōgai gakushū shinkōka*) which includes the Offices of Special Training College Education Promotion and Educational Businesses; the Social Education Division (*Shakai kyōikuka*); the Education Media and Learning Resources Division (*Gakushū jōhōka*); the Youth Education Division (*Seishōnen kyōikuka*); and the Women's Education Division (*Fujin kyōiku-ka*).[12] Also pertinent to social education is the advisory Lifelong Council and numerous non-governmental organizations that fall under the Monbushō's jurisdiction.

Broadly defined, "lifelong learning" means formal schooling as well as non-formal education, higher education, professional/vocational training, cultural activities, hobbies, volunteer activities, and sports. Associated with lifelong learning but with a narrower definition is "social education" (*shakai kyōiku*). This concept is somewhat vague in usage, but it basically designates non-formal education, with the added meanings of "completion of character" and "learning for enjoyment." Thus, in addition to the formal educational structure of schools, teachers, and education boards, the Monbushō oversees an extensive system of non-formal educational facilities and activities that are designed to build a "lifelong learning society."

An understanding of how the authorities view lifelong learning is apparent in what the National Council on Educational Reform (an *ad hoc* committee, 1984–7) had to say about why lifelong learning is necessary: (1) to overcome the "diploma-oriented society" (*gakureki shakai*); (2) to provide learning opportunities to respond to the growing demand for leisure-oriented learning activities; and (3) to continue learning to cope with social, economic, and technological changes. In June 1990, the Diet passed the Lifelong Learning Promotion Law concerning the Development of the Systems to Facilitate the Measures for the Promotion of Lifelong Learning, stipulating (1) the duties and roles of prefectural education authorities in the promotion of lifelong learning; (2) the establishment of national and local lifelong learning councils; and (3) special districts for the promotion of lifelong learning with preferential taxation for the private suppliers designated by the prefectural authorities and approved by the national authorities.[13]

Why is the Monbushō interested in social education? Fearful of losing its *raison d'être* due to a declining student population, the Monbushō is utilizing and creating various lifelong learning programs as a means of extending its bureaucratic operations (*cf.* Fujioka 1994a: 69; 1995). Some criticize the Monbushō for using lifelong learning to make profits through the "education, culture, and sports industry" and to unify the ideology of the citizens (e.g. traditional gender roles, "Japaneseness," good workers) (Higashi 1992: 260). Facilities and activities connected to lifelong learning appear to be state attempts to supplement the functions of formal schooling and provide numerous venues in which additional knowledge building transpires. Auxiliary sites of state education/socialization are notable because they are attempts to support traditional gender and generational norms and augment worker training.

Table 6.1 provides a breakdown of the various types of facilities used for social education. What is notable is the heavy involvement of the state in what may be called civil society. This has obvious implications for how governmental interests may shape private concerns.

In addition to these, there are about 230,000 sports facilities, many of which are school physical educational facilities. Non-school sports

Table 6.1 Types and numbers of social educational facilities as of 1990 (calculated from MTY: 116–21)

Type of facilities	Total	National	Local government	Private
Audio-visual centers and libraries	950	–	950	–
Citizens' public halls	17,347	–	17,330	17
Culture centers	1,010	–	934	76
Libraries	1,950	–	1,914	36
Museums	799	28	387	384
Youth centers, children's nature centers, cultural centers for children, and others	1,154	13	1,141	–
Women's educational facilities	214	1	87	126

facilities account for 27.4 percent and university/college facilities make up 4.2 percent. The Monbushō also maintains a number of national facilities for social education, such as the National Science Museum, National Olympics Memorial Youth Center, national youth houses, national children's centers, and the National Women's Educational Center.[14]

In order to ensure that the Monbushō's social education policies are carried out effectively, "social education personnel" are placed in the appropriate sites. These include social education officers appointed by local boards of education, officers working at citizens' public halls, librarians, public museum curators, and "leaders for social education organizations," such as PTAs, youth organizations, and women's organizations (Table 6.2). The national government encourages and assists the in-service training of these personnel at the national, regional, and prefectural levels. In 1965, the National Training Institute of Social Education was established for in-service training.

In addition to these, there are another 57,075 personnel, who are vaguely referred to as "social education leaders" (*shakai kyōiku shidō-in*). These include staff related to youth education (23,575 (women, 7,153)); women's education (1,123 (women, 733)); family education (1,551 (women, 478)); social physical education (25,719 (women, 5,407)); and others (5,107 (women, 1,253)).[15]

Social education has antecedents in "popular education" (*tsūzoku kyōiku*) of the Meiji period, which was associated with Western institutions such as libraries and museums. In the 1920s, economic rationalizing and disciplining groups and activities – such as working youth, youth organizations (*seinen-dan*), and additional technical training –

136   *The nature of the Japanese state*

Table 6.2 Types and numbers of social education personnel as of 1990 (calculated from MTY: 114–15)

Social education personnel	Number of personnel (women)
Social education advisory committee members	38,383 (6,745)
Social education officers and assistants	7,156 (n/a)
Social education leaders	6,452 (1,924)
Physical education advisors	51,913 (9,631)
Citizens' public hall directors and officers	25,847 (n/a)
Librarians, assistants and other staff	14,225 (n/a)
Museum curators, assistants and other staff	10,073 (n/a)
Women's education specialists	539 (n/a)
Youth facilities personnel	5,297 (n/a)
Total	159,885 (n/a)

were considered forms of social education. Social education was also used by the central authorities to spread information about scientific advances, industrial knowledge, hygiene, and civic education, and to inculcate an appreciation of labor. And as Higashi (1992) points out, many social education programs were directly tied to the ideological excesses of Japan's totalitarian past and used for "moral" training. By the late 1920s and early 1930s, social education leaders (*shuji*), assistant social education leaders (*shuji hosa*), and youth education officers (*shōnen kyōiku-kan*), were put in prefectural administrations, and the authorities encouraged municipal governments to set up boards of social education. In 1924, a division for social education was established in the General Education Bureau, and in July 1930, the Social Education Bureau (*Shakai kyōiku-kyoku*) was established from elements of the former bureau, and contained Youth Education (*Shōnen kyōiku-ka*), Adult Education (*Seijin kyōiku-ka*), and Movie Divisions (*Eiga-ka*). During the war, elements of the Religious Affairs Bureau were transferred to the Social Education Bureau, and after the war, elements from the Physical Education Bureau were moved to the Social Education Bureau. In 1949, the Social Education Law was enacted and, significantly, an amendment to this law in 1959 permitted national and local governments to grant subsidies to voluntary organizations.[16] Previously, such money had been prohibited in order to avoid government control over voluntary organizations. In July 1988, the Lifelong Learning Bureau was established out of elements of the former Social Education Bureau.

JAPANESE FORMAL EDUCATION: AN "ABILITY-TESTING DEVICE"

Elementary and Secondary Education Bureau

The Elementary and Secondary Education Bureau (*Shotō chūtō kyōiku-kyoku*), with 206 employees, is the second largest bureau in terms of personnel. It is headed by a director-general (*kyokuchō*), school inspectors, a planning director, and senior textbooks specialists. This bureau forms the heart of Japan's basic educational system, monitors the content and standards of each educational level, and authorizes and distributes educational materials. This bureau's seven divisions are the High School Division (*Kōtō gakkō-ka*), which contains the Office of Upper Secondary Education Reform; the Middle School Division (*Chū gakkō-ka*), which contains the Office of Information Technology in Education; the Primary School Division (*Shō gakkō-ka*); the Kindergarten Division (*Yōchien-ka*); the Vocational Education Division (*Shokugyō kyōiku-ka*); the Special Education Division (*Tokushu kyōiku-ka*);[17] and the Textbooks Division (*Kyōkasho-ka*).

It is worth tracing the institutional lineage of the Textbooks Division, since textbook authorization has been a primary means of bureaucratic control over the contents of education and ideology. The control of textbooks can be traced back to September 1871, when the Publications Division (*Shoseki-ka*) was established (later called the *Shoki-ka*, and in September 1872, the *Junkoku-ka*). In June 1875, this division was transferred to the Ministry of Home Affairs. However, a Books Bureau, formed from elements from within the Monbushō's secretariat, existed intermittently (from October 1897 to November 1898, and from May 1911 to June 1913), and in April 1921, a more permanent Books Bureau (*Tosho-kyoku*) was set up. In the late 1930s, due to tighter ideological controls, the work load of the Books Bureau increased dramatically, as did its personnel (called "textbook authorization officers; *tosho kanshū-kan*). In November 1943, the Textbook Bureau was absorbed into the National Education and Higher Educational Affairs Bureaus. In October 1945, the Textbook Bureau (*Kyōkasho-kyoku*) was re-established but was eventually disbanded before being reborn in its current institutional incarnation as the Textbooks Division and the textbook authorization (*kentei*) system.

Within the Monbushō, the earliest antecedents of elementary and secondary education can be traced back to the Education Affairs Bureau, established in 1886 under the cabinet system. This bureau was divided into the Specialized Education (*Senmon gakumu-kyoku*) and the

General Education Bureaux (*Futsū gakumu-kyoku*) in October 1887. During the war, these latter two bureaux were combined, along with elements from the Vocational Educational Affairs Bureau, to form the School Education Bureau. In 1949 the Elementary and Secondary Education Bureau was established and headed the General Affairs, Elementary School Education, Secondary Education, Vocational Education, and Hygiene Divisions. This bureau, perhaps because it was regarded as the core functional unit of the Monbushō, was given more responsibilities and in 1952 was expanded so that it included the Finance, Local, Textbook, Elementary School Education, Secondary Education, Vocational Education, and Hygiene Divisions, and the Special Education Office.

Schools everywhere examine, screen, select, sort, and shunt students, integrating them into politico-economic structures. But some educational systems perform these rationalizing roles better than others, and on this score, Japan has been notably successful. However, in the words of Dore, education in Japan works "provided one thinks of it as an enormously elaborated, very expensive intelligence testing system with some educational spin-off, rather than the other way round" (1976: 48–9).

Japan's educational system may be pictured as a multi-tiered pyramid. One must pass an examination at each level in order to move toward the pyramid's apex, but as one moves up the pyramid the testing becomes harder and the slots available for successful candidates fewer. The beauty of this system is that those who fail at some level do find a position in the socio-economic hierarchy. After students take examinations at the high school level, they are sorted out into five or six levels of high school. From this level in the pyramid, the best students aim for the best universities. The good ones set their sights on the medium-rank universities, and the less able settle for the junior colleges or the many vocational schools. Companies recruit from the top universities, on down the line, following a gradation. Depending on their test and mock test scores, students are able to predict with surprising accuracy what their chances are of getting into a good university. One's future position in life is decided by examination results in a thoroughly rationalized manner. The pyramid of examinations is highly rationalized, efficient, and successful at producing individuals equipped with certain forms of knowledge. But it is also ruthless in its operation, and though one can make the argument that eventually it furnishes everyone with a spot on the economic ladder, it offers few alternatives and fewer second chances. This is why talk of "holding back" (*ryūnen*) students who cannot keep up with their classmates and "grade skipping" (*tobikyū*) is still considered radical. The official goal of "fairness" and "equality" precludes any tracking according to ability, but this policy, in fact, is an aspect of a very rationalized philosophy of education in which falling behind is blamed on a lack of effort on the student's part, not an inflexible system. Such a hyper-rationalized system of education has created a profitable industry of preparatory schools, cram schools, and guidebook and teaching-aid publishing.[18]

At the apex of the pyramid are the university entrance examinations, described by Rohlen as "the dark engine driving high school culture."[19] Qualification, not knowledge acquisition, becomes the secret to ascending the pyramid of examinations. Thus, the "exam-oriented Japanese students become virtual information junkies, drinking in as many facts as possible" (1983: 316). Many charge that students are "separated into slices" (*wagiri senbetsu*) too early and certain skills and talents overlooked, resulting in a formulaic learning style which trains students to think and respond in clichés. The consequence is "ability-ism" (*nōryoku shugi*). Any subject, learning activity, or school experience that does not contribute to passing tests is devalued (*cf.* Dore 1976: 61). In Japan, mathematics, science, and Japanese language receive great attention, while history, social studies, foreign languages, and the arts receive less.

Japan's educational system is comprised of kindergartens (*yōchien*), primary schools (*shō gakkō*) (six years), middle schools (*chū gakkō*) (three years), high schools (*kōtō gakkō*) (three years), and universities, junior colleges, and graduate schools (Table 6.3).[20] There are several other types of institution whose roles in Japan's educational system are often overlooked by observers outside Japan. These include colleges of technology (*kōtō senmon gakkō*), which unlike universities or junior colleges require only the completion of middle school for admission. They have programs in engineering and mercantile marine studies and last five years, after which a student receives an associate degree. Special training schools (*senshū gakkō*), established in 1976 under the amended School Education Law, offer courses in vocational and technical education, as well as in general education. Actually, many schools that were formerly private "miscellaneous schools" (*kakushu gakkō*) became special training schools after 1976. They offer programs of one year or more, and students may enter after completing either middle or high school, depending on the program. Though special training schools do not offer degrees, students can transfer from a special training school to a university or junior college if they meet certain requirements. Many students, called "double schoolers," enroll in both universities or junior colleges and special training schools (or miscellaneous schools). This phenomenon seems to indicate that universities and junior college

Table 6.3. Important statistics of Japan's formal education (numbers in parentheses indicate correspondence courses (MTY: 2–9))

	Total number of schools	Number of students	National government schools	Local government schools	Private schools
Kindergartens	14,958	1,907,110	49	6,205	8,704
Primary schools	24,676	8,768,881	73	24,432	171
Middle schools	11,292	4,850,137	78	10,578	636
High schools	5,501	5,010,472	17	4,164	1,320
Colleges of technology	62	55,453 (157,003)	54	5 (69)	3 (22)
Junior colleges	595	530,294 (42,341)	37	56	502 (9)
Universities	534	2,389,648 (184,425)	98 (1)	46	390 (12)
Graduate schools (master and doctorate levels)	359	122,360	98	26	235
Special training Schools	3,341	859,173	161	198	3,072
Miscellaneous schools	3,055	366,536	3	75	2,977

education do not satisfy the educational demands of students. Miscellaneous schools (*kakushu gakkō*) have various admission requirements, depending on the school, and programs that last for one year or more, though some have programs that last only three months. Like special training schools, they do not offer degrees. Here it is worth noting junior colleges (*tanki daigaku*). Though usually compared with American community colleges, these schools offer both general and vocational education. They are notable because of their highly gendered nature; in 1994, 91.8 percent of their students were female (see McVeigh 1997a). Also, they are predominantly private; in 1994, 502 out of 595 were private (MTY: 2–3).

In general, the government (both national and local) has seen the need to establish schools at the lower levels, i.e. primary and middle schools, and to a lesser degree, high schools. At the tertiary level, however, government involvement becomes less significant. This is especially true of the highly gendered junior colleges, reflecting an official lack of interest in female postsecondary education. It may be stated that the state has devoted its resources to the educational institutions in which the rationalizing functions of socialization, selection, and safekeeping become salient. As already mentioned, only the practical subjects of the education function – mathematics, Japanese language (for reading), and science – receive close attention. The more advanced forms of knowledge that are usually associated with secondary and postsecondary education receive less attention. As many Japanese are apt to point out, employers do not expect universities to teach students, because they expect to train graduates themselves in company-run programs.

Japanese schooling has as its goal training, grading, and filtering productive workers, not expanding an individual's educational horizons. The outcome is that "The Japanese are producing an average adult citizen who is remarkably well suited to four requirements of modern industrial society: (1) hard, efficient work in organizations; (2) effective information processing; (3) orderly private behavior; (4) stable, devoted child rearing" (Rohlen 1983: 305). However, Rohlen writes that Japan's high school experience (and I would argue the lower levels as well) "provides no intellectual roots, it turns out students long on information and short on intellectual understanding" (*ibid.*: 267).[21]

Local Education Support Bureau

The Local Education Support Bureau (*Kyōiku josei-kyoku*), which has ninety-six employees, is headed by a director-general, school inspectors, and a planning director. It has five divisions: the Financial Affairs Division (*Zaimu-ka*), which includes the Office of Local Financial Management; the Local Affairs Division (*Chihō-ka*); the Teacher Training Division (*Kyōshokuin-ka*); the Overseas Japanese Children Education Division (*Kaigai shijo kyōiku-ka*); and the Local Buildings and Equipment Aid Division (*Shisetsu josei-ka*).

The Local Education Support Bureau was assembled in June 1984, and its organizational antecedents can be traced to the former Management, University, Science and International Affairs Bureau and the Elementary and Secondary Education Bureau.

Higher Education Bureau

The Higher Education Bureau (*Kōtō kyōiku-kyoku*), which employs 138 personnel, is headed by a director-general, three higher education advisors, inspectors, and a planning director. It is composed of five divisions: the Planning Division (*Kikaku-ka*), which includes the University Council Office; the University Division (*Daigaku-ka*), which includes the Offices of Teacher Training University and University Entrance Examinations; the Technical Education Division (*Senmon kyōiku-ka*); the Medical Education Division (*Igaku kyōiku-ka*), which includes the University Hospital Supervision Office; and the Student Affairs Division (*Gakusei-ka*).

Under the Higher Education Bureau is the Private Education Institution Department (*Shigaku-bu*), which employs thirty-five personnel and is headed by a director-general. It has three divisions: the Private Education Institution Administration Division (*Shigaku gyōsei-ka*); the Private Education Institution Management Division (*Shikō hōjin chōsa-ka*), and the Private Education Institution Aid Division (*Shigaku josei-ka*).

The Higher Education Bureau has its origins in the Specialized Education Bureau (*Senmon gakumu-kyoku*), formed when the Education Bureau split into the latter and the General Education Bureau (*Futsū gakumu-kyoku*) in October 1887. For one year (1897–8), the Specialized Education Bureau was called the Higher Education Bureau (*Kōtō gakumu-kyoku*). In 1945, the Specialized Education Bureau split into the School Education Bureau (*Gakkō kyōiku-kyoku*) and the Science Education Bureau (*Kagaku kyōiku-kyoku*). The latter became the University Educational Affairs Bureau in June 1949, absorbing elements of the School Education Bureau. In 1974, the University Educational Affairs Bureau was split into the University and Science and International Affairs Bureaux. Currently, it is called the Higher Education Bureau and contains the Private Education Institution Department. The latter was formed with elements from the former Management Bureau.

Science and International Affairs Bureau

The Science and International Affairs Bureau (*Gakujutsu kokusai-kyoku*) is notable in how it brings together and places under one organ science and international affairs, presumably because science (i.e. technology) has traditionally been associated with things foreign and has come from overseas. This bureau, which employs 131 personnel, is headed by a director-general, twelve science advisors (*kagakukan*), a planning director, and a senior specialist in scientific research. It has seven divisions: the Science Division (*Gakujutsu-ka*), which includes the Science Policy Planning Office; the Research Institutes Division (*Kenkyū kikan-ka*); the Research Aid Division (*Kenkyū josei-ka*), which includes the Offices of Research Cooperation and Grant-in-Aid Planning; the Science Information Division (*Gakujutsu jōhō-ka*); the International Affairs Division (*Kokusai kikaku-ka*), which includes the Offices of Educational and Cultural Exchange and Foreigners'

Education; the International Scientific Affairs Division (*Kokusai gakujutsu-ka*); and the Student Exchange Division (*Ryūgakusei-ka*), which includes the Student Exchange Planning Office.

Between 1868 and 1872, about 500 Japanese students were sent to America. The establishment of the Department of Education in 1871 gave some order to Japan's overseas study efforts, and by 1875 the department was awarding loan scholarships, which continued until the outbreak of the Pacific War. In order to mobilize scientific and technological research for the war effort, the Science Division (*Kagaku-ka*) was formed from elements of the Arts and Sciences Division (*Gakugei-ka*) in the Higher Educational Affairs Bureau in February 1940. Two years later, the Science Division was expanded to become the Science Bureau (*Kagaku-kyoku*), and eventually it was renamed the Science Education Bureau (*Kagaku kyōiku-kyoku*). In March 1942, positions for "science officers" (*kagaku-kan*) were instituted. This bureau coordinated communication between the various research institutes, monitored scientific and technological developments, and acquired and disseminated scientific literature from overseas, as well as administering the operating expenses of scientific research. In February 1943, the creation of a Research Mobilization Division within the Science Education Bureau reflected the extent to which the government viewed the vital importance of science and technology for the war effort. Also, directly under the Monbushō, institutes were set up in the fields of resource sciences (1941), electronic physics (1942), ethnology (1943), and statistics (1944), and many other institutes were established directly related to the war effort. In 1949, the Science Bureau became part of the University and Science Bureau (*Daigaku gakujutsu-kyoku*), and in 1974, this latter bureau was split into the University Bureau and the Science and International Affairs Bureau.

Physical Education and Sports Bureau

The Physical Education and Sports Bureau (*Taiiku-kyoku*), which employs seventy-one personnel, is headed by a director-general and a physical education and sports supervisor. It has four divisions: the Physical Education and Sports Division (*Taiiku-ka*); the Sports-for-All Division (*Shōgai supōtsu-ka*), which includes the Office of Industries and Businesses in Sports; the Competitive Sports Division (*Kyōgi supōtsu-ka*); and the School Health Education Division (*Gakkō kenkō kyōiku-ka*).

The concern for the physical well-being of students can be traced back to the employment of school health technicians (*gakkō eisei gishi*) in the mid-1920s. Starting in 1931, physical education leaders (*taiiku undō shuji*) were employed at the prefectural level. In addition to mobilizing minds for war, the Monbushō also devoted its efforts to mobilizing bodies. Thus, in order to promote student hygiene and physical exercise, the National Physical Strength Law was promulgated in April 1940, and the Physical Education Bureau (*Taiiku-kyoku*) was established in January 1941 from parts of the secretariat. In July 1945, the Physical Education Bureau became part of the Student Mobilization Bureau (*Gakuto dōin-kyoku*) (which was abolished in September 1945). By 1949, this bureau had been absorbed into the Social Education Bureau, but it re-emerged in May 1958, formed from older elements of the Social Education, Management, Elementary, and Elementary and Secondary Education Bureaux.

AGENCY FOR CULTURAL AFFAIRS: BUILDING JAPANESE IDENTITY

The Monbushō has one external organ, the Agency for Cultural Affairs (*Bunkachō*).[22] This organ, which employs 739 personnel, is headed by a commissioner (*chōkan*) and a deputy commissioner (*jikan*), who oversee the commissioner's secretariat, which has two divisions: General Affairs (*Sōmu-ka*), which includes the Cultural Policy Planning Office; and Budgeting and Accounts (*Kaikei-ka*). This agency has two departments.

The Cultural Affairs Department (*Bunka-bu*) is headed by a director-general (*buchō*) and has five divisions: the Cultural Development Division (*Bunka fukyū-ka*), which includes the Regional Culture Office; the Arts Division (*Geijutsu-ka*); Japanese Language Division (*Kokugo-ka*); the Copyright Division (*Chosakuken-ka*), which includes the International Copyright Office; and the Religious Affairs Division (*Shūkyō-ka*).[23]

The other department is the Cultural Properties Protection Department (*Bunkazai hogo-bu*). It is headed by a director-general, a councilor of cultural properties (*bunkazai kansakan*), and a planning director and has four divisions: the Traditional Culture Division (*Dentō bunka-ka*); which includes the Diffusion and Subsidy Office; Monuments and Sites Division (*Kinen butsu-ka*); the Fine Arts Division (*Bijutsu kōgei-ka*); and the Architecture Division (*Kenzōbutsu-ka*).

There are four advisory councils attached to the Agency for Cultural Affairs: Japanese Language; Copyright; Religious Juridical Persons; and Protection of Cultural Properties. Institutions under the jurisdiction of the Agency for Cultural Affairs include the National Language Research Institute; National Museums (three); National Museums of Modern Art (two); the National Museum of Western Art; the National Museum of Art, Osaka; the National Research Institutes of Cultural Properties (two); and the Japan Art Academy.

The management of culture

It is worthwhile examining the Agency for Cultural Affairs (*Bunka-chō*), an external organ of the Monbushō, because it provides a window into the state's view of what it means to be Japanese and how the state attempts to define various spheres of living. This is illustrated in the term *bunka gyōsei*, which literally means the "administration of culture" but more concretely denotes how the central authorities support, manage, and direct activities associated with matters cultural. More fundamentally and perhaps less explicitly, it means how the state defines what is "good" for society. In WBBG, "the role and direction of culture administration" is explained: (1) to make arrangements for the expansion of the cultural base (*bunka kiban*). Culture administration is necessary for and includes the arrangements for a general system and organization to promote culture; the collection of information that is related to culture and its presentation; the fostering of the organization of cultural groups; the arrangement of the material base for cultural facilities; and training artists and talented individuals who are responsible for culture; (2) to encourage and aid artistic activities and in-service training; (3) to expand opportunities so that citizens can enjoy culture and participate in cultural activities; (4) to plan the utilization and preservation of cultural assets. "These cultural assets are indispensable for correctly understanding our nation's culture and history"; and (5) to promote the international exchange of cultures (WBBG: 25–7).

Culture administration is part and parcel of a political philosophy that draws a thin line between public interests and personal belief. Part of this agency's responsibility is to keep track of religious organizations and activities in Japan. A point repeatedly made in WBBG is that a system of collaboration and cooperation (*renkei kyōryoku taisei*) and the coordination of communications (*renraku chōsei*) between national and local governments (prefectural and municipal), boards of education, and private organizations is necessary, and "while respecting the independence of each [private] organization, it is necessary to maintain relations of close cooperation and provide guidance, advice, and assistance" (*ibid.*: 59).

According to the Agency for Cultural Affairs, through returning to tradition, one can "discover peace of mind," "search for the starting point of our national characteristics" (*kokuminsei no genten*), and realize our "national identity " (*kokumin no aidentītī*) (*ibid.*: 21). Culture is important for another reason. "Presently, the lack of effort in cultural exchange has brought about economic friction among the various Europe, American, and Asian countries, and this can be regarded as one cause that has given birth to misunderstanding and distrust toward our country [Japan]" (*ibid.*: 53). Making efforts to teach other countries about Japanese culture can "confirm Japan's position in the international community" (*ibid.*: 53). Using "cultural misunderstandings" as an excuse for international economic problems is a good example of a political use of culture, and has been a common tactic of Japanese trade negotiators and official agencies.

Since the Meiji period, modern Japanese culture has been "formed by interweaving the warp (*tate ito*) of Japanese traditional culture and the woof (*yoko ito*) of European and American culture" (*ibid.*: 17). Though non-Japanese influences are acknowledged, these influences appear to be layerings over a deeper Japaneseness. Thus, Japanese identity is built by contrasting it with what it is not (foreign influences), establishing distinctions which are evident in much of everyday Japanese life. These distinctions follow the basic principle of Japaneseness (old/traditional/past) versus non-Japaneseness (new/modern/present).

The meaning of "culture"

In Japanese, the word "culture" is composed of two Chinese characters; *bun*, which originally meant "pattern" or "figure," and *ka*, which means "to change into." *Bunka* means something or someone that has acquired or been molded into a pattern, similar to what "civilize" has meant in the Western tradition. Rohlen elaborates:

> Writing, texts, and civilization are of a single piece to the Japanese, and the single character for writing and literature (*bun*) expresses this critical relationship. Culture (*bunka*), civilization (*bunmei*), literature (*bungaku*), and learning and the liberal arts (*bungei* and *bundō*) are all linked to together. The Ministry of Education is literally the "ministry of *bun*" [though sharing the same character, *bun* is also pronounced *mon*] Many of Japan's historical heroes were people of culture (*bunkajin*), and the government awards prestigious prizes to contemporary culture heroes in the arts and literature.
>
> (1983: 260)

How the word "culture" itself is used in the official literature deserves comment. Its meaning is extensive and includes learning, knowledge, leisure, learning, sports, and religion. Cultural may be artistic (*geijutsu*), traditional (*dentō*), or spiritual (*seishinteki*). The Agency for Cultural Affairs sees its responsibility as fostering a cultural life (*bunkateki seikatsu*), cultural environment (*bunkateki kangyō*), and cultural identity (*bunkateki shutaisei*). In Japanese society at large, schools, neighborhoods, and other organizations often sponsor "culture festivals" (*bunka-sai*) in the autumn. These events are opportunities to show the creative energies of the group and its solidarity.

Because culture is often associated with science, technology, and utilitarian concerns, it often possesses a positivist ring. Thus, people should, with government advice and support, elevate (*takameru*), encourage (*susumeru*), accelerate (*suishin suru*), and promote (*sokushin suru*) culture. The promotion of culture (*bunka kōshin*) requires a positive, active (*sekkyokuteki*) attitude and planning (*hakaru*). Official treatments of Japan's "cultural level" (*bunka reberu*) use charts, graphs, and statistics of increases in the number of performances, artists, museums, etc. to demonstrate advances being made, as if culture were an industrial product (e.g. see WBBG).

Early Monbushō involvement in the arts is seen in its announcement of the Fine Arts Exhibition Regulations in June 1907, and its sponsoring of exhibitions. Institutionally, the Agency for Cultural Affairs has its origins in the April 1956 formation of the Cultural Affairs Bureau (*Bunka-kyoku*). This bureau was formed by combining the Arts and Copyright Divisions of the Social Education Bureau with the Japanese Language, Religious Affairs, and International Culture Divisions of the Survey Bureau (*Chōsa-kyoku*), abolished in 1952.[24] In 1967, the Agency for Cultural Affairs was established by combining the Cultural Affairs Bureau with the Committee for the Preservation of Cultural Assets (*Bunkazai hogo i-inkai*). This committee, composed of the General Affairs and Preservation Departments, had been an external unit of the Monbushō and was formed from parts of the Social Education Bureau in August 1950.

BOARDS OF EDUCATION

In Japan, standard works on education define a board of education (*kyōiku i-inkai*) as an administrative agency (*gyōsei kikan*) established by a local government that manages education at the prefectural or municipal level. Education boards follow national guidelines laid down by the Monbushō. Prefectural and municipal boards of education are charged with the establishment, maintenance, and abolition of schools; curriculum design and revision in accordance with Monbushō guidelines; adoption of textbooks; in-service training for teachers and other personnel; and administering affairs related to social education, cultural activities, and physical education and sports. As of 1991, there were 3,471 boards of education. The vast majority of board members are male: 83.3 percent for prefectural and 90.9 percent for municipal boards. In 1991, 34.4 percent of members had had previous teaching experience. Basically, there are two types of boards of education, prefectural and municipal, though in some cases a local governing body may establish joint boards for special purposes.

The history of Japan's boards of education (*kyōiku i-inkai*) indicates how the state has historically viewed local schools as requiring centralized monitoring and control. On 11 November 1948, the government enacted the Board of Education Law, whose general purpose was to democratize and decentralize education, but more specifically, to elect local educational officials and eliminate bureaucratic inflexibility. This law provided for prefectural and municipal boards of education that would: (1) have the same rank; (2) be independent of local assemblies, executives, and the Monbushō (except in some cases determined by law); (3) have seven members on prefectural and five on municipal boards, who would be elected, except one who would be chosen by the local assembly; and (4) not be independent financially, but would have to work out a budget and submit it to the local assembly. Regular elections for boards of education were held in 1948, 1950, and 1952.

The Monbushō, however, resisted this Occupation-designed law (though many Japanese supported it), because it felt that: (1) national guidance and control would be needed for a long and indeterminate period; (2) the people of Japan were not ready to accept the responsibility for education; (3) there was a danger that the general public would be indifferent and that education could fall, at the polls, into the hands of selfish, special-interest groups; (4) local control should mean local financial responsibility; (5) educational reforms were more likely to be undone in the future by school boards; and (6) education standards would decline (Kayashima 1993: 104–5). Thus, along with other "reverse course" changes of the 1950s and in the face of intense opposition by teachers and educational experts, the Law concerning the Organization and Functions of Local Educational Administration was passed on 30 June 1956. This law undid the Board of Education Law, essentially integrating local educational structures into the Monbushō's centralized hierarchy through appointment rather than election of board members. The following sections detail how education boards link state and local levels of education.

Prefectural boards of education

The prefectural governor, with the consent of the prefectural assembly, appoints the five members of the prefectural board of education. Members, who hold office for four years, appoint a superintendent (*kyōiku-chō*) with the Monbushō's approval.[25] The superintendent oversees the board's secretariat, which is usually staffed by supervisors (*shidō shuji*), social education directors (*shakai kyōiku shuji*), and other administrative and technical staff. There are some prefectural boards of education that do not have supervisors or social education directors, but most prefectural secretariats will have divisions for personnel, guidance, and social education, and these may be staffed by officials sent by the Monbushō. Out of the five members on prefectural boards of education, no more than two can belong to the same political party.

The Monbushō provides prefectural boards of education with guidance, advice, and assistance. It also sends them notifications. These boards have the following additional functions: (1) appointment and dismissal of public school principals and assistant principals (*kyōtō*); (2) appointment of teachers and other personnel; (3) transfer of teachers; (4) issuing of teaching licenses for public and private schools; (5) enactment of regulations of the prefectural board of education; (6) requiring municipal boards to submit reports and to make necessary improvements or corrections concerning their activities; (7) establishing attendance districts for public high schools; and (8) school visits. Prefectural boards of education publish various guides, manuals, and handbooks, and holds conferences and workshops for teachers. They also participate in conferences, workshops, and meetings sponsored by the Monbushō. Supervisors on the prefectural boards of education provide guidance on curriculum, teaching, and other educational matters.

Municipal boards of education

Mayors and the heads of municipalities appoint, with the consent of the municipal assembly, the three or five members of each municipal board of education. Members, who hold office for four years, appoint a superintendent (*kyōiku-chō*) with the approval of the prefectural board of education. The superintendent oversees the board's secretariat, which is usually staffed by supervisors, social education directors, and other administrative and technical staff. Out of the five (or three) members on municipal boards of education, no more than two (or in the case of three-member boards, one) can belong to the same political party.

Prefectural boards of education provide guidance, advice, and assistance to the municipal boards. They also send them notifications. Municipal boards have the following functions: (1) compilation of register of school-age children; (2) adoption of textbooks; (3) enactment of school holidays; (4) enactment of regulations of the municipal board of education; (5) enactment of regulations concerning administration of schools; and (6) school visits. Supervisors on municipal boards of education provide guidance on curriculum, teaching, and other educational matters. Officially, municipal boards of education provide guidance, advice, and supervision for municipal elementary and middle schools. These schools have the following functions: (1) class composition; (2) allocation of total class hours to each subject; (3) approval of graduation; (4) school regulations and uniforms; (5) making and presenting of school reports; and (6) making and managing of permanent school records (attendance, absence, evaluation of learning achievements, behavior, and character).[26]

Technically, Japan's boards of education are not parts of the central educational bureaucracy in Tokyo. However, from the point of view of the officials working in the Monbushō, they are the connecting links to local educational institutions, and as such, they are mid-level units of the central administration. Thus, though originally established to decentralize educational administration, boards of education have in practice become "externalized agencies" (*gaikyoku-ka*) of the Monbushō, increasing the latter's direct control (Yamamoto 1992: 61). Like other ministries, the Monbushō uses the "transfer" (*shukkō*) system in which officials who have worked in its central offices for seven or eight years are sent to work on prefectural boards for about two years, after which they return to Tokyo. Therefore, some superintendents, heads of educational sections, and heads of guidance divisions are actually Monbushō officials. According to one observer, these officials "perform the role of the advance guard for the Monbushō's rule" (*ibid.*: 61–2). In this way, the mentality of educational bureaucrats has thoroughly permeated the local educational system. Caught between Monbushō regulations and local pressures, local administrators have generally reinforced the Monbushō's bureaucratic conservatism, been resistant to reform, and, being so dependent on the Monbushō, adopted a passive attitude (Schoppa 1991: 136–8). The reasons usually given why the national, prefectural, and municipal educational administrations should be united and require "collaborative cooperation" (*renkei kyōryoku*) are because of strong public demand to make national standards fair and to free education from local partisan concerns.

STATE AUTHORIZATION OF EDUCATIONAL ACTIVITIES

In Chapter 4, I discussed the role of special corporations in the interstices between state and society (Figure 6.2). Here I provide information about the eight (as of 1995) special corporations under the auspices of the Monbushō, which employ 2,105 personnel.

1   Japan Learning Promotion Society (*Nihon gakujutsu shinkō kai*). Established on 21 September 1967, under the supervision of the Science Division of the Science and International Affairs Bureau, this special corporation has a staff of fifty. In 1993, its operating expenses exceeded 9,096 million yen. This society is charged with funding the development of learning. Recipients must be chosen by an official government council (*shingikai*) and then authorized by the minister of the Monbushō. This society's institutional lineage can be traced back to December 1932, when a donation from the emperor established the Japan Society for the Promotion of Science. Much of its work was geared toward military-related research, and before the war, it had an annual budget ten times the amount that the Monbushō allocated for scientific research. In addition to supporting domestic research, the Japan Learning Promotion Society is involved in joint international programs.

2   Japan Artistic Culture Promotion Society (*Nihon geijutsu bunka shinkō kai*). Established on 1 July 1966, under the supervision of the Traditional Culture Division of the Cultural Properties Protection Department, the General Affairs Division in the Commissioner's Secretariat, and the Cultural Development Division of the Cultural Affairs Department of the Agency for Cultural Affairs. In 1993, it had an operating budget of 4,342 million yen and 322 personnel. This society aims to promote and preserve Japan's traditional arts. It had its start in 1966, when the National Theater (special corporation) was merged with several institutions that had all been established to preserve Japanese traditional arts.

3   Private School and Teachers Mutual Benefit Association (*Shiritsu gakkō kyōshokuin kyōsai kumiai*). Established on 1 January 1954,

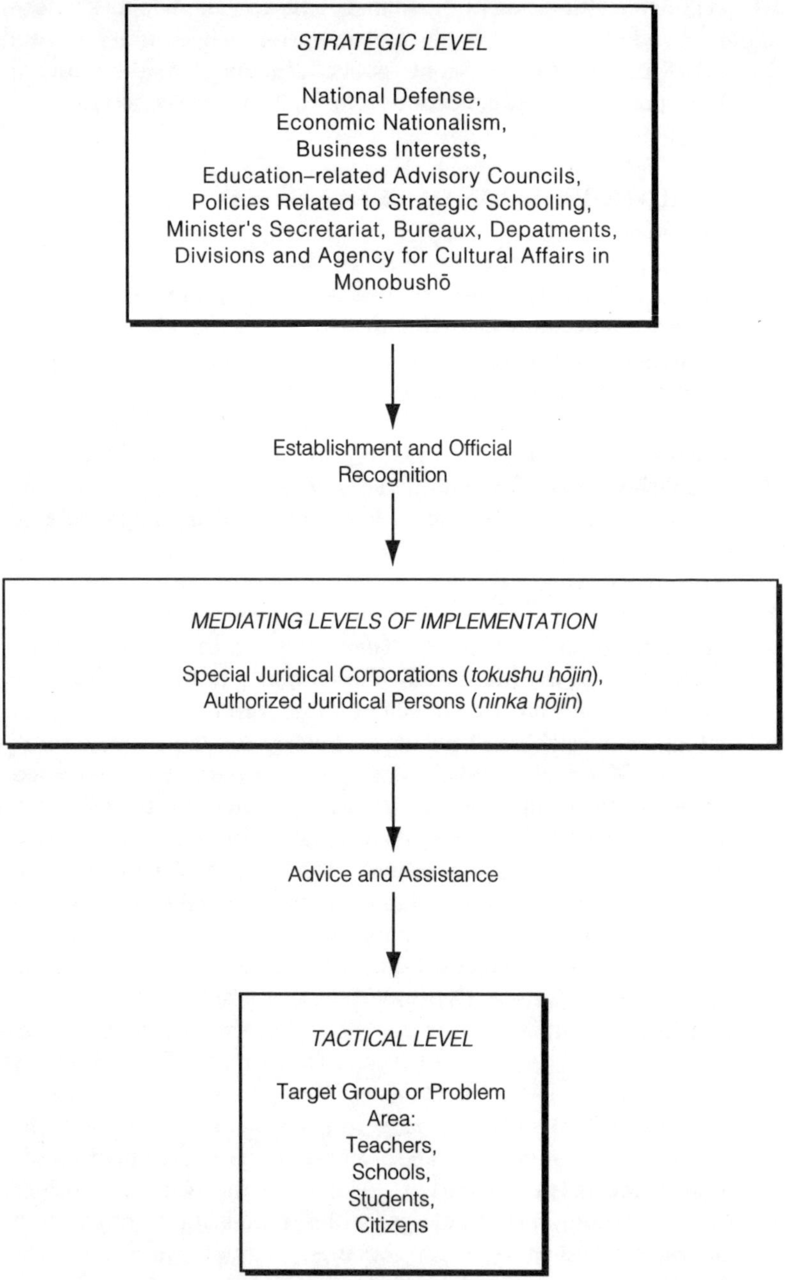

```
┌─────────────────────────────────────┐
│           STRATEGIC LEVEL           │
│                                     │
│          National Defense,          │
│        Economic Nationalism,        │
│          Business Interests,        │
│  Education–related Advisory Councils,│
│  Policies Related to Strategic Schooling,│
│ Minister's Secretariat, Bureaux, Depatments,│
│   Divisions and Agency for Cultural Affairs in│
│             Monobushō               │
└─────────────────────────────────────┘

                  │
                  ▼
       Establishment and Official
              Recognition
                  │
                  ▼

┌─────────────────────────────────────┐
│  MEDIATING LEVELS OF IMPLEMENTATION │
│                                     │
│ Special Juridical Corporations (tokushu hōjin),│
│ Authorized Juridical Persons (ninka hōjin)│
└─────────────────────────────────────┘

                  │
                  ▼
           Advice and Assistance
                  │
                  ▼

        ┌──────────────────────┐
        │    TACTICAL LEVEL    │
        │                      │
        │ Target Group or Problem│
        │        Area:         │
        │       Teachers,      │
        │       Schools,       │
        │      Students,       │
        │       Citizens       │
        └──────────────────────┘
```

Figure 6.2 The role of special corporations and authorized juridical persons in Japan's strategic education

under the supervision of the Education Personnel Benefits Division of the minister's secretariat. In 1993, its revenues totaled 503,100 million yen and its subsidies exceeded 25,823, million yen, and it had 264 personnel. This association is charged with aiding and providing welfare and other benefits to teaching personnel employed at private schools and their families.

4   Japan Private School Promotion Foundation (*Nihon shigaku shinkō zaidan*). Established on 1 July 1970, under the supervision of the Private Education Institution Aid Division of the Private Education Institution Department of the Higher Education Bureau. In 1993, its subsidized operating expenses were 262,818 million yen and it had 114 personnel. This foundation supports teaching and research at private schools. Between 1955 and 1965, many private universities and colleges were in dire financial straits, and this organization was established in order to offer them financial aid.

5   University of the Air Educational Institution (*Hōsō daigaku gakuen*). Established on 1 July 1981, under the supervision of the Lifelong Learning Promotion Division of the Lifelong Learning Bureau, the Planning Division of the Higher Education Bureau, and the First Business Division of the Broadcasting Administration Bureau of the Ministry of Post and Telecommunications. In 1993, its subsidies totaled 7,698 million yen and it employed 305 personnel. This institution of distant education, composed of an administrative office, a library, research offices, and a broadcasting station, reaches students via television and radio, providing Monbushō-accredited courses and academic programs.

6   Japan Scholarship Foundation (*Nihon ikuei kai*). Established on 20 April 1944, under the supervision of the Student Affairs Division of the Higher Education Bureau. In 1993, it distributed 199,100 million yen in loans and had 506 personnel. This foundation is probably the best-known scholarship-granting organization in Japan. It awards funds from the government to students who have financial difficulties.

7   National Stadium and School Health Center of Japan (*Nihon taiiku-gakkō kenkō sentā*). Established on 1 March 1986, under the supervision of the Physical Education and Sports Division and the School Health Education Division of the Physical Education and Sports Bureau. In 1993, its subsidies totaled 9,284 million yen, and it had 457 personnel. This center has three purposes: (1) managing national sports facilities; (2) school lunch programs; and (3) promoting the safety of schoolchildren. Its history is one of amalgamations. In 1982, the Japan School Lunch Association became

part of the Japan School Safety Association (*Nihon gakkō anzen-kai*, established in 1960), and then this association was amalgamated with the Japan School Health Association (*Nihon gakkō kenkō-kai*). In 1986, this association was further combined, along with the National Stadium, to form the National Stadium and School Health Center of Japan.

8   National Education Hall (*Kokuritsu kyōiku kaikan*). Established on 4 June 1964, under the supervision of the Financial Affairs Division of the Local Education Support Bureau. In 1993, its subsidies totaled 834 million yen, and it had eighty-seven personnel. This institution was set up to conduct research and training related to education. It also collects, organizes, and exhibits materials related to education.[27]

In addition to the special corporations there are the many authorized juridical persons (*ninka hōjin*) (see Fujioka's list of the forty-five most important; 1994a: 81). Though these groups represent a wide range of interests that are not rooted in the central educational bureaucracy (teachers, principals, professors, boards of education, education superintendents, parents, PTAs, etc.) it must be stressed that they are "official" in the sense that the Monbushō is. Again, it is not always clear where the state ends and society begins.

III: THE TACTICAL LEVEL

Under the direction of the boards of education (and less directly, the Monbushō's bureaux and divisions) are the thousands of tactical, ground-level units: the individual schools. Within each of these units disciplinary practices, organizational structure, and administrative control vary to some degree in accordance with local conditions and pressures. The sheer administrative weight of the state educational apparatus, its several layers bearing down on each school, shapes an educational atmosphere that is orderly, efficient, spartan, and largely successful in its aims.[28] Consequently, "Japanese schools teach a buttoned-down sense of time and space not unlike what one finds in the military" (Rohlen 1983: 316).[29] Such an environment fosters ritualized hierarchies between teachers and students and between senior students and junior students. What is striking about education in Japan is the wide authority educators enjoy, inside and outside school. Teachers are expected to monitor student behavior off school premises (this includes the home), and Japanese schools are well-known for their detailed regulations, uniforms, and occasional physical abuse of students.[30] Such authority reflects the extent of the state's reach and points to issues of public/private distinctions. The school is considered primarily a moralizing and socializing organization, and secondarily a teaching institution. Thus, educational activities are divided into (1) regular subjects; (2) moral education (the topic of the next chapter); and (3) special activities (classroom activities, student councils, club activities, and school events such as ceremonies, presentation programs, events related to health, safety, physical education, school excursions and community service activities).

SCHOOL ORGANIZATION

As a tactical unit, a school and its administration are positioned under prefectural and municipal boards of education, whose superintendents stand over school principals. Though many Japanese say that, ideally at least, a principal should be a leader of the teachers and represent the school, in actuality, principals serve a "personnel administrative function" of the authorities. They are, in fact, the "advance bases" (*zenshin kichi*) of the Monbushō's bureaucratic control of the schools (Sakamoto 1992: 300–1). Below the principal is the assistant principal (*kyōtō*), and next are *shunin* (teacher-managers), teachers in positions of responsibility (e.g. heads of instruction, grades, departments). Reforms in the mid-1970s made these formerly unofficial positions into official mid-level management positions, qualifying them for a salary bonus. From the Japan Teachers Union viewpoint, the *shunin* system was a government attempt to create a teachers corps supportive of the state. In any case, the *shunin* system reflects a creeping bureaucratization. Here it is useful to quote Rohlen on the dominant organizational principles of Japanese high schools: "(1) a strong emphasis on faculty supervision; (2) the organization of individuals into small groups; (3) an emphasis on a few long-term group memberships rather than on choice and fluidity; (4) an absence of formal reward and control systems to steer teacher behavior; and (5) a heavy dependence on peer pressure and faculty leadership to motivate and guide conduct" (1983: 206–7).[31]

As for students, the homeroom is the key organizing unit.[32] Each student is also a member of a grade (*gakunen*) and a group (*kumi*). In other words, students are organized into "rows" and "columns," so that in addition to being in a grade, a student will belong to a group that cuts vertically through different grades, further integrating a student into a school's group life. Student governments add to the well-organized, regulated atmosphere of school life. "Every aspect of the students' lives – from the milk they drink to the clothes they wear – is supervised and managed by some committee or section," and "For each teacher section, there is usually a corresponding student committee, and students are assigned specific tasks, such as delivering the kerosene to the art room in winter. Moreover, senior students are expected to instruct junior students in the correct way to carry out their tasks" (LeTrende 1994: 53). Students and teachers also spend a considerable amount of time on club activities, which are regarded as indispensable for socializing students. It is in these clubs that students acquire an understanding of the significance of junior/senior (*kōhai/senpai*) relations.

The effects of Japan's strategic education, premised on top-down, hierarchical organizational patterns, is visible in the classroom. Memorization, test taking, and student role performance are the primary goals of the classroom experience. Little direct appeal is made to students as individuals with something original to contribute (though many argue that this is true only in middle and high schools), and as a result, there is a tendency for teachers to distance themselves from the students, often asking questions by calling out student numbers rather than names. And, contrary to the image of quiet, well-disciplined students, "chatting students" (as one teacher told me) are a constant problem. In fact, from my own observations, both teachers and students appear to have a high tolerance for noise, a toleration that continues through university. Many teachers state that Japan's overly bureaucratized education is responsible for producing students who they describe as *shiji machi ningen* (people waiting for instructions) and *mannyuru ningen* (manual people: i.e. individuals who require manuals on how to do everything). This passivity produces students who "learn to adjust to social 'givens' with no illusion that they could help generate a society partly of their own making" (Rohlen 1983: 206–7, quotation marks in original).[33]

CONCLUSION: THE "PRODUCTIVENESS OF THE MASSES"

To conclude, there are four basic organizational pillars at the intermediate level that in no small measure have supported the state strategic educational goals. These pillars, or organizational methods, are institutional arrangements that connect grand goal-setting organs of the state with local-level schools and individual subjectivities. Above I delineated these linking institutions: (1) the central institutions are the Monbushō's bureaux, divisions, and one external organ (Agency for

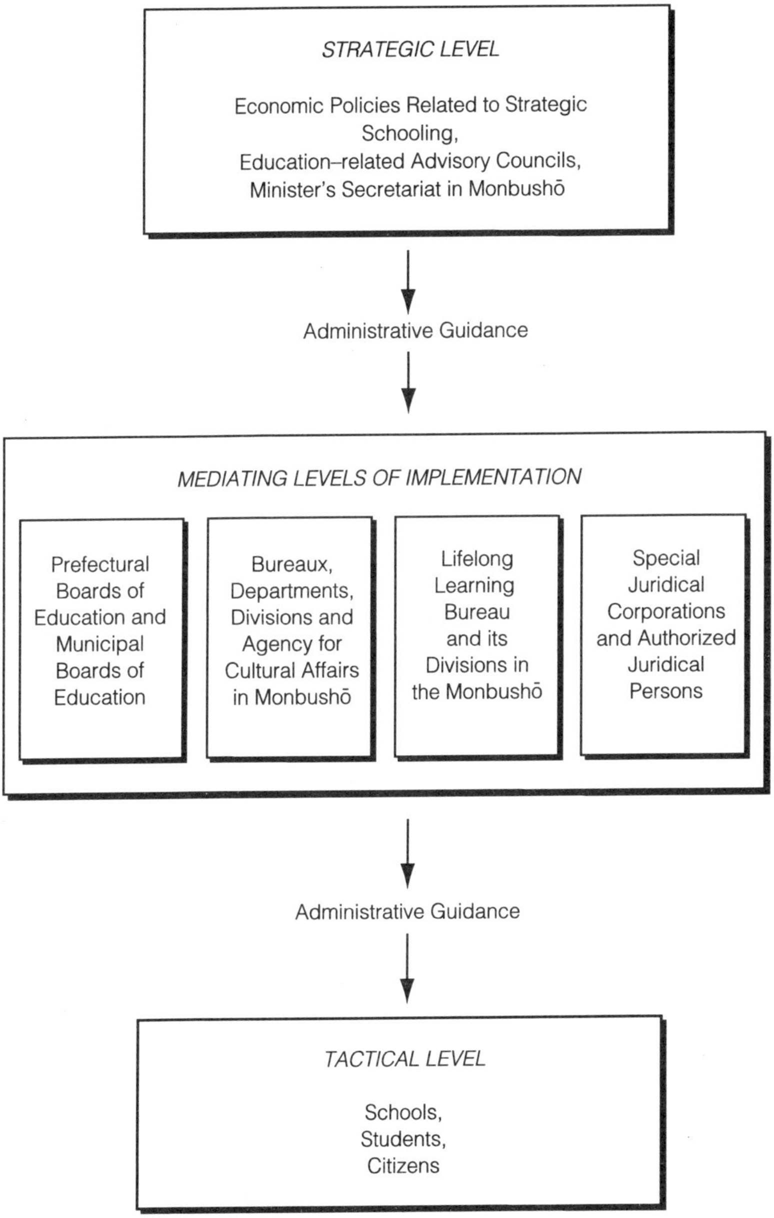

STRATEGIC LEVEL

Economic Policies Related to Strategic
Schooling,
Education–related Advisory Councils,
Minister's Secretariat in Monbushō

Administrative Guidance

MEDIATING LEVELS OF IMPLEMENTATION

Prefectural Boards of Education and Municipal Boards of Education	Bureaux, Departments, Divisions and Agency for Cultural Affairs in Monbushō	Lifelong Learning Bureau and its Divisions in the Monbushō	Special Juridical Corporations and Authorized Juridical Persons

Administrative Guidance

TACTICAL LEVEL

Schools,
Students,
Citizens

Figure 6.3 Four methods of Japan's strategic education

Cultural Affairs) that are involved with formal schooling; (2) the Life-long Learning Bureau (which has counterparts in prefectural and municipal boards of education) and its divisions. These organs, related to endeavors commonly called "social education," are targeting new areas of economic exploitation and state involvement; (3) the prefectural and municipal boards of education, which ensure that state policies are administratively secure; and (4) special juridical corporations and authorized juridical persons (Figure 6.3).

In spite of Japanese criticisms of their own schooling system (its mediocre level, individuality-crushing standardization, suicide-inducing bullying, and relentless "exam hell") we would do well to keep in mind that from the perspective of those who designed the Japanese educational system – politico-economic elites and their bureaucratic allies – schooling in Japan has achieved success. Japan's education must be viewed in the context of rapid industrialization, which was "part of a deliberate, state-directed, policy of 'catching-up' modernisation" and used education to solidify "the loyalty and the productiveness of the masses" (Dore 1976: 35).

Observers have been impressed with the quality of Japan's work-force, and bookstores in Japan have shelves filled with works about company life and practices.[34] Whatever quality Japan's workers have, it is socialized into them through the educational system, and much of this socialization involves training in rationalization (i.e. hierarchiza-tion, categorization, and routinization) and instilling "loyalty," not to a specific company, but to whatever work site they are placed in. In the next chapter, I continue this examination of the tactical level of educa-tion by analysing "moral education," the state's attempt to instill within students a rationalizing, ritualizing, and bureaucratizing mentality, which is absolutely necessary for ensuring the "productiveness of the masses" and economic growth.

7 The rationality of moral education

The state's vision of civil society

LINKING CIVILITY AND RATIONALITY THROUGH MORAL EDUCATION

Rohlen writes that Japanese high schools "are best understood as shaping generations of disciplined workers for a technomeritocratic system that requires highly socialized individuals capable of performing reliably in a rigorous, hierarchical, and finely tuned organizational environment" (1983: 209). This is true in other industrialized societies, though the designers of Japan's educational system seem particularly concerned with turning out students who acquire the skills necessary for a highly rationalized environment, both natural and social. If students come to believe in the inherent goodness and commonsensical nature of hierarchy, in-group/out-group distinctions, and the value of general orderliness, then daily routines become the training necessary for technocratic employment. A key link between good manners and economic interests is formed.

In this chapter I examine how the state, as agent, turns its objectives into subjective structures, or more specifically, how conviction in elite economic interests is reproduced. The state equals rationality equals common sense, and as I described in Chapter 2, common sense in Japan often means "morality." I will attempt to demonstrate these connections by showing how moral education is implicated in and the linkages between: (1) bureaucratic mentality: rationality and rituality, or the psychology that hierarchizes, categorizes, and formalizes the sociopolitical environment, and is used to structure and interpret sociability; (2) civility: the codes and practices that encourage a group-based and group-oriented sociability; and (3) subjectivity: the particular sentiments and conceptions that buttress a sense of rationality and rituality. My premise is that individual subjectivities – constructed through social forces – become the building blocks of civil society. More than a description of actual behavior, this chapter focuses on prescriptive texts that are state-ordained. If nothing else, this chapter furnishes an idea of how certain state elites envision the ideal Japanese society, the state's attempt at building a "civil society," and the meaning of "public" in Japan.

The word *dōtoku* literally means the "way" (*dō*) to "virtue" (*toku*). The Japanese Ministry of Education mandates that all students in primary (ages 1–6) and junior high schools (ages 7–9) receive thirty-five hours of moral education (*dōtoku kyōiku*) every year.[1] Westerners often equate "morality" with a religiously tainted "inner voice," but in Japan, *dōtoku* has a more secular flavor, with an accent on how best to interact with others in a group setting rather than on individual conscience. It is associated with etiquette, concrete and observable actions, and the actual methods that shape moral beings, expressed in the word *shitsuke* (training, breeding, discipline) (*cf.* Hendry 1986). That moral training is regarded as a central component of the good citizen is evident in the Fundamental Law of Education, in which the "completion of character" is promoted. The great significance attached to moral education is evident in how it is explained that it should be the cornerstone on which all educational activities rest. Thus, moral education, at least in primary schools, is one of the three main functions of a school, the other two being regular classes and special activities (SGTH: 5).

Moral education offers an idiom that the average Japanese finds understandable, acceptable, and desirable. Most Japanese accept that some form of instruction in moral matters is necessary, and there is no shortage of teaching materials, guidebooks, and academic works on this topic.[2] However, the content, goals, and methods of moral instruction are disputed, and the postwar contention between the Ministry of Education and the Japan Teachers Union over moral education reflects its highly contested nature. The former views moral education as a humanistic endeavor designed to foster good citizens, while the latter has often associated it with a return to prewar nationalistic indoctrination.[3]

Whatever the average Japanese may think about moral education, it is inextricably bound up with state control and images of civil society, and all state-issued guidebooks on moral education have prefaces warning about problems among today's misbehaving youth. Issues concerning moral education regularly appear in the media: due to an increase in school violence, bullying, and student absenteeism, the Ministry of Education asked prefectural boards of education to "conduct surveys on moral and ethics education at all private and public primary and middle schools" ("Government Seeking Moral Education Surveys," DY 23 June 1993: 3). The point is that school authorities do devote attention to issues of "character." For instance, the Ibaraki prefectural government's Office of Education introduced "a new screening system for prefectural high schools that involves evaluating student character traits." Students will be evaluated in twelve areas, such as disposition, ambition, environmental appreciation, and daily habits ("Schools to Assess Student Character," DY 23 June 1993: 3).

Though teachers and local governments choose privately published texts for moral education classes, these must be authorized by the Ministry of Education. Teachers supplement their moral education classes with educational television programs, videos, students' essays, exemplary biographies, literary writings, classics, and class discussions. Officially, the government lacks the authority to advocate a particular morality, and "ideological indoctrination is rarely encountered in high schools" (Rohlen 1983: 210).[4] Materials used in moral education that concern political or religious matters should be impartial (SGDK: 68). The ministry, however, does publish a list of guidebooks on teaching methods that, if carefully examined, does espouse an ethnomorality. It also recommends its own series of texts, which consist of readings.[5] Much of this chapter analyses the contents of these materials, which assert that moral education is necessary and its purpose is to teach people "how human relations should be" (*ningen kankei no arikata*), to perfect "human nature" (*ningensei, ningen-rashisa*) or "the goodness of human nature" (*ningen-rashī yosa*), and "the formation of character" (*jinkaku no keisei*), so that one becomes a *ningen-rashī ningen* (a humane person). Moral education, as "the formation of character" (*jinkaku no keisei*), is a form of self-cultivation, and as such it is a lifetime endeavor that ideally never ends.

Before proceeding, some caveats are in order. First, this chapter does not concern the problem of to what degree students accept and endorse this ethnotheory as a comprehensive set of beliefs that is applied to all aspects of life.[6] Most Japanese I have asked described moral education classes as boring and useless. However, there are many different kinds of knowledge, and knowing something is rarely a case of either belief or its lack. There are degrees of acceptance, diversity of interpretations, and differences in knowledge utilization. The point is that, in spite of its largely negative evaluations, moral education does succeed in furnishing to some degree at least a repertoire of values that inform certain practices.

Second, there are many angles from which moral education can be approached and there are numerous social variables that shape any understanding of moral education, such as gendered versions, age differences, class distinctions, occupational variability, regional diversity, and individual interpretations. For the purposes of this chapter and because space precludes their treatment, these angles and variables are glossed over. However, suffice to say that in a more detailed account of moral education, these variables cannot be ignored. It should also be mentioned that though the Ministry of Education does have considerable power *vis-à-vis* local school authorities, the latter often reinterpret, modify, and occasionally disregard central bureaucratic orders.[7]

Third, I pay particular attention to the actual language of the texts that teach moral education because words often carry culture-specific valuations that are sometimes missed if too readily glossed. The assumption that words point to some underlying "real reality" that transcends all societies and historical periods is blind to the subtleties and hues that color specific cultural constructs.

THE HISTORY OF MORAL EDUCATION

The roots of moral education can be traced to prewar courses in *shūshin*, a type of moral training that stressed values that supported nationalism and an imperialistic ideology.[8] *Shūshin* was originally a Confucian expression that encapsulated an entire political philosophy: proper self-cultivation results in family harmony, which leads to effective governing of the nation and ultimately the world.

Lanham notes that a glance at *shūshin* and *dōtoku* texts "reveals sufficient continuity to confirm that one is still in the same culture" (1979: 5). The values of patience, perseverance, diligence, orderliness, and hard work appear in both types of text. However, differences between *shūshin* and *dōtoku* texts far outweigh their similarities. Ancestor worship, loyalty to the emperor and state, Shintoism, stories about war heroes, and unconditional obedience to one's father are no longer part of moral education.

Postwar educational reforms abolished *shūshin*. For the first ten years after the war, there was no official course on moral education, though some schools did attempt to incorporate moral instruction into the general curriculum. In 1958, the Ministry of Education introduced and recommended a moral education course, and in 1962 made it a required part of the curriculum. Since then, the ministry has revised the contents of moral education about every ten years.

THE MORALITY OF RITUALITY: BUILDING CIVIL SOCIETY

In the next four subsections I explore some major themes of moral education: how it should ideally (1) constitute a collaboration between the school, home, and local community; (2) consist of a set of specific norms; (3) be actively enjoined by teachers; and (4) convince students to express their commitment to values in visible form.

The common purpose of school, neighborhood, and home

The guidebooks repeatedly emphasize that school authorities should "look for ways to have school, family, and the local community cooperate" (SGO: 24). Both SGD and CGD have chapters entitled "Training Related to Cooperation and Association between Homes and the Local Community," which spell out how cooperation and consensus should be built between these three arenas of socialization to ensure the proper character formation of children.

There are many activities that school authorities can do to ensure the linking of school and the local community. School authorities are advised to actively support an array of associations (i.e. PTA, promotion meetings (*suishin kaigi*), and other organizations) in order to tie educational goals, neighborhood concerns, and family interests together. The guidebooks suggest the orchestrating of an array of "activities," "movements," "meetings," and "associations." Specific examples are provided. For instance, primary schools might want to organize "greeting movements" (*aisatsu undō*) or open a "greeting street" (*aisatsu dōri*) in front of the school, where students can energetically greet passers-by, thereby sending good will to the neighborhood (SGDK: 38).[9]

Empathy, belongingness, diligence, and other core values

The Ministry of Education prescribes twenty-two values that primary and middle school students should learn. These are divided into four categories: (1) self; (2) relation to others; (3) relation to nature; and (4) relation to group and society. These categories vary somewhat according to grade level (grades 1–2, 3–4, 5–6, and junior high school each have their own versions). Below I list values (which are more elaborated and expanded versions of those taught in lower grades) for junior high school (from "Morals According to Grade Level," DKS 3: 102–3).

Values mainly relating to self

1   To acquire desirable life habits, strive to improve the health of one's body and mind, and lead a life of harmony (*chōwa*) and moderation.
2   To aim for high goals, accomplish things with aspiration, courage, and in a steadfast manner, and have a strong will.
3   To value the spirit of self-control (*jiritsu*), think independently (*jishuteki ni*), act sincerely, and be responsible for one's actions.
4   To love truth, pursue the genuine, aim to realize the ideal, and make it through life on one's own.
5   To reflect on one's self. Along with striving for one's improvement, developing one's individuality and pursuing a fulfilling way of life.

Values mainly relating to others

6   To understand the significance of etiquette (*reigi*), and be able to act and speak appropriate to the situation.
7   To pursue the spirit of warm human love, and have a grateful (*kansha*) and empathetic (*omoiyari*) heart (*kokoro*) toward others.
8   To understand the preciousness of friendship and have friends you can trust from your heart (*kokoro*). To mutually encourage (*hagemashiau*) and improve (*takameau*) each other.
9   For men and women to respect their respective characteristics, and have a healthy view of the opposite sex.
10   To respect everyone's individuality and position, and understand that there are many kinds of viewpoint and ways of thinking. To have a generous heart (*kokoro*) that humbly learns from others.

Values mainly relating to nature and the sublime

11   To love nature and have a rich heart (*kokoro*) that is moved by beautiful things. To deepen one's reverence toward things that transcend human power.
12   To understand the preciousness of life, and respect one's own irreplaceable life and that of others.
13   Though people have weaknesses and defects, one should believe that they also have the strength and dignity to overcome their weak points. To endeavor to discover the joy of living as a human.

Values mainly relating to group and society

14 To deepen one's understanding concerning the significance of the various groups with which one is affiliated. To be aware of one's responsibility and role, and endeavor to cooperate together (*kyōryoku shiau*) and improve group life (*shūdan seikatsu*).

15 To understand the spirit of the law, and respect one's own rights and those of others. Along with steadfastly fulfilling one's duty, endeavoring to improve social order and discipline with a sense of public spirit (*kōtokushin*).

16 To hold justice in esteem and be fair and impartial to others. To endeavor and strive for the realization of a better society without discrimination and prejudice through the spirit of social solidarity.

17 Along with understanding the preciousness of labor, to deepen the sentiment (*kimochi*) of service to society. To endeavor and strive for the development of society and the public (*kōkyō*) welfare.

18 To deepen love and respect for one's parents and grandparents, and to build a satisfying family life through an awareness that one is a family member.

19 To be aware that one is a member of a class and a school. To deepen one's love and respect toward one's teachers and those at school, and to cooperate and establish a better school atmosphere (*kōfū*).

20 To be aware that one is a member of a local community, and deepen one's gratitude (*kansha*) and respect toward the elderly and predecessors who have devoted themselves to society. To endeavor and strive for the development of one's home town.

21 To love the nation through an awareness of being Japanese. Along with devoting oneself to the development of the nation, to endeavor to benefit from the creation of new culture and the transmission of superior traditions.

22 To be aware of being Japanese in the world. To endeavor to contribute to the welfare of mankind and world peace from an international perspective.

Below I list and discuss the core values that appear in the guidebooks.

Omoiyari. This word has already been discussed in Chapter 3. The importance of this concept is evident in its frequent appearance in Ministry of Education materials. Two ministry guidebooks are devoted to this value: *Shō gakkō: omoiyari no kokoro o sodateru shidō* (Guidance for Cultivating a Heart of Empathy in Primary School) (SGO), and *Chū gakkō: omoiyari no kokoro o sodateru shidō* (Guidance for

Cultivating a Heart of Empathy in Junior High School) (CGO). *Omoi-yari* is called the "foundation of morality" and is something that should be expressed in everyday life (SGO: 7). It is a sentiment that is tied to love of family, friends, the nation, and respect for the law (SGO: 89).[10] One guidebook states that *omoiyari* means (1) to guess, infer, or imagine (what others are thinking or feeling); (2) being aware of others, namely, consideration; and (3) comparing one's own with another's position (CGO: 90). This is why "it is important to cultivate hearts that understand the pain in the hearts of others, and to make them think about and take the position of others." Besides meaning "sympathy," (*dōjō* or *kyōkan*), *omoiyari* also has an active aspect: one should "give (*yaru*) thought (*omoi*) to others" so as to ascertain what another thinks or feels (SGO: 86–7). Thus, empathy depends on one's "power of imagination" (*sōzōryoku*).

An example of naturalizing and essentializing an ethnotheory of human relations is evident in a guidebook that declares that people are endowed from birth with the foundation (*moto*) for an "empathetic heart" (*omoiyari no kokoro*). But it must be stressed that, "Although people are born possessing this good quality, if it is not correctly and richly cultivated, they soon dry up (*kokatsu suru*) and become people lacking in 'empathy'" (CGO: 88, quotation marks in original). It should be stressed that being empathetic toward others is usually regarded not so much as a universal but rather as an intragroup-oriented value. Thus, rather than extending one's consideration outward toward even unknowns (inclusive), *omoiyari* strengthens group solidarity (exclusive).

Belongingness.   Learning to privilege the group begins in school (*cf.* Hendry 1986, Peak 1991). Students should acquire "love of one's school" (*aikōshin*) and "local patriotism" (*kyōdoai*). Terms such as "group living" (*shūdan seikatsu*), "mutual understanding" (among group members) (*kyōtsū no rikai*), and "cooperation" (*kyōryoku*) are used liberally throughout the guidebooks. Students are admonished to "respect the rules of the group" and to acquire an "awareness as a member of a group." Belongingness is emotionalized through "feelings of belonging" (*shozokukan*) and "feelings of unity" (*ittaikan*), and teachers are advised to establish a "school tradition and spirit" (*gakkō no dentō ya kōfū*) (SGDK: 19). Belongingness strengthens the social boundaries between inner (*uchi*)/outer (*soto*) and the entailing concepts of "behindness" (*ura*)/"outwardness" (*omote*). These boundaries are erected and maintained by *tatemae*.

Rohlen points out that in Japanese schools "Neither ideology nor law is emphasized as the foundation of social order or meaning," and "Morality is based on a consciousness of social relations, an awareness of being interdependent" (1983: 256). The culture of Japanese schools, then, encourages an array of small "societies" that students join voluntarily or to which they are assigned. Examples of the former are clubs, special event committees, and cliques.[11] Examples of the latter are grade level and "homerooms" (*hōmurūmu*), in which students take the same classes together. Being a member of one of these small societies demands loyalty. One becomes a member in one club and does not ordinarily join other clubs. Belongingness comes about through active participation in groups, which "is assumed to be natural, healthy, and proper. Nonparticipation, it is assumed, is accompanied by loss of self-confidence and self-worth" (*ibid.*: 203), and the whole point of participating in school events is to learn how to cooperate in large groups.

As for acquiring respect for more inclusive collectivities beyond family, students in the third grade should have their awareness of being a member (*sei-in*) of a local community fostered, and develop an attitude that regards their local community as important. In the fourth grade, they should acquire an attitude that "desires the development of their local community" and considers the life of the local community from a broad view. In the fifth grade, students should have an interest in the industrial development of Japan and are encouraged to acquire love (*aijō*) of their nation. By the sixth grade, students should have feelings (*shinjō*) that give importance to their nation's history and tradition and have cultivated a sense of responsibility and awareness as Japanese in the world (SGSH: 8). In order to inculcate these "civic qualities" (*kōminteki shishitsu*) and a "law-abiding spirit" (*junpō no seishin*), materials should be carefully selected (*seisen suru*).

Though the guidebooks do mention the importance of "patriotism" (*aikokushin*), public concerns about a return to prewar nationalism appear to mitigate too much attention to this topic.[12] However, though postwar sentiments about Japanese nationality have been officially shorn of their prewar excesses, students are still socialized to possess a cultural nationality, one premised on Japaneseness. Morality, civility, and ethnic identity are all intimately linked. "Social ethics is grounded ultimately in something greater than the individual. It is not religion, but national tradition" (Rohlen 1983: 264).[13] Several guidebooks mention, using the same phrases over and over again, the need for students to become "Japanese who have a sense of identity" (*shutaisei no aru nihonjin*). It is explained that "Japanese who live in an international society" must have their understanding of "Japan's culture and tradition" strengthened. Specifically, students should learn about how their identity is rooted in the distant past. For example, students should study the "ancient Japanese imperial court" (*Yamato chōtei*) and how it unified the country, how the life of ancestors is related to their present life, and the value of cultural assets and heritage. Also, teachers are advised to have students "notice that our nation has a different culture" (SGSH: 74), and "it is necessary to have them consider the importance of making foreigners understand Japanese culture" (SGSH: 75). Another way in which cultural national identity may be constructed in the schools is through learning *kokugo* (national language; "Japanese"). Japanese is mandatory during primary (six years) and junior high (three years) school. For students who proceed to senior high school (three years), more advanced classes in Japanese are required. Since a literate workforce is essential for economic productivity, school authorities stress the learning of Japanese (*cf.* Duke 1986: 51–79).

Japan's national flag and anthem, controversial symbols because of their militaristic associations – have crept back into official guidance. In the most recent guidebooks, they are discussed in a context of "international understanding" and "world peace." It is explained that in order to respect the flags and anthems of other nations, Japanese must possess an attitude of "respect" (*sonchō*) toward their own flag and anthem and understand their "significance" (*igi*). In an apparent effort to answer concerns that Japan's national flag and anthem lack a legal basis, SGSH points out that "In our country the Hinomaru is the national flag and the Kimigayo is the national anthem. Being recognized by the people as customary (*kankō*) for a long time, our country's national flag and anthem have widely taken root" (81–3). The anthem, after all, is a song "filled with the desire to see our country prosper [*hanei suru*]." The flag and anthem are linked to the emperor and the constitution, and students should deepen their "understanding, respect, and affection" (*rikai to keiai*) for the emperor (SGSH: 80–1).

As if to stress the theme of unity and togetherness, compound verbs – composed of a main verb stem plus the verb *au* (bring together) – appear throughout the guidebooks: *kyōryoku shiau* (cooperate together); *fureau* (come in contact with); *shiau* (do together); *mitomeau* (see another's point of view); *wakariau* (understand together); *hanashiau* (consult with); *hagemashiau* (encourage one another); *manabiau* (learn together); *yomiau* (read together); *tasukeau* (help each other); *rikai shiau* (understand together); *renraku shiau* (contact each other); *toiau* (ask together); *dashiau* (contribute together); *miau* (exchange views); *kakawariau* (be related to); *itawariau* (take care of each either); *hibikiau* (reverberate together); and *tsutaeau* (communicate with each other).

Diligence. The guidebooks are filled with words such as "to endeavor" (*tsukusu*), "to exert" (*doryoku suru*), and "to be diligent" (*tsutomeru*). Students should acquire the perseverance and mental stamina needed to prepare for the rigors of the examinations, but persevering is also a value that connects one to others: one should exert oneself for the group (school grade, homeroom, club, etc.), thereby strengthening belongingness. "To be patient" (*shimbō suru*), "persevere (*gambaru*), and "endure" (*gaman suru, shinobu*), in fact, are cultural desirables in themselves, and are often heard outside of educational settings, as in cheering somebody on (*gambatte;* usually glossed as "good luck" but actually meaning to "hang in there").[14]

Self-control. The guidebooks stress that students should acquire "autonomy" (*jichiteki*), "independence" (*jiritsu*), "self-restraint" (*jisei*), and "self-reliance" (*jishu*). They should learn how to do things "freely" (*jiyū ni*) and "voluntarily" (*jihatsuteki ni*). "Although an American may read personal freedom and individualism into these words, for Japanese preschool teachers they refer almost exclusively to the need to have children learn to put aside their expectations of maternal assistance and assume responsibility for the activities required of them within the new world of *shūdan seikatsu* [group living]" (Peak 1991: 71).

Sunao. Meaning "obedience," this is another central cultural value in Japan, but it is employed toward both children and adults and it carries a heavier semantic load than the English word "obedient." It may mean submissive, gentle, meek, receptive, tractable, compliant, and coopera-tive. In a pedagogical context, White writes that this is used to describe the "good child" and possesses connotations of open-mindedness, non-resistance, being truthful, naivete, naturalness, simplicity, mildness, and straightforwardness. It strongly implies active cooperation and engagement in the activities of a group (1987: 28). It also strongly implies positive acceptance of what one is told. Being obedient points to and reinforces another important value: respecting those above one, or the idea of "occupying one's proper place" (Lebra 1976: 67–8).[15] Consequently, vertical relations are stressed, such as *kōhai/senpai* (junior/senior) and *seito/sensei* (student/master).

Other values. Other cultural desirables that make an appearance in the guidebooks are "reflection" (on one's behavior) (*hansei suru, furikaeru*) and a sense of indebtedness, often expressed through "gratitude" (espe-cially toward one's parents, superiors, and teachers) (*kansha*).

To conclude this subsection on core values, it is worth noting Naitō's observation that Japanese morality is characterized by two fundamental themes: (1) an emphasis on harmony (*chōwa*), which is grounded in empathy; and (2) relativism or particularism. However, "the concept of harmony excludes universalistic rules because harmony ought to be created and sustained not by universal rules but by careful consideration of situation factors." These concepts work against attempts to teach more universal norms, since students generally come to regard trans-situational values as too idealistic and removed from real life (Naitō 1990: 33–4). As I discuss on p. 174 ("Ritualizing experience through emotion"), "situational factors," – as elements in "situations" (*bamen*) and the "atmospheres" of schools, homerooms, and clubs – are charged with emotion, thereby strengthening social structures.

Administrative guidance and the active role of teachers

I have already introduced the term "administrative guidance." In educational materials prepared by the Ministry of Education, *shidō* (guidance, leadership, instruction, or coaching) is by far the most ubiquitous word, with many guidebooks having *shidō* in their title.[16] Indeed, "administrative guidance" seems to capture the spirit of how the state's educational institutions should relate to their charges: as parental authorities at the apex of the political system, they should guide students along the correct path (Figure 7.1). LeTrende notes that "There was no debate over whether students *should* be guided to a set of beliefs, only *which* beliefs to inculcate and how much autonomy the teacher should have in determining these beliefs" (1994: 45, italics in original).

There is an earnest and urgent feel to the discourse about how educational practices should be executed. The guidebooks are replete with terms such as "planning" (*keikaku suru, hakaru*), "improvement" (of teaching methods) (*kaizen*), "how to move forward with training" (*kenshū no susumekata*), and the need to "promote" (*suishin suru*) and make moral instruction "effective" (*kōkateki*). Moral education should be "deliberate" (*keikakuteki*) and "developmental" (*hattenteki*).

Like students, teachers themselves require "constant evaluation" by senior school authorities, as a section called "What should be done in planning to improve guidance, motivation, and understanding of the teacher's role in moral education?" explains (CGD: 21). Another guidebook advises that in performing their duties, teachers should "steadily carry out the flow of planning, execution, and evaluation," with each stage of teaching carefully examined (SGD: 15).

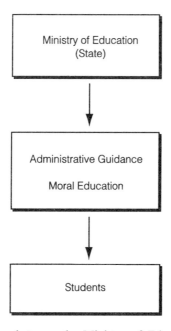

Figure 7.1 The relation between the Ministry of Education, administrative guidance, and students

Vis-à-vis students, a teacher should have students "internalize" (*naimenka suru*) "the ability to make moral judgments" (*dōtokuteki handanryoku*), a "moral attitude" (*dōtokuteki taido*), and a "moral consciousness" (*dōtoku ishiki*). They should make efforts in training, recognize their position's responsibility, set themselves up as models, and respond to the citizens' expectations as public servants (CGD: 4). They have an active role to perform toward the students, which is seen in the use of causative verb endings: teachers should "make" [or more softly, "have"] [students] acquire [morals]" (*mi ni tsukesaseru*); "make consider" (*kangesaseru*); "make understand" (*rikai saseru*); "make aware of" (*kizukaseru*); "make conscious of" (*jikaku saseru*); and "have [students] evaluate themselves" (*jiko hyōka saseru*).

Being observed and making morality visible

Vigilance of student behavior and appearance is an important theme in the guidebooks. Students should have their "actual condition" (*jittai*) investigated through measuring their attitudes. Specifically, reports of daily life, description of impressions, questionnaires about school events, and journals kept by students in charge of school activities or chores should all be monitored (SGD: 38). Rules about uniforms, hair length and style, posture, and positioning of the body should be carefully observed. In particular, complex sociolinguistic practices (*aisatsu*) receive a considerable amount of attention, and publications entitled "Greetings and Language" (*Aisatsu to kotoba*), "Honorific Language" (*Keigo*), "Language Training" (*Kotoba no shitsuke*), and "Speech" (*Kotobazukai*) are written for pedagogical purposes.[17]

Occupying one's proper social standing is part of the strategy used to prevent *faux pas*, so that Japanese have a tendency to signal clearly – through proper attire, uniforms, sociolinguistic behavior, and other forms of etiquette – their social standing and role. Manners preclude miscues. Anticipating the wishes of others and protecting their feelings (*omoiyari;* see above) then, are accomplished through etiquette, which in theory should make morality visible through manners. Also, displaying an engaging, enthusiastic attitude – by being "cheerful" (*akarui, yōki*) and acting "positively" (*sekkyokuseiteki ni*) – is highly desired because it firmly signals one's heartful acceptance of the group or displays one's devotion to the task at hand. It is also a way of symbolizing obedience (*sunao*) to one's superiors.[18]

RITUALIZING MORALITY AND MORALIZING RITUALITY

"It is through a socially acquired sense of ritual that members of a society know how to improvise a birthday celebration, stage an elaborate wedding, or rush through a minimally adequate funeral" (Bell 1992: 81), or manipulate codes of civility in order to negotiate a social landscape. A sense of ritual is rooted in the culturally informed body, along with the other senses:

> These senses include the traditional five senses – which never escape the structuring action of social determinism – but also the sense of necessity and the sense of duty, the sense of direction and the sense of reality, the sense of balance and the sense of beauty, common sense and the sense of the sacred, tactical sense and the sense of responsibility, business sense and the sense of propriety, the sense of humor and the sense of absurdity, moral sense and the sense of practicality, and so on.
>
> (Bourdieu 1977: 124)

In the next four subsections I discuss how moral education inoculates a sense of rituality, which governs the Japanese perspective on civility. This is accomplished by (1) ritualizing bodies through mundane and concrete practices; (2) emotionalizing experience; (3) "totalizing" moral instruction; and (4) permeating the very design of pedagogic practices with rituality. Taken together, these socializing activities (5) identify moral education as a practice that elicits an inherent human nature.

The practice and habitualization of morality

The guidebooks repeatedly emphasize that there is nothing abstract about moral education. Accordingly, there is much discussion of "moral practice" (*dōtokuteki jissen*), "ability to practice morally" (*dōtokuteki jissenryoku*), "practical activities" (*jissen katsudō*), and "moral action" (*dōtokuteki kōi*). Morality should be an everyday, observable practice, acquired through "training" (*kenshū*), and related to "concrete life habits" (*gutaiteki na seikatsu shūkan*). The term "to embody" or "make [values] concrete" (*gutaika suru*) is commonly used. Teachers should avoid abstract discussions and relate the training to concrete guidance (CGD: 20). They should also foster "the will to act [morally]" (*jissen iyoku*) and an "attitude to act [morally]" (*jissenteki taido*). To ensure that morality becomes a "way of living" (*ikikata*), it is necessary to "habitualize" (*shūkanka suru*) and have students constantly "repeat" (*hanfuku suru*) morally charged practices. As one guidebook explains it, "Until basic behavioral patterns reach the point of becoming unconscious and fixated, repetition is necessary" (SGD: 80). Peak, in fact, notes the ubiquity of the phrase "basic habits of daily life" in materials for preschoolers (1991: 65). Daily routines (eating habits, proper speech, personal hygiene, being punctual, etc.) are taught early and considered vital to character development because it is recognized that managing the body teaches and reinforces a host of norms (e.g. *uchi/soto* and *ura/omote* distinctions, shame, the meaning of *omoiyari* and *seken*, proper sociolinguistic behavior (*aisatsu*)).

This focus on seemingly insignificant actions resonates with what Bourdieu calls *habitus*, "which designates a way of being, a habitual state (especially of the body) and, in particular, predisposition, tendency, propensity, or inclination" (1977: 214, parentheses in original). Acquiring habits often constitutes accepting, or at least apprehending, an ideology:

The whole trick of pedagogic reason lies precisely in the way it extorts the essential while seeming to demand the insignificant: in obtaining the respect for form and forms of respect which constitute the most visible and at the same time the best-hidden (because most "natural") manifestation of submission to the established order.

(*ibid.*: 94–5, quotation marks and parentheses in original)

The most obvious place to look for the embodiment of socialization is the body. Hendry judiciously discusses the cultural management of the body in her examination of Japanese preschoolers (1986). It is this corporeal locus where state interests, educational mandates, and other sociopolitical forces impress themselves. The body is expected to emit certain sounds (*aisatsu*), position itself, move in certain ways (e.g. bowing), drape itself with age-, gender-, and group-identifying attire, and, as discussed in the following subsection, internally experience appropriate feelings.

Ritualizing experience through emotion

Attempts at mobilizing bodily experiences as a strategy for naturalizing an ideology are also evident in discussions of emotion. Teachers are advised that morality should not just be "external behavioral patterns," since there is an "emotional aspect" (*shinjōteki no sokumen*) to character. "Feelings" (*kimochi*), "being moved" (*kandō suru*), and "joy" (*yorokobi*) are parts of the discourse of teaching morals. This is why teachers should teach students to have "moral feelings" (*dōtokuteki shinjō*), "intellectual sentiments" (*chiteki jōsō*), and "esthetic sentiments" (*biteki jōsō*). Students should also learn about the importance of experiencing a "satisfied feeling" (*jūjitsukan, manzokukan*) and "feelings of achievement" (*jōjukan*). Among their peers, students should learn "feelings of solidarity" (*rentaikan*), thereby reinforcing belongingness. They should also develop "feelings of familiarity" (toward teachers) (*shinkinkan*).

That moral education should ideally be a deeply emotional and moving endeavor is apparent in the use of *kokoro*. This is a key term with powerful associations in Japanese, and may mean heart, mind, will, intention, or feelings. Indeed, moral instruction is sometimes called "education for the heart" (*kokoro no kyōiku*), so teachers are told to "move" (*kandō saseru, ugokasu*) the hearts of their students.

In the classroom and during school activities, teachers should make efforts to "bring about the proper atmosphere" (literally, "breed the atmosphere," *funiki o jōsei suru*), thereby emotionally charging a venue or situation so that it becomes conducive to learning. This is because "In the process of acquiring habits, the influence of the environment is significant." Things that students come into contact with on a daily basis "can make deep impressions on their hearts without them knowing it" (*shirazu shirazu no uchi ni kokoro ni fukaku kizamareru*) (SGDK: 33). Thus, establishing the proper "living environment" (*seikatsu kangyō*) or "situations" (*bamen*) is necessary. Also "it is important to make efforts to create a desirable atmosphere so that school and classes, as groups, come to have a sense of unity" (SGD: 81). After all, students are able to learn "unconsciously" (*muishiki no uchi ni*) from their surroundings (SGDK: 30). This is why "it is said that a good school atmosphere [*kōfū*] fosters good students. History and tradition, sweat and tears, joy and sorrow, and the desires and thoughts of people accumulate so that a school atmosphere is fomented, and students are influenced by all of these" (CG: 86).

Moral instruction as a total education

Teachers are repeatedly advised to design and think in terms of "total plans" (*zentai keikaku*) and how to integrate "organically" (*yūkiteki ni*) moral education into the curriculum. All teachers should keep their colleagues and superiors informed of their teaching plans, and there is a concern for "uniform" (*kakuitsuteki*) planning. CG and SGDK are replete with organizational diagrams, flow charts, calendars, sample schedules, and "guidance plan forms" (*shidō keikaku no pēji*) that record if students are acquiring the targeted values. There seems to be a sense that moral instruction can somehow be mechanically engineered into students' heads. The concern for details and planning appears to be an attempt to organize and regulate every aspect of teacher–student interaction, so that methods themselves carry totalizing messages about the role of teachers.

The guidebooks repeatedly state that moral education should be taught not just in regular moral education classes but should be present in other classes and permeate all school activities. Moral values, in a phrase that occurs repeatedly in SGDK and CG, should supplement, deepen, and be integrated (*hojū, shinka, tōgō suru*) into all school activities. For example, teachers are advised to "clearly point out those instances when special activities possess moral education" (CGD: 29). Special activities, the importance of which is clear in publications such as *Shō gakkō shidō sho: tokubetsu katsudō hen* (Primary School Guidance Manual: A Compilation of Special Activities), may be grade activities, group activities, club activities, or school events, and are needed to foster desirable human relations, to form basic living habits and an attitude that is careful about health and safety. They are also needed to deepen one's awareness as a member of a group, the significance of being Japanese, and to foster a spirit of public service (SGTH: 2).

Also, even simple events should be afforded great significance. For instance, one guidebook discusses in detail the role of cleaning activities for socializing students. Through "experiencing the guidance of cleaning activities" students learn how the most mundane practices carry moral messages (SGD: 84–5).

Moreover, any guidance provided by teachers to students should be based on moral principles. Schools should be regarded as total institutions where morality is to be cultivated in all curricular and extracurricular activities. In mathematics, Japanese language, physical education, and other classes, and in matters related to health, safety, the school cafeteria, using the library, and before and after vacations, moral guidance should be given: "the role that moral education plays in school subjects is wide-ranging. It educates children rich in a humanism that possesses a harmony of intellect, morals, and the body" (SGD: 6). An example of how wide-ranging moral education should be is evident in a guidebook that suggests how music classes can be utilized to teach key values (in a section entitled "Using Guidance for the Choir to Make the Harmony of Friendship Reverberate") (CGO: 41–5).

The significance of saturating the environment with messages is that whichever way one turns, the same reality is confronted. In this way an ideological house of mirrors is built that convinces its inhabitants of an omnipresent, "natural," and "commonsensical" normative world view.

Messages in the method: learning to ritualize social life

It is not surprising that Japanese often perceive social reality in a "framed" manner because they live in a culture with a high sense of rituality.[19] It is also therefore not surprising that compartmentalizing and ritualizing experience is a socializing/educating technique. Sano (1989) discusses how day-care educators create an alternating rhythm of work and play by initiating "feeling" or "mood change" (*kibun tenkan*) among children, and Hendry explains how, through the use of music, this alternating rhythm segments temporal periods in kindergartens and day nurseries (1986: 134–43).[20]

The appropriate place to look is in the important concept of knowing how to *kejime o tsukeru* (discriminate). Lebra notes that the Japanese tendency to distinguish, carefully and clearly, between different spheres of social situation is expressed in this word. This type of knowledge is highly regarded since the individual who cannot make proper *kejime* is considered immature and not to be relied upon. "This concern for maintaining *kejime* may contribute to the Japanese person's keen awareness of the discrepancy between *honne* and *tatemae*" (Lebra 1976: 136).[21] The complex social transformations that a social actor initiates using *omote/ura* and *uchi/soto* all pivot around *kejime*, which in the words of Bachnik, acts as a "meta-index" (1992: 26): *kejime* "can index *how much* discipline, submission of self, or boundedness and, conversely, *how little* emotion, self-expression, or spontaneity is appropriate in a given situation" (Bachnik 1992: 11, italics in original).[22]

How is the Japanese predilection for ritualizing and segregating experience taught in educational settings? Consider the importance afforded school functions. Japanese schools, as microcosms of Japanese society, reflect a concern for establishing a highly predictable rhythm of rites that clearly demarcates spatio-temporal boundaries, assigns everybody a role, and provides a general sense of order.[23] Some major ceremonies include entrance ceremony (*nyūgaku-shiki*); opening ceremony (*shigyō-shiki*); club guidance (*kurabu shōkai*); homeroom home visit (*katei hōmon*); student committee activities (*i-inkai katsdō*); field trips (*ensoku*); school trip (*shūgaku ryokō*); cleaning (*seisō*); closing ceremony (*shūgyō shiki*); athletic meet (*taiiku taikai*); school culture festival (*bunkasai*); graduating students farewell party (*yosenkai*); and graduation (*sotsugyō shiki*). Besides the major ceremonies, there are a host of other events that are ritualized and pressed into sociopolitical service, such as "commencement of work," "finishing of work," "completion of work," "rotation of posts," "morning meetings," and activities related to the memorial of the school's establishment. Many of these are also suffixed with *shiki* ("ceremony"), thereby indicating their ritualizing function. There are other more minor but more ubiquitous rituals and routines, such as practices associated with lunch time, cleaning, and arriving at and leaving school, greetings (*aisatsu*), teacher–student interactions, and donning uniforms, that also carry moral messages.

Japanese pedagogical thought possesses a theory of why ritual is so important (SGTH has a chapter entitled "School Events," pp. 52–7). Ceremonies and school events "are moving group activities that possess educational value which cannot be easily obtained in regular classes." Such activities "provide order and change to school life" and can "develop healthy children's minds and bodies." Because "school life can become monotonous, during every year, semester, and month, plan events that segment and provide rhythm to children's life, making for a more lively life." They make school life enjoyable and rich. Ceremonies are educational activities that "aim to develop and comprehensively demonstrate everyday learning and experiences that are found in grade activities, group activities, and club activities." They are important because they deepen a sense of unity (*ittaikan*) and a sense of belonging (*shozokukan*), foster responsibility, cooperation, and discipline, and allow students to experience the joys and sorrows of the group together. Thus, it is necessary to have the students "participate in a postive manner in the events" (SGTH: 52–7). A "desire to participate" (*sanka iyoku*) in ceremonies is made visible through control of the body. Thus, students are told to keep their hands on their laps, to sit still, not to talk, not to turn their heads, and to make a serious face.

This great concern for predictability, control, and order is also evident in preparing for school functions. Such concerns teach rationality. Rohlen notes that planning and rehearsals are just as important as the events themselves, and that "remarkable to me was the degree of detailed preparations that teachers insisted on for events that Americans would see as largely casual and spontaneous" (1983: 165). This makes sense, because "Precision in schoolwide events is another sign of a school's moral state" (*ibid.*: 201). However, "It is important to appreciate that orderliness in a Japanese school does not evoke some authoritarian image in the eyes of most, but rather is pleasant evidence of benevolence, high morale, and successful instruction" (*ibid.*: 201).[24]

Preparations, precision, and predictability are aspects of ritualization, which socializes students to perceive reality as composed of discrete units of experience and to break the social world down into well-bounded groups, clearly circumscribed scenes, and neatly defined situations, thereby reflecting and giving expression to the norms of *uchi/ soto*, *ura/omote*, and *kejime* (discrimination). What is significant about all this ritualizing is that the "form" – of school functions, events, and daily practices – is just as significant as the "content." Hidden messages of morality – as a code that ritualizes, hierarchizes, organizes, and demarcates the social world – are embedded in the method. The "way" and "how," not just the "what" of events, imparts knowledge about cultural desirables.

Naturalizing a sense of morality

"Moral sense [*dōtokusei*] is at the root of human existence" (SGDK: 10) and is something inborn. This is why teachers use a guidance that "cultivates the sprout of morality" (*dōtoku no mebae o tsuchikau*) (SGDK: 39). Accordingly, fostering morality may be called an education that makes us human and brings out the goodness of human nature" (CGD: 2). This is why teachers are advised to use their "antennae in order to feel the kindness [*yasashisa*] that children have" (SGO: 3). Presenting morality as something embedded in various institutions (school, family, and neighborhood), in all facets of school life, and in quotidian and concrete practices, is a strategy to saturate the environment with normative messages. And management of the body – how it is dressed, adorned, moved about, and the sounds it emits, are all regulated and controlled in such a way that an individual embodies and experiences normative principles.[25] Moral messages are also embedded in the very methods that teachers employ to direct and organize their pedagogical strategies. Such socializing experiences construct subjectivity. Becoming so habitual and unquestioned, such practices naturalize and essentialize a moral world view, making it irrefutable.

CONCLUSION: THE STATE'S VISION OF EDUCATION AND CIVIL SOCIETY

In Japan, civil society is rooted in nation building and maintaining an orderly, predictable, and controlled environment that is conducive to elite goals and economic pursuits. Students do learn about parliamentary government, pacifism, democracy, and respect for human rights. However, if these values are viewed within the greater sociopolitical context of Japan, they acquire a certain abstractness.[26] "Freedom is not an end, but a means to improving civilization" (Rohlen 1983: 264). Thus, observers who carelessly bandy about terms such as "democracy," "liberalism," and "individualism" should bear in mind that Japanese governmental and other elites have a notably different view of their responsibilities *vis-à-vis* their citizens. Though democratic "institutions can be integrated with others in this kind of society [Japanese]," it should be remembered that "they have no prior or higher moral weight," and indeed, "the basic democratic values as Americans understand them – individual rights, grass roots initiative, freedom, and social justice" are not emphasized in the Japanese classroom (*ibid.*: 265). Thus, we should not readily assume that as a modern industrialized state that has economically "made it," the Japanese accept and espouse Anglo-American ideas and ideals. This needs to be stressed, not to pass judgment, but to reach better understandings of the specifics of Japanese sociopolitical dynamics.[27]

8   Conclusion

Lessons from Japan about state and society

In this book, I have argued that in Japan self, society, and state are linked by rationalizing and ritualizing practices, which constitute a bureaucratic ethos, driven by an economic nationalism. This ethos shapes and is a product of public/private distinctions, state/individual relations, state structures, education (especially "moral"), political legitimacy, and "common sense." By pointing out these connections and relations, I have attempted to provide an analysis that demystifies the discourse used to understand Japan. How does such an analysis aid us in understanding the practical realities of social life in Japan? What lessons does Japan offer us about the consequences of hyper-rationalization driven by consumerist capitalism in which the state plows, seeds, and cultivates the social soil so much in its obsession with economic growth that other fruits, such as a healthy civil society, have trouble taking root? Also, what lessons can Japan teach us about social scientific methodology in general?

In this final chapter, I suggest what I believe are some important lessons that Japanese society can teach us about the directions modernity has taken and may take in other societies. The first lesson concerns what happens to a society's ability to respond to crisis when rationalization (hierarchization, categorization, and standardization) so thoroughly permeates the social body that efficiency mutates into a dangerous virus. The second lesson concerns a civil society too state-oriented and premised on an essential "Japaneseness." The last lesson concerns social scientific methodology and the need for an anthropology of state, as it relates to Japan in particular and political economic studies in general.

PROBLEMS OF A HYPER-RATIONALIZED SOCIETY

In the early 1990s, Japan seemed to be at a historical turning point. A stubborn economic recession, continuing corruption at the central and local levels, emergency rice imports due to bad weather and the pressures of a new international trade regime, and the 1993 dissolution of the LDP's dominance (the "1955 system"), all seemed to augur major changes. As if these jolting events were not enough, in 1995 and 1996 Japan witnessed natural and man-made tragedies that only increased public awareness and criticism of state officials. Below I examine the official panic and incompetence in the wake of the great Hanshin earthquake of January 1995, since it clearly demonstrates the weaknesses of an overly bureaucratized state and society. But first, consider some of the other tragedies and events of the 1995–6 period:

- The Aum Shinrikyō March 1995 gas attack in Tokyo subways was only the most public expression of this group's terrorism, which included kidnapping, murder, extortion, intimidation, and smuggling. The mystery is how this group continued to carry on criminal activities for years without police intervention, though they had been repeatedly alerted to the group's activities. The media's lurid attention to Aum and its activities took a disturbing twist when it was learned that a broadcast company (TBS) had shown Aum officials a film clip of an interview with an anti-Aum lawyer, who, along with his wife and child, were apparently killed by Aum members in 1989 (see Hardacre 1996 for a discussion of Aum and the media). Later the public would learn that officials apparently hid the fact that a policeman confessed to the attempted assassination of the chief of the National Police Agency in March 1995.
- The Science and Technology Agency failed to deal adequately with leakage at the Monju fast-breeder reactor in December 1995. Subsequently, the Power Reactor and Nuclear Fuel Development Corporation (the government agency in charge of the plant) attempted a cover-up. Video tape of the leak released to the media was actually doctored to hide the extent of the damage.
- The Ministry of Finance failed to monitor adequately the lending practices of credit unions and *jūsen* (housing loan corporations), resulting in the loss of staggering amounts of money. This occurred amidst a series of other banking and credit unions disasters and scandals (some involving the Ministry of Agriculture), some with major international implications.
- The Ministry of Health and Welfare stubbornly refused to admit its

role and responsibility in allowing the importation of HIV-contaminated blood products in the mid-1980s, resulting in the death of 400 and infecting at least 2,000 hemophiliacs and others. Apparently, in a terrifying example of state–corporate collusion, the ministry wanted to protect certain pharmaceutical companies from foreign competition. At the time of this writing, it is actually too early to know the extent of the tragedy. After Kan Naoto, the Minister of Health and Welfare, took the unusual step for a minister (who are often regarded as mere figureheads of ministries) of ordering his ministry to come clean and produce the relevant documents (which they eventually did) and offered an apology, he was criticized by certain politicians. Indeed, the ministry itself opposed Kan's apology, and even resorted to attempting to sabotage a press conference where he announced that punitive action would be taken against ministry officials and regulations governing *amakudari* tightened. Ministry officials in charge of preparing his press documents changed the wording, causing some confusion among reporters and making the minister look somewhat foolish ("Just a word to undermine Health Minister Kan," AEN 4 June 1996: 8). In late 1996, Ministry of Health and Welfare officials were charged with accepting bribes. The vice-minister, who was also charged, would eventually resign.

Most of these problems were the products of incestuous relations between state structures and private economic interests – incestuous because there was no third-party monitoring of state–society relations, no official agency with a watchdog function. Moreover, once a problem was exposed, the bureaucrats often stonewalled, denying charges with a large dose of official arrogance, even disdain for those who complained about bureaucratic bungling. It is still too early to evaluate the fallout from these problems, and as I write the media reveals new details and related facts about these incidents on a daily basis. The general perception, as seen in media reportage, is that these incidents evidence a Japan at the historical crossroads. But those who write about the nature of this imminent change in the editorials of the leading newspapers and magazines often have a short-term view that adds a superficiality to their predictions. Like any other society, Japan has always been and will always be changing. The question is how significant any change will be. If viewed in the long term, the changes that we are now witnessing do not appear so momentous. This is not to deny their significance, only to make the point that the changes that characterized the 1950s, 1960s, 1970s, and 1980s were all arguably – in their own ways – as momentous as those we are seeing now. Perhaps many commentators, obsessed with Japan's political parties, have assumed that the machinations of politicians are a barometer of profound sociopolitical upheaval. They may very well be. But in this author's opinion, it is still too early to judge if the developments of the 1990s deserve to be called a sea-change of the order of the prewar/postwar divide, as some proclaim.

SHAKING STATE AND SOCIETY: THE GREAT HANSHIN EARTHQUAKE[1]

The benefits that bureaucratization, rationalization, and ritualization have afforded Japanese society – domestic peace and order, unprecedented prosperity, and economic clout that extends far beyond the Japanese archipelago – do not need to be recounted here. The accolades, some of which border on idealization (the "Japan-as-Number-One" perspective) have been heard many times. Thus, perhaps it is more fitting to relate, in a more circumspect tone, how rationalization and its ilk did not befriend relief efforts.

Campbell writes that "Democracy and bureaucracy are fundamentally antithetical. Democracy is bottom-up political process devoted to responsiveness. Bureaucracy is top-down administrative structure devoted to rationality. Modern democratic governance is based on the premise that the two can work together" (1989: 113). The choice of the Japanese is "tilted a bit to the bureaucratic side," reflecting perhaps "the preferences of its people" (*ibid.*: 135). The Japanese themselves often note the negative consequences of such a political culture. These include pernicious passivity, an unhealthy trust of authority figures, and a lack of critical thought. A bureaucracy-led, lockstep, and over-regulated life produces *shiji machi ningen* (people who are waiting for instructions) and *manyuaru ningen* (manual people), mentioned in Chapter 6. There is little need to ask questions in a world that is predefined and controlled by unseen, unaccountable authorities. What happens when such a psychology is confronted with a world-shattering crisis?

Disasters, whether natural or human-made, reveal how the sociopolitical structure of a given society is assembled and rattle a system so that cracks radiate from its weak points while its stronger parts hold fast. On 17 January 1995, the great Hanshin (Kobe-Osaka) earthquake shook the sociopolitical edifice of Japan, exposing its strengths and weaknesses, which, during more normal times, usually go unnoticed. Over 6,000 people were killed,[2] 26,804 injured, and 290,000 left homeless, and 107,388 buildings were damaged. Reconstruction costs have been estimated at around 9.5 trillion yen. The response of the government and public to the earthquake illustrated the problems plaguing modern Japan. The calamity proved to be a tragic opportunity for all the familiar clichés about Japanese public policy to make an unwelcome appearance: a bureaucracy strangled by rigid red tape, local government incompetence, political indecisiveness in Tokyo, administrative confusion, and a general inability for crisis management. "What struck home was the observation that Japan's social institutions . . . function flawlessly under ordinary circumstances, but collapse completely when a crisis occurs" ("Japan's internal emergency management," DY 11 February 1995: 15). The same features of rationalization that had turned Japan into an economic giant and secured domestic peace and order – hierarchization, categorization, formalization, standardization – mutated into an inflexibility that cost lives.

What was striking about the weak points revealed by the massive earthquake is that they appeared at every level of the sociopolitical edifice. It should be stressed that the Japanese archipelago is no stranger to killer quakes, and is surprising that so much panic and chaos ensued after the great Hanshin earthquake. Indeed, there was an almost surreal feel to post-quake reactions: a Swiss rescue team was told that their dogs would have to be quarantined for a period while an untold number of people were still buried under rubble; the Health and Welfare Ministry would initially not allow foreign doctors to help because they lacked certification to practice in Japan;[3] victims in need of rent-free housing were told to present "sufferer's certificates" ("Housing, other services available to victims," JT 22 January 1995: 4); someone, obviously aware of the disorganization, volunteered to donate mineral water, juice, blankets, and foodstuffs to anyone, *except* "an authority/association" (DY 25 January 1995: 3); while victims suffered, volunteers were asked to wait for instructions ("Volunteers get into action," JT 22 January 1995: 2); and nine days after the quake, the headlines of the *Daily Yomiuri* read "Police decide to aid illegal foreigners," as if an inordinate amount of consideration had to be given to the issue (26 January 1995: 1).

LESSONS FROM A HYPER-RATIONALIZED SOCIETY

The great Hanshin earthquake presents a paradox. Japan is a nation that, defying its dearth of natural resources, rebuilt itself after total defeat in World War II into an economic colossus by utilizing its genius for bureaucratic organization and efficiency. It is also a nation that has prided itself on high-tech answers to the daily necessities of life. Add to this a history that has witnessed countless *tsunami* (tidal waves), typhoons, and earthquakes, instilling in the Japanese people a resiliency to and preparedness for natural calamity. Why, then, with all the advantages of a post-industrial society that has made rationality a state religion, did the Japanese polity react so chaotically to the Kobe-Osaka disaster? Could it be that Japanese society, so relentlessly cultivated for economic development, organization, and systemization, has been strangled by the weeds of hyper-rationalization? Could it be that "The Government seems unable to react promptly to any event that isn't in its long-term industrial plan" (Reiko Hatsumi, "'I Am Sure Help Will Come,'" *New York Times Weekly Review*, 22 January 1995: 7)? The political ineptitude evident in response to the earthquake is actually part of a larger problem that is inextricably woven into the fabric of modern Japan's society: a hyper-rationalizing and over-bureaucratizing of the national psyche. Rationalizing practices are certainly not unique to Japan and are found anywhere. However, the question is to what degree these practices are implemented, and to what degree people place faith in them. The argument could be made that in Japan, rationalization has mutated into hyper-rationalization, a monster hatched from Japan's exacting, though successful, drive toward economic power. Rationalization is characterized by stable lines of hierarchy, procedures based on precedent, and relatively fixed modes of classification. Hyper-rationalization, however, may be characterized as the search for hierarchy even if not stipulated, the usurpation of reasoned judgment by precedent, and categorization so rigid it paralyzes thought. Hyper-rationalization steals self-initiative and personal responsibility. When all decision making becomes dominated by authorization and formalism suppresses flexibility, personal volition is regarded as a hindrance to some greater, more authoritative prerogative. A top-down-oriented sociopolitical system discourages self-assertiveness, and responsibility is traded for vacillation. The upshot is a dangerous passivism. To students of human organization these lessons are so well-known that they seem trite, but in light of the human-made problems made apparent by the great Hanshin earthquake, the unreflective bureaucratic impulse cries out for attention.

THE CENTER SHAKEN

From the start, the political leaders and ministries appeared oblivious to the severity of the disaster. Prime Minister Murayama, who first learned of the tragedy from television, did not visit Kobe until almost three days after the earthquake.[4] Lack of effective communication between the periphery and the center hindered rapid decision making. And according to one observer, the bureaucracy, "which thinks it controls prime ministers and governors," was primarily at fault for the government's initial paralysis. "Bureaucrats were responsible for the loss of many lives that could have been saved" ("Arrogance quake response under fire," DY 27 January 1995: 13).[5]

If chaos gripped the central government, matters were not much better at the local level. Officials in the area apparently saw little need to prepare for a major quake.[6] Some Kobe citizens were angry that they saw no police or official rescue for a day or two after the quake ("Survivors rebuild lives amid the rubble," JT 28 January 1995: 19). The most glaring example of confusion and indecisiveness at the local level was the time it took to dispatch the Self-Defense Forces (SDF). Even though the SDF had repeatedly asked the Hyogo prefectural governor and Kobe mayor for a prompt request for the dispatch of troops, it was not until four hours after the quake that a request came from the Hyogo prefectural governor's office. A request to the Maritime Self-Defense Forces was not made until more than twelve hours after the disaster struck ("Delay in calling out SDF rescuers comes under fire," DY 20 January 1995: 3).

The imperial family's official response (or the initial lack of) deserves comment. On 20 January, three days after the earthquake, the crown prince and princess left for an eleven-day, three-nation tour to the Middle East,[7] and the emperor and empress did not visit the devastated area until a full two weeks after the earthquake.[8] Perhaps the Imperial Household Agency (a unit of the Prime Minister's Office) was fearful that the imperial family members, as sacred and idealized symbols of Japan, would be sullied if associated in any way with disaster, even if shown expressing compassion for the victims. Though the crown prince and princess did cut their trip short, their departure from Japan several days after the quake – together with the dilatory imperial visit – left some Japanese feeling insulted.

Sometimes, the authorities' response could only be described as arrogant. Not long after the quake, Osaka Governor Kazuo Nakagawa criticized quake victims for not doing more to help themselves: "they think they can all be helped by others" ("Death toll from quake tops

2,600," JT 19 January 1995: 1–2). Perhaps the best example of official imperiousness was the press conference given by Itō Kazutoshi, the director of the National Land Agency's disaster prevention co-ordination division, who, during the interview, "smoked, glared and virtually screamed at reporters." He "lashed out in response to questions about whether Japan should change its [crisis management] system," deflecting criticism with the curious claim that stronger central government action to process foreign aid offers quickly could lead to a "revival of Japanese militarism. . . . After the hour long briefing, in which Itō impatiently interrupted questioners and yelled at one to leave the room for smiling hello to a friend, he stalked out, saying, 'I'm very busy. I have no time to deal with critics'" ("Official lashes out over quake criticism," JT 28 January 1995: 2).[9]

THE GRIP OF RACIAL CATEGORIZATION: DEALING WITH OUTSIDERS

From the perspective of overseas observers, perhaps the most enigmatic side to the government's reaction was its initial refusal of foreign aid. Five days after the earthquake, there was still no official response ("Countries offer to help but govt fails to respond," DY 23 January 1995: 2). The familiar excuses were offered as to why outside help was turned down, centering on the key classification of Japanese/non-Japanese: "language problems with foreigners"; Japan's "island mentality"; and "foreigners would not like Japanese food." Others simply said that the refusals were rooted in an arrogance that Japan could take care of itself ("Kobe's citizens forced to endure the unendurable, again," JT 28 January 1995: 19).[10] The Foreign Ministry said that it required concrete requests from local governments before it could respond to offers of international aid ("Countries offer to help but govt fails to respond," DY 23 January 1995: 2).

It is worth noting the role the foreign media played in shaping how the quake was perceived in Japan, especially since, at least initially, Japanese journalists seemed to have had a very different view of the quake's political reverberations. According to a Japanese media critic, Yoichi Matsuzoe, Japanese journalists were at first not looking for confrontational stories; i.e. they shied away from criticizing the government for responding slowly and being unprepared. However, after the foreign press had criticized the Japanese government, "the Japanese media picked it up and started hitting the government hard themselves" ("Dramatic and distant views of the quake," JT 4 February 1995: 21).

I also heard from Japanese acquaintances who volunteered to assist in the recovery that the media suppressed stories about small riots triggered by hoarding and stealing food. Also, the leader of the Swiss rescue team, while criticizing the Japanese government's slow response, had his interview inexplicably cut short by the government-affiliated television network ("'I Am Sure Help Will Come,'" *New York Times Weekly Review*, 2 January 1995: 7).

A PASSIVE CITIZENRY

The great Hanshin earthquake cracked opened and exposed several major structures that define the Japanese sociopolity. One is the relation between the local and central authorities. Another is the relation between Japan, non-Japanese, and the rest of the world. I have already discussed these issues, but now I want to examine still another aspect of the Japanese sociopolity: the relation between state (government) and society (citizenry) in Japan. This concerns "civil society" and "legitimacy."

Japan has all the markings of what in the Euro-American context are called civil society; freedom of expression, non-state associations and groupings, and a general respect toward non-kin and strangers. However, the great Hanshin earthquake exposed the nature of Japan's version of civil society, revealing how, to a large degree, it is premised on a moral authority that is top-down and state-ordained, rather than bottom-up and popularly advocated. Being so tied to the bureaucratic center, Japan's civil society is in some ways weakened by hyper-rationalization. For instance, not long after the earthquake, Japanese who volunteered their efforts were baffled by the official treatment they received. Some were turned away and told to come back when order had been restored; others were informed that their help was unneeded; and still others were told to fill out complicated forms ("Volunteers get into action," JT 22 January 1995: 2).

The Kobe-Osaka earthquake illustrated what happens when people are so used to taking orders that they become apathetic; when all decisions are made by referring to a manual; and when life is so regulated and organized that any unpredictability elicits not reaction but panic. Though the foreign media were impressed by the quake victims' stoicism and composure, closer to home, some Japanese derided the victims' passivity and indifference to fellow sufferers. In a letter to the editor, a Japanese noted a lack of solidarity, and how the mass media "showed healthy grown men cowering in the emergency shelters, whining about how hungry and cold they were, without lifting a finger to join in helping the emergency rescue operations. Add to this the chaos caused by private automobile traffic going about their personal business and obstructing rescue operations" ("Quake has exposed deeper problems," JT 22 January 1995: 18). While it may be argued that the familiar refrains heard from victims – *shō ga nai* or *shikata ga nai* ("it can't be helped") – should be admired as a type of stoic maturity directed at nature, it is just as easy to contend that this attitude reflects an unhealthy obeisance to authority (i.e. indecisive leaders, incompetent officials, unaccountable bureaucrats). Though Osaka Governor Nakagawa's remarks that quake victims were not doing enough to help themselves were certainly cold and cavalier under the circumstances, they do point to a disconcerting over-dependence on authority. Though the public certainly complained and the government made an easy target for criticism months after the disaster, there was, nevertheless, a remarkable lack of outrage toward officialdom. This, perhaps more than anything else, says much about how average Japanese view their relationship with the government. No demand for resignations, no sustained, organized assaults on government incompetence, and no great realization that someone, somewhere, was accountable for delayed action. One interpretation of this attitude is that the Japanese citizenry simply do not expect too much from their government, or that the government should not be criticized any more than nature should, since both are immovable and unassailable.

THE LESSONS OF MODERN JAPAN: WHEN THE STATE SUBORDINATES SOCIETY

In this work I have cast my net wide – rationality, political structures, belief in the state, education, moral training, civil society – in order to argue that these aspects of Japanese sociopolity are interwoven in ways that are not always obvious and form one ideological tapestry. The many different threads come together in a given individual's subjectivity, constituting the invisible institutions that shape Japan's particular political system. Do these linkages have lessons for us about the nature of sociopolity in other places? To those who still seriously discuss whether Japan is too "unique" to be of relevance to other societies, I would suggest that indeed Japan does have lessons to teach us. These lessons are about what happens to the way people live when the totalizing power of politico-economic macro-structures dominates the nooks and crannies of society; about the effects of rationalization on the human psyche; and the increasing intertwining of state, society, and self within the projects of late capitalist development. In short, Japan teaches us about how modernity bureaucratizes subjectivity. What should be remembered is that Japan, contrary to what some observers believe, does not teach us about how "tradition" and the past are in conflict with or balanced against modernization. Japan is patently futuristic in spirit, and while images of rice paddies, festivals, kimonos, and Shinto shrines may ease the rush of modernity, they cannot erase the effects of computers, bullet trains, digitization, and bureaucratic structures. The so-called "traditional" aspects of Japan are pressed into service for the distinctly modern projects of state goals, elite domination, rationalized economics, positivist assumptions, and building "Japaneseness." "Tradition" is not a historical ghost haunting Japan's techno-bureaucratized landscape: the "two seemingly contradictory languages – a language of rationalization and a language of nostalgia" (Kelly 1986: 604; *cf.* Ivy 1995), are two sides of the same coin.

There are many ways in which the state and its allied economic endeavors subordinate non-state spheres of social life. For example, consider *sābisu zangyō* ("service overtime"; "service" denoting something done or given for free), meaning unpaid overtime (see "*Zangyō*: Just whose life is it anyway?" JT 23 May 1996: 14). Though good statistics are difficult to compile, unpaid overtime is rampant and considered part of normal corporate culture. Related to this is *karōshi*, or death from overwork. Though the state (specifically, the Ministry of Labor) has officially encouraged *jitan* (shorter working hours and more paid holidays) and has, to some degree, recognized *karōshi* as a legitimate problem, workers are still expected to devote a remarkable amount of time to the workplace. One can wonder what such an occupied work schedule does to the time needed for the activities indispensable to sustaining civil society. Or, consider a recent ruling of the Tokyo High Court, an institution that ostensibly should defend the individual's rights from encroachment by others or officialdom. This court ruled that the "company has a right to decide a new post without the consent of the individual and have the employee accept it," meaning in effect that companies have the right to transfer employees far from home (i.e. spouses and families). Those who protest against such transfers run the risk of being fired. According to the judge, "Society has not yet matured enough to accept the idea of giving priority to family life" ("Firms can order transfers, court rules," JT 31 May 1996: 2). That the judiciary, as an extension of the state apparatus, can imperiously decide that society "has not yet matured enough" speaks volumes about the paternalistic attitude of officialdom. Such a court system does little to encourage an opening between the state – together with its supporting corporate structures – and the private sphere, allowing the growth of a healthy civil society.

If all of a society's sociopolitical structures are tied to state authority and national identity, then non-statist and non-nationalist sources of legitimacy are weakened, and there may be no perceived need for a civil society positioned between officialdom and the citizens. Perhaps this is why, lacking a sanctioned buffer zone between state and society, a general paranoia *vis-à-vis* the powers that be may arise.[11] Thus, after the great Hanshin earthquake and the Aum Shinrikyō gas attack in 1995, more than one Japanese expressed the fear that these terrible events would be used as excuses to increase state power.[12]

Though it can certainly be argued, in the manner of Gramsci, that civil society ultimately supports the state and its projects, the case can also be made that it furnishes a space relatively free from official controls, allowing the de-essentializing and de-naturalizing of rationalism and "common sense" that form the subjective foundations of state structures and practices. Thus, "Once bureaucracy itself is seen as an issue, rather than as simply a fact of modern life or a neutral method of organizing activity, questions about it appear in a fundamentally different light" (Ferguson 1984: 6).

CREATING CIVIL SOCIETY: DEMYSTIFYING THE "NATURALNESS" OF "JAPANESENESS"

In East Asia, the pattern of state/society relations historically differs notably from the modern Western pattern, and the distinctive features of the East Asian pattern do not simply disappear after industrialization or democratization. In East Asia, the states are organizationally pervasive, without clear-cut boundaries. Their powers and functions are diffuse, and they pay little respect to due process. Consequently, the lines between public and private, political and personal, formal and informal, official and non-official, government and market, legal and customary, and between procedural and substantial, are all blurred.

(Ding 1994: 317)

Ding notes that the above assessment is true not just of China and Taiwan, but "in democratic Japan" as well (*ibid.*: 317). What is the relation between state and society in Japan? Are there spaces between official structures and non-official spheres? Discussion of what kind of civil society Japan has is not a purely academic exercise, and an examination of public life in Japan offers us two major lessons. The first concerns the relation between state and society. Before the war, any spontaneous public life that existed was jealously monitored by officialdom. After the war,

> A better approximation of the Western model of civil society resulted, but the struggle to remake the Japanese people into a nation of individuals failed. Without the historical weight of the European Renaissance, Reformation or Enlightenment behind it, such a programme of political re-education was never likely to succeed, and only the *naïveté* of the policymakers of the Occupation encouraged the attempt.
>
> (Williams 1994: 115)

Civil society is directly related to the autonomy of an active citizenry and whether this citizenry feels committed to a watchdog function. The apparent unconcern of many Japanese citizens with official corruption and incessant scandals indicates that an essential ingredient of civil society is not functioning (*cf.* Abe *et al.* 1994: 201–12). This is not because the Japanese state controls or governs society in any direct way; rather, it affects and influences society in a multitude of more or less minor but no less significant ways (e.g. administrative guidance). Because there is usually no direct and easily discernible control by the state that can be pointed to, the state's influence over the private is actually more profound than direct dominion.

As discussed in Chapter 3, civility in Japan means high levels of rituality and expressions of etiquette that implicate certain sociopolitical dynamics: (1) social practices that construct a buffer zone between individuals, thereby upholding a type of publicness (i.e. *tatemae*); (2) the salience of shame; (3) the need for empathy; (4) the emergence of hierarchy; (5) self as intensely private or highly dramatized; and (6) in-group/out-group boundary maintenance. These dynamics evidence a civil society that, rather than being part and parcel of egalitarianism as in Euro-American polities, is so interwoven with state structures, and consequently official hierarchies, that it is deeply related to bureaucratization, rationalization, and ritualization. The consequences are predictable, such as limited communication between groups and the avoidance of direct contact between groups (and individuals).[13] But whatever the demerits of segmenting society, bureaucratic organizations (as in many other societies) successfully achieve the results that Japanese demand of them, and the oft-heard conservative Japanese counterview is that problems in Euro-American societies spring from "too much freedom" and "democracy." Nevertheless, Japan teaches us about how a state can rationalize civil society out of existence.

The second lesson concerning civil society relates to "being Japanese." It is not surprising that – in a society ordered and fragmented by rationalized categories, bureaucratic formalities, and ritualized hierarchies that inhibit the formation of spontaneous collectivities – highly abstract conceptualizations (examined in Chapter 5) such as the emperor, the "uniqueness" of Japanese culture, the "homogeneity" of the Japanese, and "Japaneseness" become attractive because they transcend factionalism and provide a unifying function. Though "Japaneseness" is as much a political (citizenship) and ethnic (cultural heritage) issue as it is a racial one (categorizing individuals according to physical traits), it is often in the latter sense that Japanese identity is primarily defined. Granting so much weight to physical appearance for defining identity is certainly not unique to Japan, but the salience of racialist ideology is often ignored because "nationalism" or "xenophobia" are the adjectives of choice for many commentators (the latter terms register a less negative gut reaction, at least for this English speaker, than "racism") (*cf.* Fallows 1994: 431–5). At times, racism is even sugarcoated by excuses about "culture," "tradition," "language" (*cf.* Miller 1982), and in the economic domain, "protectionism." But by sidestepping the role and power of racialist thinking in Japan, we neglect a key element in the sociopolitical arrangement of Japanese and non-Japanese identities. Befu notes that

> no modern state can base its citizenship purely on ethnic primordial sentiments. Japan is no exception. Its government has introduced civic sentiments calling forth universal values such as political freedom, democracy, civil rights, human dignity, equality, and the like that can presumably be shared equally by all groups, majority and minority. But these civic sentiments are only superficially overlaid on more deeply seated primordial sentiments spelled out in Nihonjinron, which excludes Koreans and other minorities from being part of the fold.
>
> (1993: 129)[14]

A healthy civil society may mean many things. One thing that it hopefully means is an acknowledgment of the fact that one's physical appearance, ethnicity, and state affiliation (citizenship, or "nationality"[15]) are not inherently indivisible.[16] "Japaneseness," for many Japanese, blurs physical appearance, ethnicity, and citizenship.

But "Japaneseness" is an aggregation of different identities assembled by sociopolitical design (i.e. it is socially "artificial" in the sense used by Heller (1990)). If one regards oneself as a racially immutable, essentialized entity, then the differences seen in others will also be attributed to prepackaged, racially determined differences. Tester's point about the development of civil society in Euro-American societies is relevant here: "The reciprocity assumed by the modern order of things was symmetric to the extent that it was presumed that, irrespective of surface appearances, all individuals counted the same and, indeed, actually were the same" (1992: 126). Japaneseness is to a large degree premised on a naturalist or essentialist view of "being physically Japanese." While certainly less venomous than the prewar variety, nationalism based on physical appearance and tightly tied to statism can only dampen diversity and popular spontaneity. Many of the components that constitute Japan's civil society are firmly linked to a state that shows evidence of conflating citizenship, cultural heritage, and physical appearance. The state's encouragement (or at least its lack of discouragement) of a race-based form of identity for being Japanese does not encourage a vibrant, tolerant civil society. Creating a social space in which individuals are encouraged to drop racialist categorization and assume a truly civic outlook would only be welcome.

RE-ORIENTING AND DE-ORIENTALIZING KNOWLEDGE

"Scholarship on Japan is frequently criticized as isolated and uninformed by general theoretical constructs and comparative research" (Haley 1991: 4). The reasons for this are complex, but one reason is that many researchers have either assumed that Japan is too "exotic" for useful comparisons, or that it is just like any other G-7 nation-state once its "cultural layering" is ripped off (the premise being that all such societies are somehow fundamentally the same). But I contend that Japan, as a highly "statized" society, does indeed have lessons to offer us concerning political economy and social science in general, since it epitomizes certain social phenomena: e.g. the relation of the state to late capitalist development, transnational capitalism, elite control, state-managed lifestyles, mass society, hyper-consumerism, urbanization, and over-administered education. Any one of these topics makes a tempting target for those interested in the impact of state structures in modern times.

In this work, I have attempted to highlight the significance of the state for understanding Japan (not because the state is necessarily less significant in any other society), but my approach could be applied to any state society. Considering the hegemonic role the state plays in the everyday lives of so many people, it is surprising that anthropology has not devoted more attention to the state (not as distant policy-making institutions, but as ubiquitous sociopolitical processes). After all, "never before have so few, by their actions and inactions, had the power of life and death over so many members of the species" (Nader 1972: 284). What does "an anthropology of the state" entail? Below I offer some suggestions.

Investigating the cosmologies of states

First, it demands that we accept Arnold's statement that "Basic economic beliefs are religious in nature" (1964: xxiii), and then proceed to question the presuppositions and "cosmology" of modernity underlying politico-economic ideologies and assumptions (invisible institutions), such as positivism, progressivsim, a mathematicized world-view, etc., and that most stubborn object of analysis hidden in *le quotidien* (*cf.* De Certeau 1984), "common sense":

> As a frame of thought, and a species of it, common sense is as totalizing as any other; no religion is more dogmatic, no science more ambitious, no philosophy more general. Its tonalities are different, and so are the arguments to which it appeals, but like them – and like art and like ideology – it pretends to reach past illusion to truth, to, as we say, things as they are.
>
> (Geertz 1983: 84)

Thus, the concern with the ordinary "leads the fieldworker to take notes of matters . . . that to other social scientists may seem trivial but that the fieldworker knows may turn out to be crucial to an understanding of the anthropology of everyday life and hence of not-so-everyday life" (Fallers 1974:11).

The particularness of each state

Second, an anthropology of state demands a recognition that – regardless of the remarkable similarities between the different cosmologies found in post-industrial societies, each sociopolity possesses its own particular historical and cultural context that must be confronted. Migdal *et al.* note that "In contemporary social science writing, where states and societies have been portrayed with broad brush strokes, different states and societies have had an uncannily uniform look. So much contemporary scholarship blurs the rich diversity produced in various societies' multiple arenas" (1994: 23). The truth is that no two socio-economic systems are the same, and even their methods of rationalization differ. Some societies may be more similar than others, but researchers should start with the assumption that differences count. The differences observed in Japan are just more salient if compared with Euro-American – specifically Anglo-American – countries (presumably differences in other Asian societies will become more obvious as their economies expand). Conviction in the truthfulness of some transcendent rationality that all societies must follow is naive and simply untrue once local particulars are taken into account: "I think that the word *rationalization* is dangerous. What we have to do is analyze specific rationalities rather than always invoking the progress of rationalization in general" (Foucault in Dreyfus and Rabinow 1983: 210, italics in original).[17] It is easy to criticize the Japanese for their claims to "uniqueness" and ethnic exceptionalism. However, there is just as much danger in having faith in universalism, as many Americans do.

The impact of state projects and policies

Third, an anthropology of state demands careful attention to the actual impact of state policies and projects on individuals or specific groups. Researchers should not regard the immediate field site as "self-sufficient isolates or as scaled-down models of the larger society of which they are parts" (Fallers 1974: 11). Rather, localities are intimately tied to and shaped by central state authorities. Furthermore, the relation between state policies (both explicit and implicit) and academic training should always be scrutinized. Institutions of higher education should ideally turn out liberally informed individuals, not well-trained policy technicians. A pursuit of policy studies for the sake of policy studies leads to a sort of "elitist academics" in which scholarly centers come to see their mission as the maintenance and improvement of status quo power arrangements (state projects and economic interests), rather than the careful analysis and critique of power wielders. It is interesting that state elites and certain researchers are both attracted to the same vision of "rationalizing" society; the former desires control and the latter understanding, but both appear remarkably interested in predictability, planning, and measuring, both as practices and methodologies.

Detailed descriptions of state structures

Fourth, an anthropology of state demands an indication and description, in terms as concrete as possible, of the relevant state structures. For the most part, anthropology has paid little attention to the state, and when it has, it has usually done so in a perfunctory manner, so that it becomes "the State" (distant, abstract, immovable, and monolithic), rather than "a state" (immediate, concrete, constituted, contested). Indeed, the very methods of anthropology – close, personal, even participatory – seem to impede analysis of the state, which is often regarded as impersonal, translocal, and unapproachable. However, though much of anthropological theorizing developed from the study of "stateless societies" (or "state-like" societies), the view that anthropological concepts and methods are especially suited to "traditional" societies, "while those of political scientists and sociologists are more appropriate to 'modern' societies," is misguided and inaccurate. According to Fallers, "This is a relic of nineteenth century typological and evolutionary thought which has inhibited the necessary synthesis" (1974: 17). How should the state be studied from an anthropological perspective? Britan and Cohen (1980) offer six concrete methodological pointers for tackling bureaucratic organizations, but their advice applies equally well to studies of the state.

The nature of appropriate analytic units: "A first task is to draw up a structural chart of the organization, locating all offices and positions and their relations to one another. A temporal dimension should also be included – a history of the organization and its structural development." Also, "Smaller subunits, such as agencies or departments, must be heuristically isolated for analysis, just as more traditional fieldwork chooses a particular community or village for study."

Formal and informal rules: "All organizations have both written and unwritten rules. The written rules can be obtained easily from the legislation, constitution, or operations manual of the organization. The unwritten rules must be obtained from observations and interviews." Moreover, "rule conflict, ambiguity, and selective enforcement are important aspects of organizational dynamics."

Input/output functions While studying the history of an organization, the researcher "must consider its formally planned inputs, their (ideal) processing, and the manner in which outputs are then provided for clients, the public, markets, etc."

Everyday activities   "Once an organization's formal structure, rules, and planned input/output are recorded and understood, research can focus on everyday organizational life" (i.e. "common sense" and *le quotidien*).

Informal networks   Because informal networks and relations have "very important effects on how the organization decides, plans, and carries out its functions, it is essential to obtain a picture of the informal networks that exist within the formal structure and that cut across other agencies and the wider society."

Environmental relations   The external relations of the organization must be analysed e.g. "formal and informal social and political linkages," "cultural continuities and discontinuities," and "the degree of dependability, monitoring, and corruption of personnel" in order to place the organization within its broader context (*ibid.*: 20–2).

One final point that deserves mention is that ethnographically oriented students of the state cannot rely on fieldwork alone: "One cannot study an elephant armed only with a microscope. Much of the data must come from documentary sources and from highly specialized interviewing" (Fallers 1974: 20).

The state is a human institution, not a variable

Finally, an anthropology of state demands that we carefully weigh the pros and cons of a substantivist versus a formalist approach (*cf.* Polanyi 1957). The latter attempts to construct abstract models with general applicability and is premised on the role of decision making. Whatever the strengths of the formalist approach, it encourages the age-old mistake of naively attempting to force social reality into methodological frameworks borrowed from the natural scientific paradigm and a consequent fixation on "variables" (often ripped from their local context), "models" (sometimes used for inapplicable comparative analysis), and a fatal attraction to trendy academic movements (e.g. "rational choice"). Formalism is rooted in the Western political philosophy of individualism and consequently idealizes individual choice, as if all social and economic reality could be reduced to autonomous individuals.

The substantivist approach does not privilege a rarefied plane of analysis above concrete human relations and institutions but relies on description and detailed empirical data. It is particular social actors, their activities, and subjectivities that matter:

The bare-bones summary of the anthropological method as the unadorned collection of empirical data, its ordering, abstraction and testing, understates the formidable difficulties involved. These challenge the modern tendency to belittle the laborious business of describing, accurately and fully, any complex dimension of an alien society.

(Williams 1996: 25)

But being knowledgeable about the empirical nuts and bolts of a particular society should not preclude a historically informed and cross-cultural view, which grants a healthy intellectual perspective and thereby respects the diversity of the human condition.

Specifically in the case of Japan, respecting the diversity of the human condition means "de-orientalizing" our thinking. Williams writes that "Asian experience has not informed the science of economics" (*ibid.*: 153). Though his assertion is disputable and seems intended to arouse interest rather than state a fact, the implication is that we would do well to take seriously the modernities unfolding in Asia on their own terms. This is the message of *Japan and the Enemies of Open Political Science* (1996), a work in which Williams pulls no punches in his argument that because of Euro-American-centric blindness and biases inherent in the methodologies used to understand Japan, the remarkable achievements of modern Japanese civilization are not appreciated. Thus, according to Williams, we lack a Japanese canon of classic works comparable to what the West has produced over the last several centuries in the social sciences. Though Williams is basically interested in Japan's genius at bureaucratic management of its society and economy, he notes that "The academic mainstream of Western social science and philosophy has not only ignored the assertion that Japan is the most significant political system of our time, but it has also rejected Japanese claims to importance of any kind" (*ibid.*: 52). He gives many reasons why this is so, including methodologies premised on textual classicism, empiricism, positivism, and especially orientalism (*cf.* Said 1985).[18] Indeed, Williams argues that ethnocentric arrogance on the part of the Euro-American tradition deserves much blame. Because some regard Japan as merely a highly successful avatar of Euro-America's (particularly America's) politico-economic institutions (i.e. capitalism, markets, legislature, and a liberal democratic tradition), they feel no need to take a serious look at the Japanese experience on its own terms. This is orientalism, conceited and complacent. Neither Japan nor any other society will benefit from such a view.

Notes

1 Introduction: where rationality and rituality meet

1 According to one observer, even activities that are usually regarded as enjoyable are highly formalized: "A rigid web of formulas covers areas of life and activities, such as sporting events, parties and honeymoons, for which spontaneity would be considered an essential ingredient in other societies" (Van Wolferen 1989: 332).

2 The counterpart of the "Japan, Inc." view, sometimes heard among Japanologists, is the "Japan as the rudderless state."

3 *Cf.* Mills's use of "bureaucratic ethos" (1963: 226). Also *cf.* Ellul's discussion of "technical civilization," in which the "rule of technique" dominates social life (1964: 97).

4 The literature that discusses and employs these terms, in English and Japanese, is too vast to cite here, but the reader is directed to Bachnik and Quinn (1994) for recent and updated treatments.

5 There are many ways to define rationalization and bureaucratization. For recent works, see Scott, Meyer *et al.* 1994 and Meyer *et al.* 1994: 181–2.

6 I do not mean to suggest that Japanese society possesses a "unique" cultural trait (rituality) absent in other societies. However, in relative terms, rituality is salient in Japan, though it should be stressed that, in spite of the emphasis on rituality in Japan, there are spheres of social life where de-ritualization is the norm, as in intimate situations (*cf.* Lebra 1976).

7 *Cf.* Crozier, who argued that bureaucratic forms of organization exist in every sphere of life in France (1964). Also see Blau 1963, Jacoby 1973, Merton 1968, and Whyte 1957.

8 *Cf.* Sakakibara, who writes that Japan has a "mixed" economy, and goes so far as to call Japan's system "non-capitalist" (1993).

9 *Cf.* Bennett's discussion of the nature of political myths: "a. The absence of explicit, formally drawn logical connections between political beliefs and values and political understandings about specific issues. . . . b. The presence of implicit psychological support for standardized political formulae due to the capacity of familiar political symbols to evoke unarticulated mythical understandings. . . . c. The capacity of individuals to hold divergent, even contradictory, myths with nearly equal intensity, which promotes tolerance for a range of possible outcomes yet imposes a rigid

consensus about the limits of legitimate debate and acceptable policy" (1980: 169).

10 *Cf.* Kertzer: "In many studies, politics is examined as a give-and-take in which people simply follow their material interests. These material interests are often taken to be self-evident. In other studies, people are viewed as consumers in a public relations market, or as empty slates socialized to reproduce the political views of their parents, peers, or neighbors" (1988: 7).

2 Demystifying a discourse: the misuses of "Japanese culture" and the production of rationality

1 For an anthropologist's view of "culture" who studies Japan, see Smith's "The Cultural Context of the Japanese Political Economy" (1992).

2 For a discussion of the meanings of "rice" in the building of Japanese identity, see Ohnuki-Tierney 1993.

3 *Cf.* Williams' definition of "essentialism": "The doctrine of cultural studies that holds that cultures have an identifying essence which precedes and governs any factual or textual manifestation of that culture" (1996: xxv).

4 Also *cf.* Haley: "whatever aspects of Japanese life that do not seem to conform to occidental expectations of model behavior are labeled 'traditional' and left at that without much further analysis or thought" (1991: 17).

5 The "revisionist" – or, depending on one's perspective, "Japan-bashers" – are ostensibly those who are overly critical of Japan. The debate for the most part takes place within the parameters of Japan–US relations. According to some (e.g. "Critics not always bashers," JT 1 August 1992: 20), accusations of "Japan-bashing" are ways of deflecting criticism and discouraging analysis of how power is organized in Japan. Well-known "revisionists" include Chalmers Johnson, James Fallows, Clyde Prestowitz, and Karl Van Wolferen.

6 To be fair, Reed admits that "the holistic, mystical concept of culture is considered a straw man in most academic writing" (1993: 33). However, he discusses it because he feels many still have outdated notions of what "culture" means. However, some of his own understandings of how the culture concept is actually employed by social scientists reproduce other misconceptions.

7 McCormack and Sugimoto point out that twice in the past half-century Japan's leaders (specifically, Premier Tōjō Hideki in 1942 and Ōhira Masayoshi in 1979) have attempted to define historical progress without resorting to Western models. On both occasions, the modernizing projects have been defined from above "by elements most committed to increased productivity and ceaseless rationalization, maintenance of central bureaucratic control, and of Japanese might in relation to the world economy" (1989: 13).

8 Here it is pertinent to refer to Tanaka's treatment of how Japanese historians of the late nineteenth and early twentieth centuries devised an "orient" (1993). Because Japanese at the time were attempting to become "modern," some felt compelled to avoid being characterized as "oriental" since this term was associated with "backward" Asia, particularly China. Thus, in an attempt to maintain Japan's own, non-Western identity, Japanese scholars

invented the term *tōyōshi* (oriental history or studies) to grant Japan an identity that was both Asian and modern.

9 Mouer and Sugimoto outline what they believe to be the three main points of *nihonjin-ron*: (1) the uniqueness of Japan and the Japanese; (2) the importance of group orientation. This point is usually part of related arguments that view the Japanese as emphasizing vertical relationships within the group and "subordinating themselves to the demands of a fairly structured set of patron–client or hierarchical relationship"; and (3) the role of consensus (1986: 406). These arguments, often used to explain the cause of economic problems and trade friction, are similar to the discourse about "internationalization" since they have as their basic premise the Japanese/ non-Japanese categorization. "If only the non-Japanese could understand us," the thinking seems to go, "our trade problems would be taken care of." See Peter Dale's *The Myth of Japanese Uniqueness* (1986) for an analysis and critique of the major theorists and proponents of *nihonjin-ron*. Also, see Befu 1993 and Minami 1973.

10 Faith in "convergence" is often misplaced. See Henderson, who discusses the role of nationalism in Japan's political economy and the pitfalls of thinking that they (i.e. the Japanese) are "becoming just like us" with regard to problems that foreign acquisitions and takeovers face in Japan (1995).

11 While some rejected the "Japan-is-unique" hypothesis, they nevertheless attempted to integrate "tradition" into Japan's economic success in a more sophisticated fashion. However, an essentializing tendency was still present. For example, Cole refers to "tradition" throughout his book, which he defines as "the legacy of preindustrial values or patterns of behavior (social structure) found in industrial society" (1971: 8). But values that constitute "traditions" do not just linger around, like some historical hangover, and to think that they do essentializes them into existence. It may be convenient to historicize human motivation, but to do so distracts us from recognizing how values are constantly constructed by present-day socioeconomic forces. See also his 1979 and 1989 works, particularly "Borrowing and Culture" (1989: 105–27).

12 I was once authoritatively told at a conference that "political scientists study institutions, and anthropologists study values. So, anthropologists don't really study power relations."

13 "Rational choice" studies are an example of political scientism.

14 *Cf.* Kertzer: "Symbols cannot be satisfactorily studied in quantitative terms, nor through surveys or electoral analyses. In emphasizing such methods, analysts have a tendency to assume that those aspects of politics that cannot be easily quantified must be unimportant. To complete the vicious circle, the resulting empirical studies then reinforce the view that modern politics is determined by rational action" (1988: 7).

15 Reed also uses the terms "psychological" and "structural approach" (1993: 47), and later asks "where is culture – inside people's heads or in the society?" (*ibid.*: 59). Such dichotomization, as if culture can be spatially localized, only serves to mystify the culture concept.

16 Though not in the mainstream tradition, there are political scientists who employ a symbolic analysis. Good examples include Aronoff 1977, 1980, 1986; Bennett 1975, 1977, 1979, 1980; Edelman 1964, 1971; and Laitin 1986. Also, see Arnold, who notes that politics and economics constitute not

"collections of truths," but "symbolic thinking and conduct which condition the behavior of men in groups" (1962: xiv).

17 See Cohen 1974, 1979, 1981 and Kertzer (1988: 1–14), who both recognize and argue for the need to apply anthropological methods (specifically, ritual and symbolic analysis) to industrialized societies.

18 *Cf.* Taussig: "Time, space, matter, cause, relation, human nature, and society itself are social products created by man just as are the different types of tools, farming systems, clothes, houses, monuments, languages, myths, and so on, that mankind has produced since the dawn of human life. But to their participants, all cultures tend to present these categories as is they were not social products but elemental and immutable things. As soon as such categories are defined as natural, rather than as social, products, epistemology itself acts to conceal understanding of the social. Our experience, our understanding, our explanations – all serve merely to ratify the conventions that sustain our sense of reality unless we appreciate the extent to which the basic 'building blocks' of our experience and our sensed reality are not natural but social constructions" (1980: 4).

19 Goffman's work (e.g. 1959) and ethnomethodological approaches (Garfinkel 1967) are more explicit examples of studies that have examined the precariousness and provisionality of "common sense" in daily life.

20 And of course, "what people learn" is precisely what anthropologists mean by culture, though learning itself is not simply a matter of filling heads with commonsensical facts, but is rather mediated through cultural forms.

21 *Cf.* Meyer *et al.* 1994 and Meyer, Boli, and Thomas 1987, who all insightfully discuss the cultural implications of rationalization.

22 "Too often . . . it is assumed that if 'primitive' societies are not organized by a strict material rationality, at least we are. So far as concerns Western society, at least we are safe in the utilitarian postulates of practical interest first elaborated by economic science and applied thence to all domains of our social action" (Sahlins 1976: 210).

23 There are many works on ritual in political science, sociology, and political anthropology. Space precludes any useful literature review. Recent and useful works include Bell 1992, who offers a review of the pertinent literature, and Kertzer 1988, who examines political rituals.

24 It is worth continuing Kertzer's thought: "Ritual action is repetitive and, therefore, often redundant, but these very factors serve as important means of channeling emotion, guiding cognition, and organizing social groups" (1988: 9).

25 *Cf.* Geertz 1980 and Cannadine and Price (1987: 19), who make the same argument that ritual enactments are sociopolitical strategies and not mere "expressive" aspects of social action.

26 *Cf.* Kertzer: "Although many political observers in the United States and other industrial nations have noted the ritual behavior associated with politics, few have ever taken it seriously. They view ritual as mere embellishment for more important 'real' political activities. But, in fact, ritual is an integral part of politics in modern industrial societies; it is hard to imagine how any political system could do without it" (1988: 3).

27 Some works in English on rituals in Japan include Ashkenazi's examination of a town's festivals (1992); Ben-Ari's analysis of the ritualized nature of worker–management relations (1990); Edwards's description of the

commercialization of weddings (1989); Hamabata's portrayal of the role of rituals in family relations (1990); McVeigh's linking of self, status, and social structure through everyday ritualizations (1994b); Raz's account of the self-presentation and performance of gangsters in ritual context (1992); Seward's description of the detailed formalities and preparations accompanying ritual suicide (*hara-kiri*) (1968); and Van Bremen and Martinez's (1995) edited collection of religious rituals in modern Japan.

28 Rationalized approaches to everyday life have a long history in Japan. Yoshino speaks of the "prefab construction" of the Edo period (1600–1867). For the "rental housing" of the urban lower classes, "the production and installation techniques were thoroughly systematized," and the builders "used ready-made products in standard sizes" (1994: 117–18).

29 A more specific example of such thinking is Japan's *kanri kyōiku* (managed education).

30 Mouer and Sugimoto note a fundamental lack of trust reflected in numerous Japanese proverbs (1986: 211–12).

31 *Cf.* Haley: "Letters of guarantee are unusually common as the prerequisite for an extraordinary variety of activities: immigration, loans, employment, and leases" (1991: 182).

32 Much has been made of *ringi* in the literature about Japanese business practices (e.g. see Tsuji 1968, Yamada 1993, and Yoshino 1968). Some have praised it as a "bottom-up" process that encourages lower-level decision making. However, its use has been misinterpreted, especially by accounts that understate the authority of leaders in an organization who often draft documents before *ringi* are circulated.

33 The reason for restrictions on overseas travel were economic: to keep Japanese currency in Japan.

34 At a research institute I frequented, copying required filling out a form that asked the researcher's name and address, title of the document to be copied, the pages to be copied, and how many sheets were to be copied.

35 Since so much money is involved, landlords do not take chances. Before I could sign a contract to rent an apartment, I had to prove that I was really who my passport, alien registration card (*gaikokujin tōrokushōmeisho*; which has the bearer's photograph and fingerprint), work ID, a letter from my guarantor, and other assorted identifications said I was by obtaining a notarized form from a consulate.

36 Company and school uniforms are a good example. As a high school student explained to me, "wearing uniforms prevents us from doing bad things – going to a game center, drinking, and smoking. Thanks to uniforms, it is easy for teachers to spot and control us" (*cf.* McVeigh 1997b).

37 A number of scholars have noted the Japanese predilection for neatly slicing up social life. Benedict described Japanese social life as "compartmentalized spheres of activity" (1989: 137). Both Bachnik 1992 and Lebra 1976 point to the importance of distinguishing clearly between different social situations, often expressed in the phrase *kejime o tsukeru* (discriminate). Hendry 1986, Sano 1989, and Tobin 1991 note how the compartmentalizing of experience becomes an effective socializing technique in educational settings. Edwards, in his study of Japanese weddings, notes a "general mode of cognition," which "consists of a tendency to separate experience into discrete contexts, isolated from each other as well as from the temporal flow,

and to focus on each context, sphere, or pose as a gestalt, a thing unto itself"
(1989: 137). Brandon *et al.* describe theatrical *kata* (technique) that
"momentarily halts the action of the play and intensifies its emotion" (1978:
84; *cf.* Ernest 1974). Lee 1982 notes the "stop-action" and the "aesthetic of
reducing motion" in Japanese artistic works.

3 The bureaucratized self: public, private, and "civil society" in Japan

1 Sections of this chapter have appeared in McVeigh 1994b.
2 My argument about private/public distinctions and comparisons are somewhat simplistic. For example, compared with the United States, Japan and
some continental European nations (where central bureaucracies have historically played an important role) are similar in certain respects (namely,
cooperation between state and businesses). However, in other more fundamental ways, such as the relation between the individual and the state,
I would argue that the United States and European countries are more
similar to each other in comparison with Japan.
3 Of course, group-centeredness, empathy, and hierarchy are relative and exist
to some degree in all societies. The question, however, is why they exist to
such degrees in Japan.
4 Perhaps the values of other Asian societies can be appreciated as well.
Discussing civil society in Korea and Taiwan, Mouzelis notes that "Perhaps
the day has come for us to shift our theoretical orientations and preoccupa-
tions. We might spend less time and energy exploring the connections
between modernity and Western values, and more on those between late
modernity (or postmodernity) and 'Eastern' values" (1995: 246).
5 Modern Western understandings of public/private resulted from complex
historical sociopolitical, economic, and religious forces. Moreover, there are
gender, class, and regional variables that shape public/private understandings within Euro-American cultures. Suffice to say that "public" was first
used in England during the fifteenth century to designate the "common
good." Not long after, the meaning of something open to general observation was added. "Private" meant privileged at a high governmental level.
Eventually, "public" "came to mean a life passed outside the life of family
and close friends; in the public region diverse, complex social groups were to
be brought into ineluctable contact," especially within in an urban setting
(Sennett 1976: 17). For a useful work on public (and private), see Benn and
Gaus 1983. For a rich historical analysis of the concept of privacy in Western civilization (the defining counterpart of "public"), see the five volumes
edited by Ariès and Duby (1990).
6 The dictates of civil society and "common sense" meet in many ways. Consider the assumption that being in public precludes staring at or touching
strangers. This is "common sense." But it is a culture-specific "common
sense" that people must learn. Goffman's "civil inattention" (politely ignoring others and avoiding facial expressions that are threatening to strangers)
and the act of positioning one's body in a "morally neutral" way when in
public (1963) are not explicitly taught, but their socialization is vital to cosmopolitan life. *Cf.* Simmel: "There is perhaps no psychic phenomenon which
is so unconditionally reserved to the city as the blasé outlook" (1988: 329).
7 Despite the many early theorists of civil society, it is Hegel who is often

associated with this notion. He argued that civil society had emerged from the interdependence and cooperative efforts of individuals, which eventually give rise to the state (1953).

8 For recent and useful works on civil society, see Cohen and Arato 1992, Hall 1995, Keane 1988, and Kumar 1993.

9 *Cf.* Simmel's "The Stranger" (1988).

10 Indeed, civil society cannot be so easily separated from the state, and many would argue that it is a servant of state interests. Though the term "civil society" has usually had positive meanings, Marx reacted to Hegel's conception of civil society by contending that the state uses civil society to defend its privileged propertied interests (1971). Gramsci regarded civil society as being in league with the state, controlling and regulating individual behavior without armed force: civil society "has become a very complex structure and one which is resistant to the catastrophic 'incursions' of the immediate economic elements (crises, depressions, etc.)." Trenchantly, he compared the superstructures of civil society "to the trench-systems of modern warfare. In war it would sometimes happen that a fierce artillery attack seemed to have destroyed the enemy's entire defensive system, whereas in fact it had only destroyed the outer perimeter; and at the moment of their advance and attack the assailants would find themselves confronted by a line of defense which was still effective" (1971: 235). Regarding political parties, Mouzelis asks whether they should be considered parts of civil society (1995: 226). Considering the length of Japan's LDP rule and its relationship to the state bureaucracy, one could certainly make the argument that this political party has been appropriated by the state. *Cf.* Migdal *et al.*, who state that the existence of civil society "reinforces the dominance of the state and allows it to rule without constant recourse to coercion or without an outlay of resources that would cripple it" (1994: 28).

11 *Cf.* Matsushita's 1971 *Shibiru minimamu no shisō* (The Ideology of the Civil Minimum).

12 This is not to say that in Euro-American polities the lines separating public and private domains are unchanging or inflexible or that there are no gray areas in Euro-American societies. Indeed, the lines between private and public, individual and government, and society and state, are constantly shifting. My point is that relative to Japan, Euro-American societies work harder to minimize any gray areas between private and public spheres.

13 *Cf.* Itō: "In Japan, it is commonly observed that while there is an official policy for dealing with farmers, there is no such policy for dealing with agriculture. This insight is very much to the point. The operational focus of the administrative apparatus of the Japanese Ministry of Agriculture and Forestry is neither the farm industry, nor its business, nor its economic functioning, but farmers and the family communities themselves. These form the objectives of policy, and the implied link is personal and direct" (quoted in Williams 1994: 70).

14 Perhaps reflecting, in the words of Doi, a "serious dearth of the type of public spirit that transcends both individual and group" (1986: 42).

15 Concerning the public's access to official information, Abe *et al.* point out that as of April 1990, 177 local governments (37 prefectures and 140 municipalities) had enacted public information ordinances, but the basic conditions of disclosure have not been worked out (1994: 188).

16 The origins of "my home-ism" are ironic. In the mid-1950s, it was part of "priority of private life (*shiteki seikatsu yūsen*)," introduced by companies to sell household appliances, and it eventually changed "from a purely commercial slogan to a new attitude toward life." However, in the early 1960s it was assaulted by critics from both the right and left, and the government itself stated that it was "harmful to public interest, national defense, and love for the native country" (Linhart 1988: 286–7). See also Hazama 1969, Morris 1973, and Tada 1978.

17 Quinn lists other associations of this culturally rich concept: bounded, nearby, enclosed, concave, dark, domestic, casual, comfortable, indulgent, free, secret, primary, privileged, special, and sacred (1994: 63).

18 This is not to deny any of the important similarities between these domains and the social landscape found in other societies. However, my focus here is to show the cultural specifics of publicness and privacy in Japan.

19 The *uchi/omote* situation does not occur.

20 Though status is usually de-emphasized when among kin and close companions, a degree of intimacy can sometimes be seen in hierarchical relations (e.g. teacher/students, employer/employees, and senior/junior students).

21 *Cf.* Goffman, who notes that ritualized-formal and intimate-familiar situations mutually define each other: "Since back regions are typically out of bounds to members of the audience, it is here that we may expect reciprocal familiarity to determine the tone of social intercourse. Similarly, it is in the front regions that we may expect a tone of formality to prevail" (1959: 128).

22 For works on *omote/ura* and *soto/uchi*, see Bachnik 1992, Doi 1973, Ishida 1984, Johnson 1980, and Lebra 1976. For a collection of sophisticated investigations of the cultural import of these concepts, see the volume edited by Bachnik and Quinn (1994).

23 Nevertheless, Goffman identifies what he calls the "outside": "It would seem reasonable to add a third region, a residual one, namely, all places other than the two already identified" (1959: 134–5).

24 However, regardless of the sociopolitical forces of hierarchy and in-group/out-group dynamics, there is a measure of negotiability and flexibility in the way an individual expresses/performs self. This is because the dictates of actively attaining a particular goal – rather than set rules – shape self.

25 Rohlen states that "Families, companies, and religious, educational, and fraternal organizations apparently create their own distinct social worlds in which order is learned and maintained" (1989: 27).

26 "Japan's experience challenges the fundamental legal dichotomy between state and societal action. Constitutional and other legal constraints designed within the context of the Western legal and political tradition to secure freedom of the individual against the state have little relevance in a society in which the principal source of restraint is the community not the state" (Haley 1991: 184).

27 Though somewhat dated, Curtis 1971 is still a useful analysis of campaigning Japanese-style.

28 See Habermas 1989 for his seminal discussion of the role of the press in the development of a public sphere in late eighteenth- and early nineteenth-century Europe.

29 Abe *et al.* explain the apolitical tendencies of TV reporting in Japan, though

they can readily be found elsewhere: " 'Isolation' refers to the taking of political and social events out of their historical and social context and the presentation of them along with episodes and attendant phenomena completely unrelated to the true nature of the event. 'Fragmentation' refers to the technique of breaking news events up into tiny bits and presenting them – in the form of news flashes, sound bites, comments, and summaries instead of imparting comprehensive understanding and evaluation of matters related to one another. And 'privatization' refers to the treating of politicians and political events without emphasizing their public significance but, rather, viewing them simply as 'private' aspects of those involved" (1994: 194).

30 See Farley 1996 for an insightful look at Japan's press and the politics of scandal.
31 See Altman 1996 and Freeman 1996 for brief discussions of *kisha*. For a general discussion of Japanese media and politics, see Pharr and Krauss 1996.
32 "Formal press conferences in Japan are stage-managed to a ludicrous degree" (Van Wolferen 1989: 95).
33 Huber writes that the press is expected by the ministries to cooperate with its economic policies and goals (1994: 7).
34 *Cf.* Jacoby, who notes that "anything of a controversial nature is regarded as disruptive in those places where everything is subject to 'impartial' regulation. With the increasing transfer of social functions to official agencies, and the officialization of all independent associations, a negative attitude develops toward the expression of *differing* opinions" (1973: 154, italics in original).
35 However, see Altman 1996, who discusses possibilities for change since 1993, when certain sectors of the broadcast news, emboldened by a series of events, challenged the government more vigorously.
36 See Westney 1996 for a comparison of the mass media as business organizations in Japan and the USA.

4 Japan's government: the bureaucratic blurring of state and society

1 *Cf.* Drifte's phrase: "cult of vulnerability" (1986).
2 See Castells 1992 for the other ingredients. He lists major commonalities of Asia's capitalist developmental states, one of which is some "emergency situation" (or "major tensions and conflicts at the international level"). He illustrates this point by discussing South Korea, Taiwan, Hong Kong, and Singapore. Though he does not explicitly mention Japan in this regard, one can easily imagine why it should be included. Johnson 1982 examines the developmental state in Japan. See also Amsden 1989, Deyo 1987, and Wade 1990 for general treatments of the developmental state. See Önis' review article of pertinent books (1991). Evans is also useful for his discussion of the role of the state in industrialization (1995: 3–20).
3 We should be wary of overlooking Japan's contributions to political philosophy. Speaking of the Ministry of International Trade and Industry, Johnson writes that "for all of Japan's alleged borrowing from abroad, the Japanese political genius rests in the identification and use of their own political assets," and that "the institutions of the Japanese developmental

state are products of Japanese innovation and experience" (1982: 322, 323). *Cf.* Williams' *Japan: Beyond the End of History*, which addresses the issue of Japan's differences with other modernized societies. Williams' statement that a "fundamental pluralism may be at work in the world's encounter with modernity" (1994: 164) seems obvious from a political anthropological perspective, but his analysis of modern Japan is incisive. See also Fallows 1994.

4 The scholarship on Japan's bureaucracy deserves at least a perfunctory treatment. One characterization that can be made is notable because it demonstrates how the political culture of scholars shapes their own research: the lack of attention that Western researchers have given to the Japanese bureaucracy: "Western political scientists, especially those working in English speaking democracies, contribute to the inflated reputation of Japanese political parties because they appear to be the most familiar feature of the Japanese political landscape" (Williams 1994: 37). Though the role of the Japanese bureaucracy is certainly not ignored in the English literature, there are relatively few monographs that deal with the bureaucracy in any comprehensive way. There are, however, important exceptions, such as Campbell's *Contemporary Japanese Budgetary Politics* (1976) and Johnson's *MITI and the Japanese Miracle* (1982). Johnson, in fact, has explicitly called for the need to study not just politicians and businesses but also Japan's bureaucracies (1975: 2–3). Other pertinent works are Craig 1975; Haley 1987; Ide and Ishida 1969; Kim's *Japan's Civil Service System* (1988); Koh's *Japan's Administrative Elite* (1989); Kubota's *Higher Civil Servants in Postwar Japan* (1969); Muramatsu and Krauss 1974; Ojimi 1975; Park's *Bureaucrats and Ministers in Contemporary Japanese Government* (1986); Pempel 1974, 1978, 1984, 1987a, 1987b; Rix 1988; Silberman 1964, 1967, 1970, 1973, 1976, 1978, 1982; Spaulding 1967; and Wade 1991. In the Japanese literature, however, there is a voluminous amount of work on bureaucracy. It ranges from academic books and articles, exposé accounts, journalistic and media reports, to government publications. In general, Japanese researchers seem more aware of the salient role of bureaucracy than their Western counterparts, even if they acknowledge democratic aspects (e.g. Inoguchi's "bureaucracy-led mass-inclusionary pluralism" (*kanryō shudō taishū hōkatsu gata tagenshugi*) (1983). Examples of academic works include Akagi's *Kansei no keisei* (Formation of Bureaucracy) (1991); Hata's *Kanryō no kenkyū: fumetsu no pāwā* (A Study of Bureaucratic Immortal Power) (1983); Honda's *Nihon neo-kanryō-ron* (The Neo-bureaucracy Debate in Japan) (1974); Ide's "*Sengo kaikaku to nihon kanryōsei*" (Postwar Reform and the Japanese Bureaucracy) (1974); Itō's *Genzai nihon kanryōsei no bunseki* (An Analysis of Modern Japanese Bureaucracy) (1980); Kawanaka's *Gendai no kanryōsei* (Contemporary Bureaucracy) (1962); Kusayanagi's *Kanryō ōkoku-ron* (The Bureaucratic Monarchy Debate) (1975); Muramatsu's *Sengo nihon no kanryōsei* (Postwar Japan's Bureaucratic System) (1981); Murofushi's *Kokyū kanryō* (National Bureaucracy) (1987); Nakajima's *Shōwashi o irodoru kakushin kanryō no jidai* (The Era of Bureaucratic Reform that Colors the History of Shōwa) (1978); Namiki's *Tsūsanshō no shūen* (The End of MITI) (1989); Sataka's *Nihon kanryō hakusho* (White Paper on the Japanese Bureaucracy) (1989); Sugano's *Gendai no kanryōsei* (Contemporary Bureaucracy) (1971); Tsuji's *Shinpan nihon kanryōsei no kenkyū* (A Study of Japanese Bureaucracy) (new edition,

1969); Yamaguchi's *Ōkura kanryō no shihai no shūen* (The End of Domination by Finance Ministry Bureaucrats) (1987); Yamanaka's *Nihon kindai kokka no keisei to kanryōsei* (The Formation of Japan's Modern State and Bureaucracy) (1974); and Yasuhara's *Ōkurashō* (The Ministry of Finance) (1974). A number of former bureaucrats have written commentaries about their experiences that provide an insider's perspective: Hayashi's *Nihon kanryō kenkoku-ron* (On State Building by Japanese Bureaucrats) (1982); Itō's *Genzai nihon kanryōsei no bunseki* (An Analysis of the Contemporary Japanese Bureaucracy) (1980); Kami's *Ōkura kanryo* (The Ministry of Finance) (1986); Katō's *Kanryō desu, yoroshiku* (I Am a Bureaucrat, Pleased to Meet You) (1983); Kawaguchi's *Kanryō shihai no kōzō* (The Structure of Bureaucratic Control) (1987); Ōkita's *Nihon kanryō jijō* (Conditions of Japanese Bureaucrats) (1984). Sakakibara's *Nihon o enshutsu suru shin kanryō-zō* (A Portrait of New Bureaucrats Who Direct Japan) (1977); and Sakakibara and Noguchi's *Ōkurashō, nichigin no bunseki* (Analysis of the Ministry of Finance and the Bank of Japan) (1977). Also see *Kanchō monogatari* (A Tale of Government Offices) (1962, Tōkyō Shimbunsha (ed.)). While still a bureaucrat, Miyamoto described working for the Ministry of Health and Welfare in *Straitjacket Society* in a critical and humorous light (1994). Journalistic accounts include Tahara's *Nihon no kanryō* (Japan's Bureaucrats) (1979) and *Heisei-nihon no kanryō* (Bureaucracy in Heisei Japan) (1990); Koitabashi's *"Sengo umare" erīto kanryō no sugao* (The Real Faces of Elite Bureaucrats Who Were "Born After the War") (1986); and four books by Kuribayashi: *Ōkurashō: ginkō-kyoku* (The Ministry of Finance: The Banking Bureau) (1988); *Ōkurashō: shukei-kyoku* (The Ministry of Finance: The Budget Bureau) (1990); *Ōkurashō: shuzei-kyoku* (The Ministry of Finance: The Tax Administration Bureau) (1991a); and *Ōkurashō: shōken-kyoku* (The Ministry of Finance: The Securities Bureau) (1991b). More recent works include Gotōda's *Sei to kan* (Politics and Bureaucracy) (1994), Murakawa's *Nihon no kanryō* (Japan's Bureaucracy) (1994); and Okada's *Gendai nihon kanryōsei no seiritsu* (The Formation of Contemporary Japan's Bureaucracy) (1994). *Kanchō zen keiretsu chizu* (Guide to the Entire Bureaucratic Network) (1994a), edited by Fujioka, provides a convenient guide to all the ministries. Recent concerns and thinking about bureaucracy are reflected in Fujioka's *Tsūsanshō no yomikata* (How to Read the Ministry of International Trade and Industry) (1994b); Igarashi and Ogawa's *Gikai: kanryō shihai o koete* (The Diet: Overcoming Bureaucratic Control) (1995); Ikuta's *Nippon kanryō yo doko e iku* (Where is Japan's Bureaucracy Going?) (1992); and *Ōkurashō dokusai* (The Dictatorship of the Ministry of Finance) (1994); Kamoshida's *Datsu "kan" no shisō; henkaku no tame no 3 tsu no kinkyū teigi* (Thoughts on Removing "Bureaucracy": 3 Emergency Proposals for Reform) (1994); *Kanryō: kishimu kyodai kenryoku* (Bureaucracy: The Creaking of Great Power) (1994, Nihon Keizai Shinbunsha (ed.)); Ōmae's *Heisei kanryō-ron* (Essays about Heisei Bureaucracy) (1994); Ōmiya's *Sekimatsu nippon no kanryōtachi* (Japan's Bureaucrats at the End of the Century) (1991); Ōtsuka's *Oyakusho to no toraburu kaiketsuhō* (How to Solve the Government's Troubles) (1994); Yoda's *Oyakusho no shikumi* (Organization of the Governmental Bureaucracy) (1994); and two supplements, *Kanryō no boyaki* (Bureaucratic Complaints (supplement no. 180, 1994) and *Ōkura kanryō no shōtai* (The True Character of the Ministry of

Finance, (supplement no. 214, 1994), both edited by Takarajima. Other useful sources in Japanese are *Jinji-in geppō* (National Personnel Authority's monthly bulletin); *Kankai* (The Bureaucratic World); *Kanpō* (Official Gazette); *Kōmuin hakusho* (White Paper on Civil Servants); *Nenji hōkokusho* (Annual Reports); and the monthly column, *Kasumigaseki konshidensharu* (Confidential Report from Kasumigaseki), in *Bungei shunjū*. Johnson's work on MITI (1982) and his thesis of the "developmental state" have generated both agreement and controversy, with many scholars using his arguments as an academic foil. For example, Calder (1988, 1993) challenges Johnson's (1982) thesis of the "developmental state" with his argument of "corporate-led strategic capitalism." He gives more credit to the free market rather than bureaucratic guidance, and argues that private companies, not the state, have orchestrated the Japanese miracle. Ramseyer and Rosenbluth (1993) also disagree with the conventional wisdom (i.e. the bureaucrats control the politicians). They emphasize the leverage that politicians have over bureaucrats: politicians can veto legislation; control bureaucrats' careers; and some ambitious bureaucrats want to become politicians in the future, so they must not ruffle the feathers of too many politicians. The volume edited by Wilks and Wright, *The Promotion and Regulation of Industry in Japan* (1991), also calls into question the bureaucracy's role in developing Japan's economy. Other works that are pertinent to this issue include Callon's *Divided Sun: MITI and the Breakdown of Japanese High-Tech Industrial Policy 1975–93* (1995); Campbell's *Contemporary Japanese Budget Politics* (1976) and *How Policies Change: The Japanese Government and the Aging Society* (1992); Friedman's *The Misunderstood Miracle: Industrial Development and Political Change in Japan* (1988); Okimoto's *Between MITI and the Market: Japanese Industrial Policy for High Technology* (1989); and Samuels' *The Business of the Japanese State: Energy Markets in Comparative and Historical Perspective* (1987). Regardless of where one stands on the state-versus-market, bureaucracy-versus-business issue, the decline in bureaucratic power since the 1970s should not be equated with its demise, and though certainly worthy of study, analyses of party and electoral politics in Japan should not eclipse an appreciation of the role of bureaucratically guided public policy.

5 The three reasons for creating a "non-political" civil bureaucracy were, in fact, highly political: (1) to defuse public criticism of the monopoly of power by two feudal domains (Satsuma and Chōshū); (2) to demonstrate their "modernity" to the West to hasten revision of the unequal treaties; and (3) most importantly, to "retain authoritarian control after 1890, when the new parliament (National Diet) opened and political parties began public campaigning for a share of power" (Johnson 1982: 37).

6 Some have argued that a host of changes in Japan's political landscape (environmental problems, consumer movement, the strength of opposition parties in local areas, the "oil shock," and the slowdown of GNP growth in the late 1960s and early 1970s) have eroded ministerial domination, so that "non-bureaucratic institutions took on increased importance in the formulation of national public services," resulting in "fragmentation, decentralization, and debureaucratization" (Pempel 1987a: 285, 287). Specifically in the areas of economics, some (e.g. Calder 1988, 1993) have attempted to balance Johnson's thesis (1982) of the bureaucratically guided

"developmental state" as an explanation for Japan's "economic miracle" by giving more credit to the private sector and the free-market "economic miracle." Others have given more credit to politicians (e.g. Ramseyer and Rosenbluth 1993). However, though other political actors and social pressures have reigned in Japan's bureaucracies during the last two decades (something Johnson does not deny, 1982), the ministries still wield considerable power.

7 This is why Johnson suggests that the real equivalent of the Japanese Ministry of International Trade and Industry in the United States is not the Department of Commerce but rather the Department of Defense, "which by its very nature and functions shares MITI's strategic, goal-oriented outlook" (1982: 21).

8 Johnson compares Japan and Germany in the late nineteenth century, during which the elite took "preemptive measures to forestall formation of mass movements that could interfere with its goals, above all the emergence of a unified labor movement." The elite also undertook diversionary activities that promoted national pride but also deflected "attention from constitutional development" (1995: 47).

9 Organs in the Prime Minister's Office include the Fair Trade Commission; National Public Safety Commission; Environmental Disputes Coordination Commission; Imperial Household Agency; Management and Coordination Agency; Hokkaidō Development Agency; Defense Agency; Defense Facilities Administration Agency; Economic Planning Agency; Science and Technology Agency; Environment Agency; Okinawa Development Agency; and National Land Agency. Among these, the Defense Agency and the Economic Planning Agency are of particular importance.

10 See *Gyōsei kikōzu* (Administrative Organization Charts) (1994) for the official explanation of governmental organization.

11 In 1985, there were 1,186,313 national civil servants. At the local level (prefectural and municipal), there were 3,406,561 civil servants (Kim 1988: 5). For an analysis of why Japanese bureaucracies are so effective, see Kim (1988: 15–16).

12 But consider one of the "customs" in the ministries. Though there is no legal basis, unwritten rules dictate that ministers should pay, out of their own pockets, from 300,000 to 400,000 yen to ministry officials, chauffeurs, bodyguards, and receptionists. During holiday seasons, secretaries and other officials expect to receive 50 percent more. A minister also pays other expenses, such as "gifts like sake and beer to be given to each section of the ministry, as well as to public and private organizations affiliated with the ministry." These "inaugural greetings" may cost about one million yen each month (about $10,000) ("Unwritten rules tax ministers: greasing bureaucrats' palms a legacy of the LDP era," JT 1 September 1994: 3). Recently, local officials have been caught up in a series of scandals, often involving misappropriation of funds (e.g. "Bureaucrats' partying costs billions," DY 20 July 1995: 1) and paying homage to Tokyo bureaucrats as a way of currying favor (e.g. "21 prefectures probe lavish entertainment," DY 14 September 1995: 1).

13 For example, see "Bureaucrats' colossal arrogance" (DY 7 June 1994: 7). Since the war, there have been numerous high-level commissions devoted to administrative reform (called "administrative adjustment" before the war)

of the ministries. Though there have been some improvements, these have been regarded by many as minimal. The Second Ad Hoc Commission on Administration (1981) advocated not just structural reform but also a change in policy direction. These reforms did "not fundamentally attack the interwoven, collusive structure of business, administration, and politics; rather, one may even say that it simply opened up new territory to be carved up, exploited, and traded on by entrepreneurs and their political cronies" (Abe *et al.* 1994: 99).

14 Ministry officials loudly criticized a proposed plan to give more hiring power to one organ above the separate ministries, suspecting that the plan was an attempt to place the ministries in a secondary position to elected politicians. See "Bureaucrats slam new hiring plan" (DY 31 May, 1996: 3).

15 Though Japan's bureaucrats may be called a "meritocratic elite," ascriptive criteria also play a role. This is because one's chances of passing the fiercely competitive examinations depend to a large degree on "the quantity and quality of preparations for entrance examinations to schools at succeeding levels that one can purchase" (Koh 1989: 253).

16 Being a law graduate in Japan does not mean one obtains a license to practise law. In order to do this, one must pass a judicial examination in which only 2 percent pass, receive two years of postgraduate training at the state-run Judicial Training Institute, and then pass its graduation examination.

17 See Park 1986 for a similar view.

18 For a discussion of recruitment, see (Kim 1988: 21–35).

19 According to one bureaucrat, specialists may incite envy among co-workers (Miyamoto 1994: 168). The generalist–specialist dichotomy is perhaps similar to some degree to the "red" (dedicated to political goals) versus "expert" (motives suspect because knowledgeable of other things) theme that has been so divisive and decisive in modern Chinese politics. Note Campbell's observation that the "careful strictures against overspecialization are aimed at excluding values and norms other than those of the organization itself" (1989: 119–20).

20 For a profile of Japanese higher civil servants, see Kim (1988: 37–50).

21 Campbell notes that "the ministries descended at various times from the prewar Home Ministry (Health and Welfare, Transport, Labor, Construction and Home Affairs) tend to have strong central staffs, while others are more likely to take an 'umbrella' form with strong bureaus; in all, however, the influence of the central staff has probably been increasing over time" (1976: 15–16).

22 Johnson notes how much of Japan's structural corruption becomes understandable once it is understood that "inside/outside" distinctions (*uchi*/*soto*) encourage "payment for access by outsiders to the bureaucratic centers where the main decisions for the society are made" (1995: 202).

23 *Cf.* Williams, who writes that "In talking about the location of Japanese political power, the proper rendering of *honne* might be 'the always obscured *locus* of true power' and *tatemae* as 'the indispensable legitimacy of certain necessarily conspicuous political forms.'" He continues: "The notion of *honne* is well-developed in Japan not because the Japanese have a penchant for mistaking appearance for reality, but because they recognize political 'forms' (*tatemae*) as being anything but superficial" (1994: 22). Williams does not expand upon this last point, but apparently he means

214 Notes

that legitimacy is as important as actual political practice. *Cf.* Johnson's discussion of important political terms (1980).

24 For their part, officials at the Ministry of Health and Welfare must learn "Dietspeak," which has its own special words and is described in a guide (Miyamoto 1994: 39–41).

25 However, "the ministry adopting this tactic may face Frankenstein's problem – the interest group may aim its pressure at its parent. Organizations do take on lives of their own" (Campbell 1976: 25). See Muramatsu *et al.* 1986 for a description of postwar pressure groups.

26 An example of governmental dominance of the non-profit sector in Japan is "bureaucratic think tanks": "These ministerial bodies wield tremendous power, control the best and the brightest intellectual resources, and have a virtual monopoly on key sources of information" (Ueno 1992: 1). For a detailed discussion of Japanese think tanks, see Suzuki (1993: 1–15). *Cf.* what Mouer and Sugimoto write about semi-official public bodies (*gaikaku dantai*): "Their research activities and publications are carefully scrutinized, and directions which will win budgetary allocations are often openly suggested by officials in the ministry responsible for overseeing their activities" (1986: 244). For more discussion on the lack of a public-interest, non-profit sector in Japan, see Ueno 1992 and "Flexing the Civic Muscles," DY 6 August 1994: 6. See also "Japan lags behind in 'brain' sector" (DY 25 October 1994: 7). For a treatment of Japanese corporate philanthropy, see London 1993.

27 Criticized in the past for being too simplistic, the concept of "Japan, Inc." appears to be making a comeback, though in a more sophisticated form, in recent research on Japan's political economy. The word heard in this connection is "network"; e.g. see Imai 1992 and Kumon 1992.

28 These terms are ambiguous. Strictly speaking, "public corporation" is *kōkyō kigyō* in Japanese, which has a broad meaning. Sometimes, "public corporation" is used in English works to refer to the more specific enterprise of "special corporations" (*tokushu hōjin*). To add more confusion, the term *kōsha* is also sometimes rendered as "public corporation."

29 There are many treatments of special and public corporations in Japanese, some put out by the government. See Fujioka 1995, Matsubara 1995, and *Tokushu hōjin sōran* (An Overview of Special Juridical Persons) 1995. Also, see the investigation of special corporations, *Tokushu hōjin o kiru* (Kill the Special Legal Entities) by Tōkyō Shinbun Tokushu Hōjin Shuzaihan (Tokyo Newspaper's Coverage Team for Special Legal Entities) 1980. In English, see Johnson 1974 and 1978, especially the latter, which offers a rich account of just how different state–business–society relations are in Japan compared to the Anglo-American model. In this useful work, Johnson provides the historical context out of which Japan's state–business relations developed.

30 For example, similar institutions in the United States are the Army Corps of Engineers, the Tennessee Valley Authority, the Port Authority of New York and New Jersey, the National Endowment for the Arts, and the Commodity Credit Corporation. The differences with their Japanese counterparts are more in form than substance.

31 This bureau administers postal savings deposits, government pension funds, and other government-sponsored funds.

32 See the article written by the Administrative Management Agency in Tsuji (1984: 43–4) for more details on the reasons for establishing special corporations.

33 The *Daily Yomiuri*, under the title of "Public Corporations: Trimming the Fat," ran a five-part series about the need for reform. A look at the following headlines indicates some of the concerns over public corporations: "Money-eating public corporations come under scrutiny of reformers" (7 December 1994: 8); "Activities of public corporations interfering in private business" (10 December 1994: 12); "Govt could gain 25 trillion yen by privatizing public firms" (9 December 1994: 16); "Murayama determined on reforms" (11 December 1994: 5); and "Finances of public corporations shrouded in secrecy" (9 December 1994: 16).

34 See "Govt to Hasten Review of Public Corps" (DY 15 October 1994: 2).

35 Regardless of what direction the public debate about *amakudari* may be taking, in 1994 a ministry official told me in a matter of fact manner that special corporations are a good idea and are needed for retiring officials.

36 Johnson explains the bureaucratic subculture and its "rewards and ranking based on strict seniority" that encourage this retirement system (1974: 958–61).

37 For treatments of *shingikai*, see Abe *et al.* (1994: 39–45), Schwartz 1993, and Sone *et al.* 1985.

38 Advisory councils are collectively known as *shingikai*, and include the following types: *shingikai, shinsakai, kyōgikai, chōsakai,* and *i-inkai.* For an official list, see *Shingikai sōran* (An Overview of Advisory Councils) (1994).

39 *Cf.* Campbell: "Appointments and staff work are controlled by the ministry, often with an eye to excluding or isolating opposition, so unfavorable reports are rare," and "many are used chiefly to mobilize and demonstrate clientele support" (1976: 24). Schwartz notes that *shingikai* are often called ministries' robots (*robotto*); cheering sections (*ōendan*); backers (*ato oshi*); tunnel organizations (*tonneru kikan*: a concealed channel of influence); sham bodyguards (*shin eitai magai*); ornaments (*kazarimono*); kept bodies (*goyō kikan*; i.e. government-controlled), and invisibility-granting fairy cloak (*kakuremino*; i.e. means of obscuring bureaucratic responsibility) (1993: 230).

40 Shiono also suggests that "administrative guidance has been fostered by paternalistic human relations in Japan" (1984: 215). There are many works on administrative guidance in Japanese (e.g. Shindo 1992, Yakushiji 1989). For a treatment in English, see Haley (1991: 139–68).

41 See McCormack's discussion of the "construction state" (*doken kokka*), in which "money flows through the system guided by the bureaucrats to benefit those who form part of the privileged national grid of politicians, bureaucrats, and business people. These are the circuits of shared interest and advantage that underlie the political economy as a whole and are centered in the 'public works' sector: the building of dams, highways, express rail lines, nuclear power stations, and the concreting of rivers and coastlines" (1996a). For more detailed discussions, see McCormack (1996b: 25–77) and Woodall 1996.

42 In Japan, laws themselves are often loosely interpreted, and consequently there is a great need for ordinances and regulations, which are written by the ministries. This rule-making function of the bureaucracy grants them

additional powers. *Cf.* Pempel: "Interpretation and administration are clearly powers; they are not politically neutral techniques that will be performed in precisely the same way by any appropriately trained bureaucratic technician. From such a perspective alone, the policymaking powers of the Japanese bureaucracy must be recognized as substantial" (1978: 83). Also, the lack of a strong judiciary in Japan that might check administrative expropriation only enhances bureaucratic power.

43 The meanings of technical terms is crucial if one is to appreciate how the Japanese bureaucracy operates. For example, Johnson points out that though *kyoka, ninka, tokkyo,* and *menkyo* all mean to permit or license, there are critical differences in meaning between them that are important for bureaucratic practice (1980: 108–9). Other words favored by bureaucrats are: *hōkoku* (report); *kakunin* (confirmed); *kensa* (inspection); *kentei* (approval); *kōfu* (granting); *ninshō* (certified); *nintei* (authorized); *shiken* (examination); *shinkoku* (declaration); *shinsa* (investigation); *shinsei* (application); *shitei* (designated); *shōdaku* (consent); *shōmei* (proof); *shōnin* (approval); *teishutsu* (submission); *todokede* (notification); and *tōroku* (registration) (*Cf.* Yoda 1994: 72).

44 There are many works on local government; e.g. see Amakawa 1987, Baxter and MacDougall 1983, Flanagan *et al.* 1980, Hoshino 1970, Kuroda 1974, MacDougall 1989, Muramatsu 1975, Purnendra 1989, Reed 1986, Samuels 1983, Steiner 1965, and Tsuji 1976.

45 Article 158 of the Local Autonomy Law specifies in detail the internal organization of prefectural government.

46 For recent examples in the media, see "Dates for govt decentralization proposed" (DY 10 October 1994: 2), and "Decentralization watchdog proposed" (DY 30 October 1994: 2).

47 "Even when the central government plays no particular role, local policies tend to vary within a very small range. The diffusion of a new program among local governments tends to be quite rapid and tends to include almost all of them. Communications among local governments (and between central and local governments) are remarkably dense. In fact, there is a single national agenda shared by the central government and all local governments." The upshot is that "Local policymaking in Japan takes place on a national stage" (Reed 1982: 163).

48 Consider how "informalilty and verticality," two features of official conflict resolution in Japan, operate in an environment lacking Euro-American legal codes: "informality limits the participants and significance of a specific dispute by stressing its particular issues rather than the underlying universal principles involved; verticality engenders dependence on government resolution of conflict by involving it in most disputes at every level" (Upham 1987: 166).

5 Rationality, bureaucracy, and belief in the state

1 Portions of this chapter have appeared in McVeigh 1996b.

2 The notion of invisible institutions resonates with Foucault's "discourse" (1979) and Gramsci's "hegemony" (1971). These notions regard the state (or at least the effects of its projects) as ubiquitous and diffuse, pervading and permeating society and subjectivity (cognition, emotions, belief,

thoughts, etc.). More specifically, some researchers such as Donzelot (1979) and Foucault (1980) examine how state projects connect to the everyday sphere (such as practices related to the family) through "soft domination." Some of Althusser's "ideological state apparatuses" are pertinent here, such as the mass media, family, commercial enterprises, and other institutions that are usually regarded as non-state structures, though in fact they serve core state objectives (other ideological state apparatuses are better charac- terized as core or para-state, such as legal systems, political parties, schools, and health and welfare services) (1971). According to Mitchell, the state should be analyzed as a "structural effect"; "That is to say, it should be examined not as an actual structure, but as the powerful, metaphysical effect of practices that make such structures appear to exist" (1991: 94; also *cf.* Mitchell 1990). Here I am just delineating the nature of the problem. A more in-depth analysis of the metaphysical effect of the Japanese state must await my next study of Japan's political cosmology.

3 *Cf.* Herzfeld: "But religions are rarely content with public rituals alone, and bureaucracy similarly requires rituals of personal commitment – practices that are sometimes less obviously ritualistic" (1992: 37).

4 The problem with this analogy is that, admittedly, it steals agency from individuals and sounds suspiciously similar to the "national character" mode of analysis (from macrocosm to microcosm). Thus, one must regard the self as an intentional social actor who uses the hierarchical, taxonomic, and formalizing schemata for a variety of purposes.

5 *Cf.* Migdal *et al.*: "In fact, those social scientists who, wittingly or unwit- tingly, exaggerate the capabilities of the state become part of the state's project to present itself as invincible. State sovereignty, the actual imposition of supreme state authority over its claimed territory, has simply too often been taken for granted" (1994: 14). Furthermore, we should be wary of forgetting that states, regardless of their power, are parts of soci- eties. In anthropological thinking the state has played a central role for those who have adopted a cultural evolutionist, materialistic approach. In any case, not enough attention is devoted to an anthropology of the state outside this latter approach. There are, however, exceptions. See Fallers 1974.

6 Indeed, in the Meiji period, early nationalism lacked a sense of popular solidarity and was a state-orchestrated elitist ideology that regarded both common people and foreigners as dangerous: "evil subjects and crafty foreigners" (*kanmin kōi*).

7 Space precludes a detailed treatment of the history of Japanese political philosophy. For an introduction in the English literature, especially on Tokugawa theorizing about bureaucracy, see Najita 1974.

8 *Cf.* Williams: "In countries heir to the Confucian tradition of elite state service, bureaucracy is often feared and criticized but rarely belittled or dismissed as ineffective. On the contrary, bureaucrats who work at the heart of East Asian states and polities are the beneficiaries of considerable pres- tige. Bureaucracy may be criticized as unresponsive and heavy-handed but rarely as unnatural or unnecessary" (1994: 38).

9 "Is Japan really democratic?" is a major leitmotif in political science on Japan. See Ishida and Krauss 1989. How ever one decides to answer this question, one must be wary of overlooking local versions of "democracy"

and assuming it to be universal. Japan's democracy, whatever it may mean, is not the Anglo-American variety that so many (especially the North American media) seem to assume it is. Abe *et al.* point out the reasons why Japan's postwar democratic reforms have had limited impact: (1) the continuation of the emperor, if only as a symbol, represented continuity with the prewar period. "At the very least, this facilitated the survival of archaic and unreconstructed popular attitudes and facilitated the continuation of old ideas of domination within a democratic institutional framework"; (2) after the war, the bureaucracy actually increased its power, "which constituted the institutional heart of the autocratic government since the Meiji era"; (3) from 1945 to 1952, the Occupation forces enacted reforms unilaterally; and (4) the change in popular political perceptions lagged behind changes in institutional reworkings (1994: 11–12).

10 Yoshino's *Cultural Nationalism in Contemporary Japan* (1992) is an excellent treatment of Japan's contemporary nationalism.

11 See D'Andrade (1995) for a history of cognitive anthropology.

12 When I have asked Japanese female students why there were no corresponding "men" offices in the bureaucracies, many responded that because women are "weak," they need men to establish and run such offices in order to care for women.

13 There are many works about how women relate to private/public distinctions. See Caplan and Bujra 1979, Elshtain 1981, Lamont *et al.* 1980, Leacock 1972, Okin 1979, 1991; Pateman 1983, 1988; and Sharistanian 1986a, 1986b, 1986c, 1986d. Moore (1984) also touches upon this topic. See Ferguson (1984) for how women relate to bureaucracy. See Lebra (1984) for a treatment of women in Japan.

14 "The state subsumes the person; therefore, in the syllogistic reasoning of nationalism under stress, the differentiation of persons (or ethnic groups) is a moral attack on the state, and invites retaliation" (Herzfeld 1992: 63).

15 Not all students accept the myths of Japaneseness, and some were quite vocal about this point. One student wrote in a report that "it is nonsense to stick to such silly theories." Another student told me that because the Japanese have felt a sense of inferiority due to their defeat in the war, they make themselves feel better by convincing themselves of such notions. Still another student explained that though Japan has become a great economic power, the average person leads a hard life. Thus, talking about the "uniqueness" of being Japanese "makes Japanese think that they are rich in a way."

16 See Twine (1991) for a treatment of the reform of written Japanese.

17 There are many works about the sociolinguistic aspects of Japanese. In English, Miller's *Japan's Modern Myth* (1982) is an excellent treatment of the sociopolitical role that the Japanese language plays in building Japaneseness.

18 For a description of how Japanese students learn *kokugo*, see Duke (1986: 51–79).

19 Here mention should also be made of the National Institute of Japanese Literature, which is attached to the Ministry of Education.

20 I believe that the sociopolitical dynamics of envy are a much overlooked aspect of Japanese society.

21 *Cf.* Fukushima: "the egalitarianism in communally oriented societies is

often restricted to the homogeneous cultural groups that tend to comprise them (1995: 253).

22 " 'Victim consciousness' (*higaisha ishiki*) is a popular euphemism in postwar and contemporary Japan, and the [nuclear] bombs occupy a central place in this consciousness. From this perspective, it can be observed that nuclear victimization spawned new forms of nationalism in postwar Japan – a neo-nationalism that coexists in complex ways with antimilitarism and even the 'one-country pacifism' long espoused by many individuals and groups associated with the political Left" (Dower 1995: 281).

23 It should be pointed out that some Japanese, while proud of Article 9, which renounces war, are disgusted with the hypocrisy and shallow understanding displayed by many Japanese who extol postwar Japan's "pacifism."

24 There are many works on the importance of public ceremony and ritual for political legitimization. For some recent and useful examples, see Binns 1979–80, Cannadine and Price 1987, Cohen 1974, and Kertzer 1988.

25 See Fujitani (1992) and Mayer (1989) for analyses in English of the meaning of the emperor in contemporary Japan.

26 The Japanese are not the only ones to confuse and conflate the meanings of state (state structures) and nation (ethnic group). This is a common mistake in much of the political science literature. See the useful articles by Connor (1994), who disentangles their definitions.

27 "In contrast to the United Kingdom, where in the planning of any local event, the possibility of some member of the royal family being present is almost always on the agenda, in Japan, any such initiative is left to the court, and the courtiers are not particularly inclined to encourage such participation" (Crump 1989: 188–9).

28 Though the Japanese learned from other continental mentors, the German example exerted strong influence, shaping administrative law, constitutional theory, military organization, economics, management of state finances, and the organization of the banking system (Williams 1994: 122–3).

29 Understandably, many of Japan's economic bureaucrats are proud of the role of the state, since it justifies their own policies and *raison d'être*. A Japanese diplomat explained to me that asking what kind of economy Japan has is not a very useful question. He said that if speaking to former Soviet Union officials, he would play up planned aspects, but if meeting Americans, he would emphasize the role of the market in Japan's economy. For what it is worth, almost all Japanese students that I discussed the nature of Japan's economy with argued that the state is heavily involved in Japan's economy. Some even explained that the state attempts to make the economy "appear" to be a free market.

30 I am not arguing that the state is necessarily the main or most important variable in explaining Japan's economic prowess.

31 See Miyashita and Russell 1994 for a recent and extended treatment of *keiretsu*.

32 The six major industrial groups are Mitsubishi, Mitsui, Sumitomo, Fuyō, Sanwa, and Daiichi Kangyō.

33 This three-level analysis has similarities with Parsons's (1960) discussion of the hierarchical structure of all large bureaucratic organizations. The first level, the institutional, corresponds to the strategic and functions as a link between the two lower levels (technical and managerial) and the larger

society. The second level, the managerial, corresponds to the intermediate, and regulates internal affairs and mediates between the lowest level (technical) and the immediate environment. The third level, the technical, corresponds to the tactical and is where an organization's practical activities are carried out. Here it is pertinent to mention Mannheim's distinction between "substantial rationality" (strategic planning; reflecting on one's actions so as to accomplish intended goals) and "functional rationality" (tactical planning, or "carrying out orders"; the consideration needed, with relatively little reflection, to execute a series of actions with predetermined goals) (1940: 53–9).

6 Japan's Ministry of Education: rationalized schooling and the state

1 Perhaps the pedagogic counterpart of the regulatory orientation may be called an *education of facilitation*. This is an academics of deducement, designed to assist and encourage students how to learn. The teacher's role is to regulate the learning environment by instructing students in how to derive knowledge. The government's role is relatively passive, and educational authorities stress the "how" of learning.
2 Since the war, the Monbushō's influence has been counterbalanced by organizations such as the Japan Teachers Union (though recently this group has reached what amounts to a rapprochement with the Monbushō, at least officially) and other groups. The role that these non-official groups have played in shaping Japanese education cannot be ignored, but because I am focusing on the state, I will gloss over them.
3 Besides the Monbushō, there are other ministries concerned with education. The Ministry of Finance must approve the Monbushō's budgeting, particularly its reform projects; the Ministry of Health and Welfare guards its control over the nursery schools from Monbushō encroachment; the Ministry of International Trade and Industry is concerned with maintaining Japan's education at an internationally competitive level; and the Ministry of Foreign Affairs attempts to make sure that the Monbushō's textbook screening process does not damage Japan's relations with its neighbors (Schoppa 1991: 93).
4 For those of us not used to state-centered political philosophies, the notion that the state can possess and actively pursue non-military strategic objectives may be foreign, even discomforting. This is especially so if the state under examination is conventionally regarded as democratic. However, democratic political impulses and centralized governments are not necessarily incompatible.
5 Two other caveats concerning my description of Japan's strategic schooling might be mentioned. First, it is admittedly too neat and should be regarded as only an approximate model. Its fit undoubtedly varies depending on particular policies and time periods. Moreover, it may not always be clear where the lines between the strategic, intermediate, and tactical levels should be drawn.
6 In the May 1995 edition of the Ministry of Finance's Publication Bureau Publication Catalog, about fifty of the approximately ninety items on education contained the word "guidance" (*shidō*) in the title.
7 Any historical data not referenced is from *Kokushi daijiten* (Great Dictionary

of National History) (1992); *Monbushō* (*Gyōsei kikō shirīzu no. 105*) (1980); and *Japan's Modern Educational System: A History of the First Hundred Years*) (1980). Any other data not referenced is from *Education in Japan: A Graphic Presentation*) (1994) and *Waga kuni no bunkyō shisaku* (Our Country's Education Policy) (1994).

8 For example, *The Essence of the National Polity* (*Kokutai no hongi*) (1937), *The Way of the Subjects* (*Shinmin no michi*) (1940), and *The Outline of National History* (*Kokushi gaisetsu*) (1940).

9 Pre-1945 Monbushō involvement in other matters ideological deserves mention. In August 1932, the Monbushō established the National Spiritual and Culture Research Institute (*Kokumin seishin bunka kenkyūjo*), which opposed socialism, progressive thinking, and any kind of liberalism. This institute was combined with the National Training Center (*Kokumin renseisho*) in January 1942, to form the Nationalism Training Center (*Kyōgaku renseisho*) in November 1943. The Monbushō also provided support and facilities for various kinds of "patriotic educational groups." In 1940, in order to unify these various groups and rationalize their activities (which reportedly carried on open disputes), the Monbushō persuaded the leaders of various youth groups to combine and form the Greater Japan Youth and Child Group (*Dai nippon seishōnen-dan*). In January 1945, the Greater Japan Congress for Instruction in Patriotism (*Dai nippon kyōka hōkoku-kai*) was set up, bringing together the social education associations with the Minister of Education as president. In February 1942, two women's groups merged to form the Greater Japan Women's Association (*Dai nippon fujin-kai*), which was affiliated to the Imperial Rule Assistance Association (*Taisei yokusan-kai*). This group concerned itself with teaching about the importance of womanly virtues, national defense, family life, the disciplining of youth, savings, and home education.

10 See Schoppa for a discussion of business attitudes toward education policy (1991: 120–48).

11 Here mention should be made of the national educational and research institutes under the Monbushō's jurisdiction: national universities (98); national junior colleges (37); national colleges of technology (54); national schools for handicapped children (1); the National Laboratory of High Energy Physics; the National Institute of Japanese Literature; the National Institute of Polar Research; the Institute of Space and Astronautical Science; the National Institute of Genetics; the Institute of Statistical Mathematics; the International Research for Japanese Studies; the National Astronomical Observatory; the National Institute for Fusion Science; the Okazaki National Research Institutes (which include the Institute for Molecular Science, Institute for Basic Biology, and the Institute for Physiological Science); the National Center for Science Information System; the National Museum of Ethnology; the National Museum of Japanese History; the National Institute of Multi-media Education; the National Center for University Entrance Examination; the National Institute for Academic Degrees; and the Center for National University Finance. There are other organs under the Monbushō's jurisdiction: the National Institute for Educational Research; the National Institute for Special Education; the National Science Museum; National Olympic Memorial Youth Center; thirteen national youth houses; fourteen national children's centers; the

National Women's Education Center; the Japanese National Commission for UNESCO; and the Japan Academy.

12 Other ministries have similar facilities and activities. Important examples include the Rehabilitation Bureau (*Kyōsei-kyoku*), particularly its Education Division (*Kyōiku-ka*), of the Ministry of Justice; the Children and Family Bureau (*Jidō katei-kyoku*) of the Ministry of Health and Welfare; the Women's Policy (*Fujin seisaku-ka*), Women's Labor (*Fujin rōdōka*), and Women's Welfare Divisions (*Fujin fukushi-ka*) in the Women's Bureau (*Fujin-ka*) of the Ministry of Labor; and the Women and Life Division (*Fujin Seikatsu-ka*) in the Agricultural Bureau (*Nōsanengei-kyoku*) of the Ministry of Agriculture. Though these various government bodies probably do not work in tandem, it can safely be said that they share enough of a common normative view that their respective operations produce a totalizing effect, thereby bureaucratically building belief.

13 Before this legislation, many prefectures already had sections or divisions for lifelong learning in their educational departments.

14 For this section, I have relied on WBS (294–310); *Education in Japan* (1994: 120–3); and MTY. See *Monbushōnai shōgai gakushū* (Lifelong Learning in the Ministry of Education) (1994); For a more detailed breakdown, see *Shakai kyōiku chōsa hōkokusho* (Survey of Social Education) (1990).

15 This information is basically compiled from MTY (114–21). Other sources in English use different terminology and present different breakdowns and statistics. Consequently, the data are not always clear. *Cf. Social Education and Its Administration in Japan* 1972; WBS (132–51); *Education in Japan* 1994; and *Shakai kyōiku chōsa hōkokusho* (Survey of Social Education) (1990).

16 Other related legislation includes: the Library Law of 1950; the Museum Law of 1951; the Youth Study Classes Promotion Law of 1953; the Law for Promotion of Youth Study Class of 1953; and the Sports Promotion Law of 1951 (revised in 1970).

17 In any population, there are individuals who for whatever reason are not readily processed by the screening, sorting, and shunting functions of the education–economic system. Rationalization excludes or dismisses what it cannot categorize and control, and individuals who are not easily classified are shunted away from what may be termed primary rationalizing to secondary or para-rationalizing structures. Thus the need for "special education" (*tokushu kyōiku*) designed for handicapped individuals in Japan. See *Waga kuni no tokushu kyōiku* (Special Education in Our Country) (1994).

18 See Tsukada for an ethnography of preparatory schools (*yobikō*) (1991).

19 It is worth providing the rest of Rohlen's opinion on this topic: "One wonders whether academic high schools could remain as orderly and serious if this pressure were absent. Without exams there would be less compliance with conventions and fewer limits on political squabbles and reform efforts. School systems and individual teachers would be more innovative and more independent of the Ministry of Education, and education itself would become more colorful and chaotic. I doubt that most Japanese would find such a development comfortable" (1983: 317). Also, note Rohlen's observation that "The Ministry of Education is unable to rule education directly through its domination of local school systems and loyal teachers, but it can

in fact control exams and textbooks. The ambition to succeed in education is the ultimate source of discipline" (*ibid.*: 266).

20 Dore 1987 and Dore and Sako 1989 provide useful accounts of the structure and dynamics of the Japanese education system.

21 See Okano or an excellent ethnography of school-to-work transition. She fills a gap in the literature by investigating "mediocre to low achievers" (1993).

22 Information about the *Bunkachō* can be found in *Waga kuni no bunka to bunka gyōsei* (Our Country's Culture and Culture Administration) (1987).

23 The Religious Affairs Bureau (*Shūkyō-kyoku*) was moved from the Ministry of Home Affairs in June 1913. In October 1945, it was absorbed into the Social Education Bureau. Later, it would re-emerge as the Religious Affairs Division in the Agency for Cultural Affairs.

24 The Survey Bureau was a descendant of the Survey and Dissemination Bureau (*Chōsa fukyō-kyoku*) (12 December 1946–30 May 1949). The Survey and Dissemination Bureau was actually rooted in the wartime Textbook Bureau (*Tosho-kyoku*) and its postwar incarnation of the same English appellation (*Kyōkasho-kyoku*) (abolished 30 May 1949).

25 Prefectural and municipal education superintendents have their interests represented by the influential Prefectural Education Superintendents Association and the Association of Local Education Superintendents.

26 Private schools are not under the jurisdiction of the municipal authorities. Rather, they are under the purview of prefectural governors, who must approve their establishment. Private schools are required to submit reports concerning their educational activities and other matters to the governor. Each prefecture has a private school council, and the governor must seek the latter's opinion if certain actions are taken *vis-à-vis* private schools.

27 Much of this information comes from Fujioka (1994a: 75–81). For more details, see *Monbushō kankei hōjin meibo* (Register of Juridical Persons Associated with the Ministry of Education) (1994).

28 *Cf.* Rohlen: "The well-intended teachers and well-behaved students put their efforts to purposes that are ultimately shallow and uninspired. The nation benefits economically. Society is well run. But it is a system without much heart" (1983: 320).

29 During the war, schools were actually militarized. In March 1944, middle- and higher-level school students were mobilized all year round in order to carry out war-related duties. On 1 April 1945, it was decided to discontinue instruction at all schools, with the exception of the first several years of elementary school. On 22 May 1945, the Wartime Education Order stipulated that each school was to organize a "student brigade." Increasingly, school buildings became used for military supply storage, evacuation hospitals and centers, and even munitions factories.

30 The darker aspect of these arrangements gives rise to bullying (along with the occasional suicide), school refusal problems, school violence, apathy, and according to many Japanese educators, a lack of creativity and political awareness.

31 For a basic outline of a Japanese middle school in English, see Teraoka 1983.

32 For a description of homerooms, see Rohlen (1983: 178–87).

33 *Cf.* Rohlen's opinion of what social studies textbooks impart to students:

"This is a society best run by technocrats who know how to adjust the gauges and values to maintain the optimal mix. The management of society is an economic, not a political science" (1983: 256).

34 There are many works on company life. One of the best is Clark 1987. See Rohlen 1974 for an anthropological perspective.

7 The rationality of moral education: the state's vision of civil society

1 Though Rohlen's research is certainly pertinent to this chapter's topic, it should be clarified that he investigated senior high schools, where moral education is not required. See his discussion (1983: 247–65) on textbooks for "social studies" subject area courses (which included ethics, geography, history, politics and economy, and contemporary society). The social studies subject area was disbanded in 1994, though currently students must study "civics," a subject area in which students must take either contemporary society or ethics plus politics and economy. Because social studies is related to questions of morality and civility, I include some materials from social studies guidebooks in this chapter.

2 Materials on moral education published in Japanese may be broadly divided into works by (1) academics and professors of education; (2) school teachers and those working for educational bureaucracies; and (3) the Japan Teachers Union. I am grateful to Satō Izumi for pointing this out to me. Many Japanese bookstores have sections devoted to moral education materials, and there are numerous book series available for classroom instruction. As an example of the kinds of stories these books contain, see Seito's *Dōtoku shidō no tame no wazai senshū* (Selected Discussion Materials for Moral Guidance) (1989).

3 Any treatment of moral education entails a consideration of the "textbook controversy": how the Japanese government portrays Japan's imperialist past and its subjugation of Asian countries in authorized history books. This contentious and complex issue is beyond the purview of this chapter. For an English treatment of the textbook controversy, see Herzog (1993: 193–207).

4 Indeed, Rohlen describes Japanese students as being politically apathetic (1983: 210).

5 See DK 1, DK 2, DK 3, DK 4, DKS 1, DKS 2, and DKS 3.

6 Much of the Japanese literature on morals is concerned with the effectiveness of moral education.

7 However, "The Ministry of Education is unable to rule education directly through its domination of local school systems and loyal teachers, but it can in fact control exams and textbooks." This is significant, because "The ambition to succeed in education is the ultimate source of discipline" (Rohlen 1983: 267).

8 For an English source, see Hall (1949) for an examination of prewar texts used in *shūshin* education. Also see Kaigo (1963).

9 The emphasis on having public institutions ("public" here meaning government and private schools) and the private domain (families) join forces to socialize/educate children also socializes parents – particularly mothers – to become more "publicly involved." Ironically, however, some nursery schools and kindergartens privatize the lifestyle of mothers, thereby

reinforcing their identity as mothers: mothers are told by preschools how to dress, feed, equip, and prepare their children for school in amazing and time-consuming detail. Peak reports that mothers of newly enrolled students were told by preschool authorities to "Feel that you are also a new student at this preschool" (1989: 59–62).

10 See Peak 1991 for a discussion of *omoiyari* in a preschool setting.

11 For a description of clubs in Japanese schools, see Rohlen (1983: 187–94).

12 As if pre-empt criticisms about Japan's wartime aggressions, "it is important to touch upon the fact that our nation caused much damage" to China and other countries (SGSH: 68–9).

13 It should be mentioned that much of the socialization about being a "good Japanese" occurs outside the classroom (via family, media, popular culture), and in ways that are not always obvious.

14 "*Gambaru*" is a core value that appears in many social contexts. For a discussion of how it relates to educational settings, see Duke (1986: 121–47), Hendry (1986: 83), and Singleton 1993. For an examination of the role it plays in Japanese society in general, see Amanuma (1987).

15 Peak (1991: 73) and Hendry (1986: 87–8, 160) report that being *sunao* is an important cultural desirable at the preschool level.

16 LeTrende discusses in detail the meaning of "guidance": (1) Knowledge is acquired in an experiential process that has mental, emotional, ethical, and physical components; (2) Teacher and learner study the same thing; i.e. there is a correct form or order to the acquisition and interpretation of knowledge – one path, one set of discoveries; (3) The teacher is expected to have already successfully completed the path, or to be more advanced that the learner; (4) The learner, not knowing the path, is dependent on the teacher; (5) The teacher will model the correct interpretation or correct skills and the learner will imitate these; (6) Exertion is crucial to knowing – the teacher may set the learner strenuous and difficult tasks; (7) Basic skills are seen as containing all the elements for complex mastery – the teacher may require a repetition of the basics at any point on the path; (8) Intense effort and a sense of appreciation of effort are necessary to successfully completing the path, but there must be balance or harmony in the learner's emotional relationship with the task at hand; (9) To sustain the learner's emotional balance, the teacher encourages an appreciation of effort and sacrifice in the learner. This is often accomplished by the teacher demonstrating his or her commitment to the learner's progress and affirming that the teacher and learner share one goal: the learner's success; (10) Reflections on past actions – success or failure – are essential for correcting and consolidating gains (1994: 55–6).

17 See Hendry's discussion of *aisatsu* and greetings (1986).

18 See Peak (1991: 73), who discusses the importance of "cheerfulness" for preschoolers.

19 For example, in his study of weddings, Edwards describes the Japanese tendency to segment this long and complex ceremony into "fixed poses." He believes that this focus on frozen action "consists of a tendency to separate experience into discrete contexts, isolated from each other as well as from the temporal flow, and to focus on each context, sphere, or pose as a gestalt, a thing unto itself" (1989: 137). As he points out himself, this "general mode of cognition" corresponds to Benedict's description of Japanese social life

as "compartmentalized spheres of activity" (1989: 137). Edwards suggests that this is in fact an example of a "basic approach to experience" that finds expression in other spheres of Japanese life, such as in the traditional theater, where maintaining a dramatic pose (*mie*) is highly appreciated (1989). An emphasis on posing is also seen among Japan's teenage bikers (*bōsōzoku*), who have a repertoire of poses that indicate (sometimes ironically) masculinity and intimidation, important themes in their subculture (Sato 1991: 88–92). Another observer notes the "stop-action" and the "aesthetic of reducing motion" in Japanese artistic works (Lee 1982: 54–5).

20 Sano also points out that *kibun tenkan* is a topic much discussed in the popular media as a special skill that successful individuals (e.g. company presidents and political leaders) employ (1989: 126–31).

21 Naitō writes that the "double structure of morality" (*tatemae* and *honne*) is behind the lack of efficacy in moral education training, because many students interpret such lessons as mere formality (*tatemae*) and stereotypical, and come to believe that moral education is not applicable to real life (1990: 31–2).

22 See also Hendry (1986: 84–5) and Tobin 1991 for discussions of *kejime* in a preschool setting.

23 LeTrende explains the rationality behind the ritualized activity at the schools: "Foreign teachers and exchange students alike have voiced their exasperation with the redundancy and inefficiency with which most tasks are carried out. Schools could be cleaned, managed, and supplied in a manner much more efficient in terms of cost and time. When I made such 'efficiency' suggestions to teachers, they pointed out that the tasks were essential to the students' education and emotional well-being. Teachers regard the various duties as a major part of education – ways to teach students how to work with others and how to care for themselves" (1994: 54).

24 Here it is pertinent to reiterate Rohlen's observation that "private ambitions of students for exam success" drives the high levels of orderly behavior in Japanese high schools (1983: 209).

25 The entire body should be encouraged to learn. Note the advice about teaching reading: "When lower level children are reading, they should use more than their eyes. It is important that they feel, know, and respond with their ears, limbs, and entire body" (SGD: 66).

26 "Students learn to be cooperative and polite with others, but not to sacrifice for them. They learn to recite the achievements of great men, but not to emulate them" (Rohlen 1983: 320).

27 There are other terms that we should use more cautiously in the Japanese context, such as "party rule," "legislative process," and "consumer interests." *Cf.* Van Wolferen's observation: "The Japanese have laws, legislators, a parliament, political parties, labour unions, a prime minister, interest groups and stockholders. But one should not be misled by these familiar labels into hasty conclusions as to how power is exercised in Japan. . . . The Japanese prime minister is not expected to show much leadership; labour unions organise strikes to be held during lunch breaks; the legislature does not in fact legislate; stockholders never demand dividends; consumer interest groups advocate protectionism" (1989: 24).

8 Conclusion: lessons from Japan about state and society

1 For a more detailed version of the post-earthquake response, see McVeigh 1996c, from which portions of this chapter are borrowed. For examples of Japanese compiled news reporting, see *Hanshin daishinsai asahi shinbun ōsaka honsha shimen shūsei* (Asahi Newspaper: Ōsaka Main Office Newspaper Compilation on the Great Hanshin Earthquake) (*Asahi shinbun-sha* (Asahi Newspaper Co.) 1995); *Kobe shinbun tokubetsu shukusatsuban hōdō kiroku* (Kobe Newspaper Special Pocket Edition News) (*Kobe shinbun-sha* (Kobe Newspaper Co.) 1995); *Gekiron teigen: Hanshin daishinsai* (Arguments and Proposals: Great Hanshin Earthquake) (*Asahi shinbun "rondan"* (Asahi Newspaper "World of Criticism") 1995); and *Hanshin daishinsai zen kiroku* (Great Hanshin Earthquake: Complete Records) (*Kobe shinbun-sha* (Kobe Newspaper Co.) 1995).

2 Eventually it would be reported that 6,414 died, including those who died of quake-related causes in hospitals (DY 26 December 1996: 2).

3 On 24 January, regulations requiring them to have Japanese medical licenses in Japan were dropped, though by then it was too late for many of the victims.

4 Legally, the prime minister has wide jurisdiction during a disaster. Under Article 125 of the Basic Law of Disaster Response, the prime minister has the authority to control economic activities, the Self-Defense Force (SDF), the MSDF (Maritime SDF), police, and firefighters. In "Japan needs crisis management system" (DY 10 February 1995: 13), former Prime Minister Hosokawa analyzes the weaknesses in the present crisis management system and how they relate to the prime minister's post. He notes that "When I entered the residence [Prime Minister's], which was built in 1928, I was surprised to find out that there was not a single computer at Japan's supreme headquarters. It is not on 24-hour alert for crisis, with the exception of the Cabinet Secretary Affairs Office, which is badly understaffed with only 24 members. The National Land Agency's Disaster Prevention Bureau is closed at 5 p.m. It is as if they believe disasters occur only during daytime."

5 The record of Japanese leadership in crisis management is far from commendable. Ironically, Kaifu, who has criticized Murayama's bungled response to the great Hanshin earthquake, was widely criticized for being slow to respond to Iraq's invasion of Kuwait when he was prime minister. The 1985 crash of a JAL airliner, which killed 520 lives, is in some ways eerily similar to the Hanshin earthquake. In both incidents, lives were lost because of bureaucratic stalling due to in-fighting; offers of help by the US military were squandered; and a governmental head appeared less than interested in making himself present at the disaster site (in the 1985 crash, Prime Minister Nakasone was on vacation 20 minutes away by helicopter from the crash site, but he did not visit the site to console survivors and encourage rescue workers) (Van Wolferen 1989: 319–20).

6 Indeed, after the dust settled, it was revealed that 60 percent of local governments lack emergency plans ("Many localities lack quake measures," DY 26 January 1995: 3).

7 They cut their trip short by two days and returned to Japan.

8 One article about the imperial visit gave the impression that the emperor

and empress do not keep up with current events: "According to their aides, the Emperor and Empress expressed a strong wish to travel to the quake-stricken area after reading of the plight of displaced people and hearing from Cabinet ministers who visited the affected area" ("Royal couple visits Kobe, views damage," JT 1 February 1995: 1).

9 But not all officials shared Itō's attitude. Self-Defense Forces Lt. Gen. Yusuke Matsushima, commander of the Chubu District Army Head-quarters, "tearfully apologized for the delayed dispatch of troops to the disaster area" ("Official lashes out over quake criticism," JT 28 January 1995: 2). See "GSDF commander defends timing of relief troop dispatch" (JT 22 February 1995: 3) for an unconvincing explanation as to why the troops took so long to respond.

10 It should also be noted that in typical Japanese fashion, comparisons were made with how catastrophes are handled in America, and the media focused attention on the US Federal Emergency Management Agency.

11 Perhaps, because there is no clearly demarcated "public" space recognized by and separate from officialdom, "ritualistic resistance" and "expressive protest" (Koschmann 1978) become acceptable as forms of opposition in Japan.

12 These sentiments are expressed in Ayako Doi's "The other poison in the air" (JT March 30, 1995: 18).

13 Fukushima has a different interpretation of Japanese society, categorizing it as a "high-trust society" in which spontaneous nonkinship-based associations easily form" (1995: 171). He compares Japan with Korea, China, Germany, Italy, France, and the United States. His assessment, though it certainly has merit, grants economic success much weight and suffers from a "bird's-eye view" of Japanese society.

14 In McCormack's terms, "Japaneseness" should become "a civic and moral, rather than an ethnic, quality" (1996b: 296).

15 "Nationality" is a confusing term. Some use it to refer to membership in a state (citizenship), others use it to mean ethnicity, while still others merge its different senses. See Connor (1994).

16 *Cf.* Heller and Tester, who argue that the "de-naturalizing" of social arrangements led to the creation of civil society. In the West before the modern period, "asymmetric reciprocity" (hierarchy) established a social milieu that was seen as inseparable from nature. Such a world view emphasized ascription and acceptance (passivity). Modernity emerged when individuals lost faith in the "naturalness of society" and began to regard human relations as "artificial" (i.e. socially constructed). "Symmetric reciprocity" took hold, emphasizing achievement and freedom (activity) (Heller 1990). Once the social world was viewed as a product of social relationships and social processes, a degree of reflexivity entered human relations that bolstered civil society (Tester 1992: 11).

17 *Cf.* Sahlin's discussion of the role that the culturally constructed notion of "rationality" plays in the West (1976).

18 See Littlewood (1996) for a treatment of how the West has portrayed Japan.

Bibliography

Abe, Hitoshi, Muneyuki Shindō, and Sadafumi Kawato (1994) *The Government and Politics of Japan*, Tokyo: University of Tokyo Press.

Aisatsu to kotoba (Greetings and Language) (1989) Agency for Cultural Affairs (ed.), Tokyo: Ministry of Finance.

Akagi Suruki (1991) *Kansei no keisei* (Formation of Bureaucracy), Tokyo: Heibunsha.

Allinson, Gary D. (1975) *Japanese Urbanism*, Berkeley: University of California Press.

Althusser, L. (1971) *Ideology and Ideological State Apparatuses (Notes Toward an Investigation in Lenin and Philosophy and Other Essays)*, New York: Monthly Review.

Altman, Kristin Kyoto (1996) "Television and Political Turmoil: Japan's Summer of 1993," in Susan J. Pharr and Ellis S. Krauss (eds) *Media and Politics in Japan*, Honolulu: University of Hawaii Press, pp. 165–86.

Amakawa, Akira (1987) "The Making of the Postwar Local Government System," in Robert E. Ward and Sakamoto Yoshikazu (eds) *Democratizing Japan: The Allied Occupation*, Honolulu: University of Hawaii Press, pp. 253–83.

Amanuma Kaoru (1987) *"Gambari" no kōzō: nihonjin no kōdō genri* (The Structure of "Persistence": A Principle of Japanese Behavior), Tokyo: Yoshiawa Kōbunkan.

Amsden, Alice H. (1989) *Asia's Next Giant: South Korea and Late Industrialization*, New York: Oxford University Press.

Ariès, Philipe and Georges Duby (eds) (1990) *A History of Private Lives* (5 vols), Cambridge, Mass.: The Belknap Press of Harvard University Press.

Arnason, Johann (1989) "Paths to Modernity: The Peculiarities of Japanese Feudalism," in Gavan McCormack and Sugimoto Yoshio (eds) *The Japanese Trajectory: Modernization and Beyond*, Cambridge: University of Cambridge Press, pp. 235–63.

Arnold, Thurman W. (1962) *The Symbols of Government*, New York: Harcourt, Brace, and World.

—— (1964) *The Folklore of Capitalism*, New Haven, Conn.: Yale University Press.

Aronoff, Myron J. (1977) *Power and Ritual in the Israel Labor Party*, Assen: Van Gorcum.

—— (1980) "Ideology and Interest: The Dialectics of Politics," in Myron J. Arnold (ed.) *Ideology and Politics, Political Anthropology*, vol 1, New Brunswick, New Jersey: Transaction, pp. 1–30.

—— (1986) "Establishing Authority: The Memorialization of Jabotinsky and the Burial of the Bar-Kochba Bones in Israel under the Likud," in Myron J. Arnold (ed.) *Ideology and Politics, Political Anthropology*, vol 5, New Brunswick, New Jersey: Transaction, pp. 105–30.

Ashkenazi, Michael (1992) *Matsuri: Festivals in a Japanese Town*, Honolulu: University of Hawaii Press.

Bachnik, Jane M. (1992) "The Two 'Faces' of Self and Society in Japan," *Ethos* 20 (1): 3–32.

Bachnik, Jane M. and Charles J. Quinn, Jr (eds) (1994) *Situated Meaning: Inside and Outside in Japanese Self, Society, and Language*, Princeton: Princeton University Press.

Baxter, James C. and Terry E. MacDougall (1983) "Local Government," *Encyclopedia of Japan*, Tokyo: Kodansha, pp. 63–71.

Befu, Harumi (1993) "Nationalism and Nihonjinron," in Harumi Befu (ed.) *Cultural Nationalism in East Asia: Representation and Identity*, Berkeley: University of California Institute of East Asian Studies Research Papers and Policy Studies, no. 39: 107–35.

Bell, Catherine (1992) *Ritual Theory, Ritual Practice*, New York: Oxford University Press.

Ben-Ari, E. (1990) "Ritual Strikes, Ceremonial Slowdowns: Some Thoughts on the Management of Conflict in Large Japanese Enterprises," in S. N. Eisenstadt and Eyal Ben-Ari (eds) *Japanese Models of Conflict Resolution*, New York: Kegan Paul International, pp. 94–124.

Benedict, Ruth (1989) [1946] *The Chrysanthemum and the Sword: Patterns of Japanese Culture*, Boston: Houghton Mifflin.

Benn, S. I. and G. F. Gaus (eds) (1983) *Public and Private in Social Life*, London: Croom Helm.

Bennett, W. Lance (1975) "Political Sanctification: The Civil Religon and American Politics," *Social Science Information* 14: 79–106.

—— (1977) "The Ritualistic and Pragmatic Bases of Political Campaign Discourse," *The Quarterly Journal of Speech* 63 (3): 219–38.

—— (1979) "Imitation, Ambiguity, and Drama in Political Life: Civil Religion and the Dilemmas of Public Morality," *Journal of Politics* 41: 106–33.

—— (1980) "Myth, Ritual and Political Control," *Journal of Communication* 30: 166–79.

Bestor, Theodore C. (1989) *Neighborhood Tokyo*, Stanford: Stanford University Press.

Binns, Christopher A. P. (1979–80) "The Changing Face of Power: Revolution and Development of the Soviet Ceremonial System," *Man* (n.s.) 14: 585–606 and 15: 170–87.

Blau, Peter M. (1963) *The Dynamics of Bureaucracy: A Study of Interpersonal Relationships in Two Government Agencies*, Chicago: University of Chicago Press.

Bourdieu, Pierre (1977) *Outline of a Theory of Practice*, Cambridge: Cambridge University Press.

Bourguignon, Erika (1980) "Introduction and Theoretical Considerations," in Erika Bourguignon (ed.) *A World of Women: Anthropological Studies of Women in the Societies of the World*, New York: Praeger.

Brandon, James R., William P. Malm, and Donald H. Shively (1978) *Studies in Kabuki*, Honolulu: East–West Center.

Britan, Gerald M. (1981) *Bureaucracy and Innovation: An Ethnography of Policy Change*, Beverly Hills: Sage.

Britan, Gerald M. and R. Cohen (eds) (1980) *Hierarchy and Society: Anthropological Perspectives on Bureaucracy*, Philadelphia, PA: Institute for the Study of Human Issues.

Buruma, Ian (1984) *Behind the Mask*, New York: Pantheon Books.

Calder, Kent E. (1988) *Crisis and Compensation: Public Policy and Political Stability in Japan, 1949–1986*, Princeton: Princeton University Press.

—— (1993) *Strategic Capitalism*, Princeton: Princeton University Press.

Callon, David (1995) *Divided Sun: MITI and the Breakdown of Japanese High-Tech Industrial Policy 1975–93*, Stanford: Stanford University Press.

Campbell, John C. (1976) *Contemporary Japanese Budget Politics*, Berkeley: University of California Press.

—— (1984) "Policy Conflict and Its Resolution with the Governmental System," in Ellis Krauss *et al.* (eds) *Conflict in Japan* Honolulu: University of Hawaii Press, pp. 294–334.

—— (1989) "Democracy and Bureaucracy in Japan," in Takeshida Ishida and Ellis S. Krauss (eds) *Democracy in Japan*, University of Pittsburgh Press, pp. 113–37.

—— (1992) *How Policies Change: The Japanese Government and the Aging Society*, Princeton: Princeton University Press.

Cannadine, David and Simon Price (eds) (1987) *Rituals of Royalty: Power and Ceremonial in Traditional Society*, Cambridge: Cambridge University Press.

Caplan, Patricia and Janet M. Bujra (eds) (1979) *Women United, Women Divided*, London: Indiana University Press.

Castells, Manuel (1992) "Four Asians Tigers with a Dragon Head: A Comparative Analysis of the State, Economy, and Society in the Asian Pacific Rim," in Richard P. Appelbaum and Jeffery Henderson (eds) *States and Development in the Asian Pacific Rim*, Newbury Park, Calif.: Sage, pp. 33–70.

Chū gakkō: dōtoku kyōiku jūjitsu no tame no kōnai kenshū no tebiki (A Primer on School Training For Realizing Moral Education in Junior High School) (1984) Ministry of Education (ed.), Tokyo: Ministry of Finance.

Chū gakkō: dōtoku kyōiku shidō jō no shomondai (Various Problems Concerning Guidance for Moral Education in Junior High School) (1990) Ministry of Education (ed.), Tokyo: Ministry of Finance.

Chū gakkō: omoiyari no kokoro o sodateru shidō (Guidance for Cultivating a Heart of Empathy in Primary School) (1986) Ministry of Education (ed.), Tokyo: Ministry of Finance.

Clark, Rodney (1987) *The Japanese Company*, Charles E. Tuttle.

Cohen, Abner (1974) *Two-Dimensional Man: An Essay on the Anthropology of Power and Symbolism in Complex Society*, Berkeley: University of California Press.

—— (1979) "Political Symbolism," *Annual Review of Anthropology* 8: 87–113.

—— (1981) *The Politics of Elite Culture*, Berkeley: University of California Press.

Cohen, Jean L. and Andrew Arato (1992) *Civil Society and Political Theory*, Cambridge, Mass.: MIT Press.

Cole, Robert E. (1971) *Japanese Blue Collar: The Changing Tradition*, Berkeley: University of California Press.

—— (1979) *Work, Mobility, and Participation: A Comparative Study of American and Japanese Industry*, Berkeley: University of California Press.

—— (1989) *Strategies for Learning: Small-Group Activities in American, Japanese, and Swedish Industry*, Berkeley: University of California Press.

Connor, Walker (1994) *Ethnonationalism: The Quest for Understanding*, Princeton: Princeton University Press.

Craig, Albert M. (1975) "Functional and Dysfunctional Aspects of Government Bureaucracy," in Ezra Vogel (ed.) *Modern Japanese Organization and Decision-Making*, Berkeley: University of California Press, pp. 3–32.

Crozier, Michel (1964) *The Bureaucratic Phenomenon*, Chicago: University of Chicago Press.

Crump, Thomas (1989) *The Death of an Emperor*, Oxford: Oxford University Press.

Curtis, Gerald (1971) *Election Campaigning Japanese Style*, New York: Columbia University Press.

Dale, Peter (1986) *The Myth of Japanese Uniqueness*, University of Oxford: Nissan Institute for Japanese Studies.

D'Andrade, Roy (1995) *The Development of Cognitive Anthropology*, Cambridge: Cambridge University Press.

De Certeau, Michel (1984) *The Practice of Everyday Life*, Berkeley: University of California Press.

Deyo, Frederic C. (ed.) (1987) *The Political Economy of the New Asian Industrialism*, Ithaca, NY: Cornell University Press.

Ding, X. L. (1994) "Institutional Amphibiousness and the Transition from Communism: The Case of China," *British Journal of Political Science* 24 (3): 293–318.

Doi Takeo (1973) "*Omote* and *Ura:* Concepts Derived from the Japanese 2-fold Structure of Consciousness," *Journal of Nervous and Mental Disease* 157: 258–261.

—— (1986) *The Anatomy of Self*, Tokyo: Kodansha.

Donzelot, J. (1979) *The Policing of Families*, New York: Pantheon.

Dore, Ronald (1976) *The Diploma Disease: Education, Qualification and Development*, Berkeley: University of California Press.
—— (1987) *Taking Japan Seriously*, London: Athlone Press.
Dore, Ronald and Mari Sako (1989) *How the Japanese Learn to Work*, London: Routledge.
Dōtoku kyōiku suishin shidō shiryō – chū gakkō: yomimono shiryō to sono riyō 1 (Materials to Promote Guidance in Moral Education – Reading Materials and Their Use for Junior High School 1) (1991) Ministry of Education (ed.), Tokyo: Ministry of Finance.
Dōtoku kyōiku suishin shidō shiryō – chū gakkō: yomimono shiryō to sono riyō 2 (Materials to Promote Guidance in Moral Education – Reading Materials and Their Use for Junior High School 2) (1990) Ministry of Education (ed.), Tokyo: Ministry of Finance.
Dōtoku kyōiku suishin shidō shiryō – chū gakkō: yomimono shiryō to sono riyō 3 (Materials to Promote Guidance in Moral Education – Reading Materials and Their Use for Junior High School 3) (1993) Ministry of Education (ed.), Tokyo: Ministry of Finance.
Dōtoku kyōiku suishin shidō shiryō – shō gakkō: yomimono shiryō to sono riyō 1 (Materials to Promote Guidance in Moral Education – Reading Materials and Their Use for Primary School 1) (1991) Ministry of Education (ed.), Tokyo: Ministry of Finance.
Dōtoku kyōiku suishin shidō shiryō – shō gakkō: yomimono shiryō to sono riyō 2 (Materials to Promote Guidance in Moral Education – Reading Materials and Their Use for Primary School 2) (1992) Ministry of Education (ed.), Tokyo: Ministry of Finance.
Dōtoku kyōiku suishin shidō shiryō – shō gakkō: yomimono shiryō to sono riyō 3 (Materials to Promote Guidance in Moral Education – Reading Materials and Their Use for Primary School 3) (1993) Ministry of Education (ed.), Tokyo: Ministry of Finance.
Dōtoku kyōiku suishin shidō shiryō – shō gakkō: yomimono shiryō to sono riyō 4 (Materials to Promote Guidance in Moral Education – Reading Materials and Their Use for Primary School 4) (1994) Ministry of Education (ed.), Tokyo: Ministry of Finance.
Douglas, Mary (1986) *How Institutions Think*, Syracuse, NY: Syracuse University Press.
Dower, John W. (1995) "The Bombed: Hiroshimas and Nagasakis in Japanese Memory," *Diplomatic History* 19 (2): 275–95.
Dreyfus, Hubert L. and Paul Rabinow (1983) *Michel Foucault: Beyond Structuralism and Hermeneutics* (second edition), Chicago: University of Chicago Press.
Drifte, Reinhard (1986) *Arms Production in Japan: The Military Applications of Civilian Technology*, Boulder, Colo.: Westview Press.
Duke, Benjamin (1986) *The Japanese School*, New York: Praeger.
Durkheim, Emile (1966) *The Division of Labor in Society* (trans. George Simpson), New York: Free Press.

Edelman, Murray (1964) *The Symbolic Uses of Politics*, Urbana: University of Illinois Press.
—— (1971) *Politics as Symbolic Action*, Chicago: Markham.
Education in Japan: A Graphic Presentation (1994) Ministry of Education (ed.), Tokyo: Ministry of Education.
Edwards, Walter (1989) *Modern Japan Through Its Weddings: Gender, Person, and Society in Ritual Portrayal*, Stanford: Stanford University Press.
Elias, Norbert (1978) *The Civilizing Process: The History of Manners*, vol. 1, Oxford: Basil Blackwell.
—— (1982) *The Civilizing Process: State Formation and Civilization*, vol. 2, Oxford: Basil Blackwell.
—— (1983) *The Court Society*, Oxford: Basil Blackwell.
Ellul, Jacques (1964) *The Technological Society*, New York: Alfred A. Knopf.
Elshtain, Jean Bethke (1981) *Public Man, Private Woman: Women in Social and Political Thought*, Princeton: Princeton University Press.
Ernest, Earle (1974) *The Kabuki Theatre*, Honolulu: University of Hawaii Press.
Evans, Peter (1995) *Embedded Autonomy: States and Industrial Transformation*, Princeton: Princeton University Press.
Fallers, Lloyd A. (1974) *The Social Anthropology of the Nation-State*, Chicago: Aldine.
Fallows, James (1994) *Looking at the Sun: The Rise of the New East Asian Economic and Political System*, New York: Vintage Books.
Farley, Maggie (1996) "Japan's Press and the Politics of Scandal," in Susan J. Pharr and Ellis S. Krauss (eds) *Media and Politics in Japan*, Honolulu: University Of Hawaii Press, pp. 133–63.
Ferguson, Kathy E. (1984) *The Feminist Case against Bureaucracy*, Philadelphia: Temple University Press.
Fiske, Shirley J. (1994) "Federal Organizational Cultures: Layers and Loci," in Hamada, Tomoko and Willis E. Silbery (eds) Anthropological Perspectives on Organizational Culture, New York: University Press of America, pp. 95–119.
Flanagan, Scott, Ellis Krauss, and Kurt Steiner (eds) 1980) *Political Opposition and Local Politics in Japan*, Princeton: Princeton University Press.
Foucault, Michel (1973) *Madness and Civilization: A History of Madness in the Age of Reason*, New York: Vintage Books.
—— (1975) *The Birth of the Clinic: An Archeology of Medical Perception*, New York: Vintage Books.
—— (1979) *Discipline and Punish: The Birth of the Prison*, New York: Vintage Books.
—— (1980) *The History of Sexuality, Vol. I, An Introduction*, New York: Vintage Books.
Freeman, Laurie A. (1996) "Japan's Press Clubs as Information Cartels," *Working Paper No. 18*, Japan Policy Research Institute (April).
Friedman, David (1988) *The Misunderstood Miracle: Industrial Development and Political Change in Japan*, Ithaca, NY: Cornell University Press.

Fujioka Akifusa (ed.) (1994a) *Kanchō zen keiretsu chizu* (Guide to the Entire Bureaucratic Network), Tokyo: Niki Shuppan.

—— (1994b) *Tsūsanshō no yomikata* (How to Read the Ministry of International Trade and Industry), Tokyo: Ohesu Shuppansha.

—— (1995) *Hitome de wakaru tokushu hōjin to kokka purojiekuto* (Special Corporations and State Projects Understood at a Glance), Tokyo: Niki Shuppan.

Fujitani, Takashi (1992) "Electronic Pageantry and Japan's 'Symbolic Emperor,'" *Journal of Asian Studies* 51 (4): 824–50.

Fukushima, Francis (1995) *Trust: The Social Virtues and the Creation of Prosperity*, New York: Free Press.

Garfinkel, Harold (1967) *Studies in Ethnomethodology*, Englewood Cliffs, NJ: Prentice-Hall.

Geertz, Clifford (1983) *Local Knowledge: Further Essays in Interpretive Anthropology*, New York: Basic Books.

Gerth, H. H. and C. Wright Mills (eds) 1958) *From Max Weber: Essays in Sociology* (trans. H. H. Gerth and C. Wright Mills), New York: Oxford University Press.

Giner, Salvador (1995) "Civil Society and Its Future," in John A. Hall (ed.) *Civil Society: Theory, History, Comparison*, Cambridge, Mass.: Polity Press, pp. 301–25.

Gluck, Carol (1985) *Japan's Modern Myths: Ideology in the Late Meiji Period*, Princeton: Princeton University Press.

Goffman, Erving (1959) *The Presentation of Self in Everyday Life*, New York: Anchor Books.

—— (1963) *Behavior in Public Places: Notes on the Social Organization of Gatherings*, New York: The Free Press.

Goodman, Roger (1993) *Japan's "International Youth": The Emergence of a New Class of Schoolchildren*, Oxford: Clarendon Press.

Gotōda Masahara (1994) *Sei to kan* (Politics and Bureaucracy), Tokyo: Kōdansha.

Gramsci, Antonio (1971) Selections from the Prison Notebooks (eds and trans. Quintin Hoare and Geoffrey Nowell Smith), London: Lawrence and Wishart.

Great Hanshin Quake, The (1995) Special Report, Tokyo: Japan Times Newspaper Ltd.

Gyōsei kikōzu (Administrative Organization Charts) (1994) Sōmuchō Gyōsei Kanrikyoku (ed.), Tokyo: Sōmuchō Gyōsei Kanrikyoku.

Habermas, Jurgen (1989) *The Structural Transformation of the Public Sphere*, Cambridge, Mass.: MIT Press.

Haley, John (1987) "Government by Negotiation: A Reappraisal of Bureaucratic Power in Japan," *Journal of Japanese Studies* 13 (Summer): 343–57.

—— (1991) *Authority without Power: Law and the Japanese Paradox*, New York: Oxford University Press.

Hall, John A. (1995) *Civil Society: Theory, History, Comparison*, Cambridge, Mass.: Polity Press.

Hall, Robert King (1949) *Shushin: The Ethics of a Defeated Nation*, New York: Teachers College, Columbia University.

Hamabata, Matthews Masayuki (1990) *Crested Kimono: Power and Love in the Japanese Business Family*, Ithaca, New York: Cornell University Press.

Handelman, Don (1976) "Bureaucratic Transactions: The Development of Official–Client Relationships in Israel," in Bruce Kapferer (ed.) *Transaction and Meaning: Directions in the Anthropology of Exchange and Symbolic Behavior*, ASA Essays 1, Philadelphia: Institute for the Study of Human Issues, pp. 223–75.

—— (1978) "Introduction: A Recognition of Bureaucracy," in Don Handleman and Elliot Leyton (eds) *Bureaucracy and World View: Studies in the Logic of Official Interpretation*, St John's, Institute of Social and Economic Research, Memorial University of Newfoundland, Social and Economic Studies No. 22, pp. 1–14.

—— (1981) "Introduction: The Idea of Bureaucratic Organization," *Social Analysis* 9: 5–23.

—— (1983) "Shaping Phenomenal Reality: Dialectic and Disjunction in the Bureaucratic Synesis of Child-abuse in Urban Newfoundland," *Social Analysis* 13: 5–40.

Hardacre, Helen (1989) *Shinto and the State (1868–1989)*, Princeton: Princeton Universtiy Press.

—— (1996) "Aum Shinrikyo and the Japanese Media," *Working Paper No. 19*, Japan Policy Research Institute (April).

Hata Ikuhiko (1983) *Kanryō no kenkyū: fumetsu no pāwā* (A Study of Bureaucratic Immortal Power), Tokyo: Kōdansha.

Hayashi Shūzō (1982) *Nihon kanryō kenkoku-ron* (On State Building by Japanese Bureaucrats), Tokyo: Gyōsei Mondai Kekyūjo.

Hazama Hiroshi (1969) "*Mai-hōmu no naka no ikigai*" ("The Reason for Living in My Home"), *Rōdō mondai* 133: 86–91.

Hegel, G. W. (1953) *Hegel's Philosophy of Right* (trans. T. M. Knox), Oxford: Clarendon Press.

Heller, Agnes (1990) *Can Modernity Survive?* Cambridge: Polity.

Henderson, Dan F. (1995) "Foreign Acquisitions and Takeovers in Japan," *Saint Louis University Law Journal* 39: 897–915.

Hendry, Joy (1986) *Becoming Japanese: The World of the Pre-School Child*, Honolulu: University of Hawaii Press.

Herzfeld, Michael (1992) *The Social Production of Indifference: Exploring the Symbolic Roots of Western Bureaucracy*, Chicago: University Chicago Press.

Herzog, Peter J. (1993) *Japan's Pseudo-democracy*, Sandgate, Folkstone, Kent: Japan Library.

Higashi S. (1992) "*Shakai kyōiku o mo shihai suru monbushō*" (The Ministry of Education's Control of Social Education), in Sakamoto H. and Yamamoto H. (eds) *Monbushō no kenkyū: kyōiku no jiyū to kenri o kangaeru* (Research on the Ministry of Education: Thinking about the Freedom of Education and Rights), Tokyo: Sanmitsu Shobō, pp. 240–61.

Hirata Kiyoaki (1987) "La société civile japonaise contemporaine" (Contemporary Japanese Civil Society), *Actuel Marx* (Marx Today) 2.

Hobsbawm, Eric and Terence Ranger (eds) (1983) *The Invention of Tradition*, Cambridge: Cambridge University Press.

Hollerman, Leon (1967) *Japan's Dependency on the World Economy*, Princeton: Princeton University Press.

Honda Yasuharu (1974) *Nihnon neo-kanryō-ron* (The Neo-bureaucracy Debate in Japan), Tokyo: Kōdansha.

Hoshino Mitsuo (1970) *Chihō jichi no riron to kōzō* (The Theory and Structure of Local Government), Tokyo: Shinhyoron.

Huber, Thomas M. (1994) *Strategic Economy in Japan*, Boulder, Colo.: Westview Press.

Ide Yoshinori (1974) "*Sengo kaikaku to nihon kanryōsei*" ("Postwar Reform and the Japanese Bureaucracy"), in *Sengo kaikaku* (Postwar Reform), vol. 3, *Seiji katei* (The Political Process), Tōkyō Daigaku Shakai Kagaku Kenkyūjo (ed.), Tokyo: Tōkyō Daigaku Shuppan, pp. 143–229.

Ide Yoshinori and Takeshi Ishida (1969) "The Education and Recruitment of Governing Elites in Modern Japan," in Rupert Wilkinson (ed.) *Governing Elites: Studies in Training and Selection*, New York: Oxford University Press, pp. 108–34.

Igarashi Takayoshi and Ogawa Akio (1995) *Gikai: kanryō shihai o koete* (The Diet: Overcoming Bureaucratic Control), Tokyo: Iwanami Shoten.

Ikuta Tadahide (1992) *Nippon kanryō yo doko e iku* (Where is Japan's Bureaucracy Going?), Tokyo: Nihon Hōsō Shuppansha.

—— (1994) *Ōkurashō dokusai* (The Dictatorship of the Ministry of Finance), Tokyo: Ohesu Shuppansha.

Imai, Ken'ichi (1992) "Japan's Corporate Networks," in Shumpei Kumon and Henry Rosovsky (eds) *The Political Economy of Japan: Cultural and Social Dynamics*, vol. 3, Stanford: Stanford University Press, pp. 198–230.

Inoguchi Takashi (1983) *Gendai nihon seiji keizai no kōzō* (The Structure of Contemporary Japan's Political Structure), Tokyo: Tōyō Keizai Shinpōsha.

Ishida Takeshi (1984) "Conflict and Its Accomodation: *Omote–Ura* and *Uchi–Soto* Relations," in E. Krauss, T. P. Rohlen, and P. G. Steinhoff (eds) *Conflict in Japan*, Honolulu: University Press of Hawaii, pp. 16–38.

Ishida, Takeshi and Ellis S. Krauss (eds) (1989) *Democracy in Japan*, Pittsburgh: University of Pittsburgh Press.

Isomura Eiichi and Kuronuma Minoru (1974) *Gendai nihon no gyōsei* (Contemporary Japanese Administration), Tokyo: Teikokou Chihō Gyōsei Gakkai.

Itō Daiichi (1980) *Genzai nihon kanryosei no bunseki* (An Analysis of Modern Japanese Bureaucracy), Tokyo: Tokyo Daigaku Shuppankai.

Ivy, Marilyn (1995) *Discourses of the Vanishing*, Chicago: University of Chicago Press.

Jacoby, Henry (1973) *The Bureaucratization of the World*, (trans. Eveline L. Kanes), Berkeley: University of California Press.

Jain, Purnendra (1989) *Local Politics and Policy making in Japan*, New Delhi: Commonwealth Publishers.

Japan's Modern Educational System: A History of the First Hundred Years (1980) Mininstry of Education (ed.), Tokyo: Mininstry of Education.

Johnson, Chalmers (1974) "The Reemployment of Retired Government Bureaucrats in Japanese Big Business," *Asian Survey* 14 (11): 953–65.

—— (1975) "Japan: Who Governs? An Essay on Official Bureaucracy," *Journal of Japanese Studies* 2 (1): 1–28.

—— (1978) *Japan's Public Policy Companies*, Washington, DC: American Enterprise Institute for Public Policy.

—— (1980) *"Omote* (Explicit) and *Ura* (Implicit): Translating Japanese Political Terms," *Journal of Japanese Studies* 6: 89–115.

—— (1982) *MITI and the Japanese Miracle*, Stanford: Stanford University Press.

—— 1995) *Japan: Who Governs? The Rise of the Developmental State*, New York: W. W. Norton and Co.

Kaigo Tokiomi (1963) "A Short History of Postwar Japanese Education," *Journal of Social and Political Ideas in Japan* 1: 15–23.

Kakinuma M. (1992) *"Zaikai ni ugokasareru monbushō"* (The Ministry of Education: Driven by the Business World), in Sakamoto H. and Yamamoto H. (eds) *Monbushō no kenkyū: kyōiku no jiyū to kenri o kangaeru* (Research on the Ministry of Education: Thinking about the Freedom of Education and Rights), Tokyo: Sanmitsu Shobō, pp. 114– 133.

Kami Ikko (1986) *Ōkura kanryo* (The Ministry of Finance), Tokyo: Kodansha.

Kamoshida Akito (1994) *Datsu "kan" no shisō; henkaku no tame no 3 tsu no kinkyū teigi* (Thoughts on Removing "Bureaucracy": 3 Emergency Proposals for Reform), Tokyo: Gendai Shorin.

Kanchō monogatari (A Tale of Government Offices) (1962) Tōkyō Shimbunsha (ed.), Tokyo: Tōkyō Shimbunsha.

Kanryō no boyaki (Bureaucratic Complaints) (1994) Takarajima (ed.), *Bessatsu* 180 (Supplement 180), Tokyo: Takarajimasha.

Kanryō: kishimu kyodai kenryoku (Bureaucracy: The Creaking of Great Power) (1994) Nihon Keizai Shinbunsha (ed.), Tokyo: Nihon Keizai Shinbunsha.

Katō Eiichi (1983) *Kanryō desu, yoroshiku* (I Am a Bureaucrat, Pleased to Meet You), Tokyo: TBS Buritanikia.

Kawaguchi Hiroyuki (1987) *Kanryō shihai no kōzō* (The Structure of Bureaucratic Control), Tokyo: Kodansha.

Kawanaka Niko (1962) *Gendai no kanryōsei* (Contemporary Bureaucracy), Tokyo: Chūō University Press.

Kayashima, Atsushi (1993) *American Democracy on Trial in Japan*, Tokyo: Ōtori Shobo.

Keane, John (ed.) (1988) *Civil Society and the State: New Eurupean Perspectives*, London: Verso.

Keigo (Honorific Language) (1991) Agency for Cultural Affairs (ed.), Tokyo: Ministry of Finance.

Kelly, William W. (1986) "Rationalization and Nostalgia: Cultural Dynamics of New Middle Class Japan," *American Ethnologist* 13 (4): 603–18.

Kertzer, David I. (1988) *Ritual, Politics and Power*, New Haven, Conn.: Yale University Press.

Kim, Paul S. (1988) *Japan's Civil Service System: Its Structure, Personnel, and Politics*, Westport, Conn.: Greenwood Press.

Kobayashi Tetsuya (1978) *Society, Schools and Progress in Japan*, Oxford: Pergamon Press.

Kogawa Tetsuo (1989) "New Trends in Japanese Popular Culture," in Gavan McCormack and Sugimoto Yoshio (eds) *The Japanese Trajectory: Modernization and Beyond*, Cambridge: University of Cambridge Press, pp. 54–66.

Koh, B. C. (1989) *Japan's Administrative Elite*, Berkeley: University of California Press.

Koitabashi Jirō (1986) *"Sengo umare" erīto kanryō no sugao* (The Real Faces of Elite Bureaucrats Who Were "Born After the War"), Tokyo: Kōdansha.

Kokushi daijiten (Great Dictionary of National History) (1992) Kokushi Daijiten Henshū I-inkai, Tokyo: Yoshikawa Kōbun-kan.

Koschmann, J. Victor (1978) "Introduction: Soft Rule and Expresive Protest," in J. Victor Koschmann (ed.) *Authority and the Individual in Japan*, Tokyo: University of Tokyo Press, pp. 1–30.

Kotoba no shitsuke (Language Training) (1990) Agency for Cultural Affairs (ed.), Tokyo: Ministry of Finance.

Kotobazukai (Speech) (1989) Agency for Cultural Affairs (ed.), Tokyo: Ministry of Finance.

Krauss, Ellis S. (1996) "Portraying the State: NHK Television News and Politics," in Susan J. Pharr and Ellis S. Krauss (eds) *Media and Politics in Japan*, Honolulu: University of Hawaii Press, pp. 89–129.

Kubota Akira (1969) *Higher Civil Servants in Postwar Japan: Their Social Origins, Educational Background and Career Patterns*, Princeton: Princeton Universtiy Press.

Kumar, Krishan (1993) "Civil Society: An Inquiry into the Usefulness of an Historical Term," *British Journal of Sociology* 44 (3): 375–95.

Kumon, Shumpei (1992) "Japan as a Network Society," in Shumpei Kumon and Henry Rosovsky (eds) *The Political Economy of Japan: Cultural and Social Dynamics*, vol. 3, Stanford: Stanford University Press, pp. 109–41.

Kuribayashi Yoshimitsu (1988) *Ōkurashō: ginkō-kyoku* (The Ministry of Finance: The Banking Bureau), Tokyo: Kōdansha.

—— (1990) *Ōkurashō: shukei-kyoku* (The Ministry of Finance: The Budget Bureau), Tokyo: Kōdansha.

—— (1991a) *Ōkurashō: shuzei-kyoku* (The Ministry of Finance: The Tax Administration Bureau), Tokyo: Kōdansha.

—— (1991b) *Ōkurashō: shōken-kyoku* (The Ministry of Finance: The Securities Bureau), Tokyo: Kōdansha.

Kuroda, Yasumasa (1974) *Reed Town, Japan: A Study in Community Power Structure and Political Change*, Honolulu: University of Hawaii Press.

Kusayanagi Daizō (1975) *Kanryō ōkoku-ron* (The Bureaucratic Monarchy Debate), Tokyo: Bungei Shunjū.

Kyogoku Jun-ichi (1993) *The Political Dynamics of Japan*, Tokyo: University of Tokyo Press.

Laitin, David (1986) *Hegemony and Culture*, Chicago: University Of Chicago Press.

Lamont, Rosette C. *et al.* (eds) (1980) *Women: The Dialectic of Public and Private Spaces – Centerpoint: A Journal of Interdisciplinary Studies* 3 (special issue).

Lanham, Betty B. (1979) "Ethics and Morals Precepts Taught in Schools of Japan and the United States," *Ethos* 7 (1): 1–18.

Leacock, Eleanor Burke (1972) "Introduction," in *Origin of the Family, Private Property and the State*, Friedrich Engels, New York: International Publishers, pp. 7–67.

Lebra, Takie Sugiyama (1976) *Japanese Patterns of Behavior*, Honolulu: University of Hawaii Press.

—— (1984) *Japanese Women*, Honolulu: University of Hawaii Press.

—— (1992) "Self in Japanese Culture," in Nancy Rosenberger (ed.) *The Japanese Sense of Self*, Cambridge: Cambridge University Press, pp. 105–120.

—— (1993) *Above The Clouds*, Berkeley: University of California Press.

Lee, O-Young (1982) *The Compact Culture: The Japanese Tradition of "Smaller Is Better,"* New York: Kodansha International.

LeTrende, Gerald (1994) "Guiding Them on: Teaching, Hierarchy, and Social Organization in Japanese Middle Schools," *Journal of Japanese Studies* 20 (1): 37–59.

Linhart, Sepp (1988) "From Industrial to Postindustrial Society: Changes in Japanese Leisure- Related Values and Behavior," *Journal of Japanese Studies* 14 (2): 271–307.

List, Friedrich (1922) [1844] *National System of Political Economy* (trans. S. S. Lloyd), London: Longman, Green and Co.

Littlewood, Ian (1996) *The Idea of Japan: Western Images, Western Myths*, London: Secker & Warburg.

London, Nancy R. (1993) *Japanese Corporate Philanthropy*, Oxford: Oxford University Press.

McCormack, Gavan (1996a) "Afterbubble: Fizz and Concrete in Japan's Political Economy" *Working Paper No. 21*, Japan Policy Research Institute (June).

—— (1996b) *The Emptiness of Japanese Affluence*, New York: M. E. Sharpe.

McCormack, Gavan and Sugimoto Yoshio (eds) (1989) "Introduction: Modernization and Beyond," in Gavan McCormack and Sugimoto Yoshio (eds) *The Japanese Trajectory: Modernization and Beyond*, Cambridge: University of Cambridge Press, pp. 1–14.

MacDougall, Terry E. (1989) "Democracy and Local Government in Postwar Japan," in Takeshi Ishida and Ellis S. Krauss (eds) *Democracy in Japan*, Pittsburgh: University of Pittsburgh Press, pp. 139–69.

McVeigh, Brian (1991a) "Gratitude, Obedience, and Humility of Heart: The

Cultural Construction of Belief in a Japanese New Religion," unpublished dissertation, Princeton University.

McVeigh, Brian (1991b) "Gratitude, Obedience, and Humility of Heart: The Morality of Dependency in a New Religion," *Journal of Social Science* 30 (2): 107–25.

—— (1992) "The Authorization of Ritual and the Ritualization of Authority: The Practice of Values in a Japanese New Religion," *Journal of Ritual Studies* 6 (2): 39–58.

—— (1994a) "New Religions, Office Ladies, and Teaching Morals in Schools: Three Expressions/Examples of Japanese Ethnomorality," paper presented at the 39th International Conference of Orientalists in Japan, Tokyo, May 12.

—— (1994b) "Ritualized Practices of Everyday Life: Constructing Self, Status, and Social Structure in Japan," *Journal of Ritual Studies* 8 (1): 53–71.

—— (1995a) "Rituals of Civility: The Role of Moral Education in Japan," paper presented at the 40th International Conference of Eastern Studies, Tokyo, May 12.

—— (1995b) "The Femininization of Body, Behavior, and Belief: Learning to Be an 'Office Lady' at a Japanese Women's College," *The American Asian Review* 13 (2): 29–67.

—— (1996a) "Cultivating 'Femininity' and 'Internationalism' through Ceremonies: Rituals and Routine at a Japanese Women's Junior College," *Ethos* 24 (2): 314–49.

—— (1996b) "Rationality, Bureaucracy, and Belief in the Japanese State," *Tōyō Gakuen Daigaku Kiyō* 4: 125–40.

—— (1996c) "Shaking State and Society in Japan: Problems of an Over-Rationalized Society," *Kenkyūshitsu dayori* 27: 75–84.

—— (1997a) *Life in a Japanese Women's College: Learning to Be Ladylike*, London: Routledge.

—— (1997b) "Wearing Ideology: How Uniforms Discipline Bodies and Minds in Japan," *Fashion Theory: The Journal of Dress, Body & Culture* 1 (2): 1–26.

Mannheim, Karl (1940) *Man and Society in an Age of Reconstruction*, New York: Harcourt and Brace.

Marshall, Byron (1067) *Capitalism and Nationalism in Prewar Japan: The Ideology of the Business Elite, 1869–1941*, Stanford: Stanford University Press.

Maruyama Masao (1964) *Gendai seiji no shisō to kōdō* (Thought and Behavior in Modern Japanese Politics), Tokyo: Miraisha.

Marx, Karl (1971) *Early Texts* (ed. and tran. David McLellan), Oxford: Basil Blackwell.

Matsubara Satorō (1995) *Tokushu hōjin kaikaku* (Reform of Special Corporations), Tokyo: Nihon Hyōronsha.

Matsumoto Sannosuke (1978) "Special Introductory Essay: The Roots of Political Disillusionment: 'Public' and 'Private' in Japan," in J. Victor Koschmann (ed.) *Authority and the Individual in Japan*, Tokyo: University of Tokyo Press, pp. 31–51.

Matsushita Keiichi (1971) *Shibiru minimamu no shisō* (The Ideology of the Civil Minimum), Tokyo: Tōkyō Daigaku Shuppansha.

Mayer, Adrian (1989) "The Funeral of the Emperor of Japan," *Anthropology Today* 5 (3): 3– 6.

Merton, Robert K. (1968) "Bureaucratic Structure and Personality," in Robert Merton (ed.), *Social Theory and Social Structure*, New York: Free Press, pp. 249–60.

Meyer, John W. *et al.* (1994) "Bureaucratizaion without Centralization," in Richard W. Scott, John W. Meyer *et al.* (eds) *Institutional Environments and Organizations: Structural Complexity and Individualism*, London: Sage, pp. 179–205.

Meyer, John W., John Boli, and George M. Thomas (1987) "Ontology and Rationalization in the Western Cultural Account," in G. M. Thomas *et al.* (eds) *Institutional Structure: Constituting State, Society, and Individual*, London: Sage, pp. 12–37.

Michels, Robert (1959) [1911] *Political Parties*, New York: Dover Publications.

Migdal, Joel S., Atul Kohli, and Vivienne Shue (eds) (1994) *State Power and Social Forces*, Cambridge: Cambridge University Press.

Miller, Roy A. (1982) *Japan's Modern Myth*, New York: Weatherhill.

Mills, C. Wright (1956) *The Power Elite*, New York: Oxford University Press.

—— (1963) *Power, Politics and People: The Collected Essays of C. Wright Mills* (Irving Louis Horowitz, ed.), New York: Ballantine.

Minami Hiroshi (1973) "The Interpretation Boom," *Japan Interpreter* 8 (2): 159–73.

Mitchell, Timothy (1990) "Everyday Metaphors of Power," *Theory and Society* 19: 545–77.

—— (1991) "The Limits of the State: Beyond Statist Approaches and their Critics," *American Political Science Review* 85 (1): 77–96.

Miyamoto, Masao (1994) *Straitjacket Society: An Insider's Irreverent View of Bureaucratic Japan*, Tokyo: Kodansha.

Miyashita Kenichi and David Russell (1994) *Keiretsu: Inside the Hidden Japanese Conglomerates*, New York: McGraw-Hill.

Monbu tōkei yōran (Summary of Statistics on Education) (1994) Ministry of Education (ed.), Tokyo: Ministry of Education.

Monbushō gyōsei kikō shirīzu no. 105 (Administrative Organization Series no. 105) (1980) Kyōikusha (ed.), Tokyo: Kyōikusha.

Monbushō kankei hōjin meibo (Register of Juridical Persons Associated with the Ministry of Education) (1994) Kanchō Tsūshinsha (ed.), Tokyo: Kanchō Tsūshinsha.

Monbushōnai shōgai gakushū (Lifelong Learning in the Ministry of Education) (1994) *Shōgai gakushū – shakai kyōiku gyōsei* (Lifelong Learning and Social Education Research Group), Tokyo: Daiichi Hōki.

Moore, Barrington, Jr (1984) *Privacy: Studies in Social and Cultural History*, New York: M. E. Sharpe.

Morris, V. Dixon (1973) "The Idioms of Contemporary Japan IV," *The Japan Interpreter* 8 (1): 121–36.

Morris-Suzuki, Tessa (1989) *A History of Japanese Economic Thought*, London: Routledge.

Mouer, Ross and Yoshio Sugimoto (1986) *Images of Japanese Society: A Study in the Social Construction of Reality*, London: Kegan Paul International.

Mouzelis, Nicos (1995) "Modernity, Late Development and Civil Society," in John A. Hall (ed.) *Civil Society: Theory, History, Comparison*, Cambridge, Mass.: Polity Press, pp. 224–49.

Murakami Yasusuke (1984) *Shin chūkan taishū no jidai* (The Era of the New Middle Masses), Tokyo: Chūō Kōronsha.

Murakawa Ichirō (1994) *Nihon no kanryō* (Japan's Bureaucracy), Maruzen Raiburari.

Muramatsu Michio (1975) "The Impact of Economic Growth Policies on Local Politics in Japan," *Asian Survey* 15: 799–816.

—— (1981) *Sengo nihon no kanryōsei* (Postwar Japan's Bureaucratic System), Tokyo: Tōyō Keizai Shinpōsha.

Muramatsu Michio and Ellis S. Krauss (1974) "Bureaucrats and Politicians in Policymaking: The Case of Japan," *American Political Science Review* 78: 126–46.

Muramatsu Michio *et al.* (1986) *Sengo nihon no atsuryoku dantai* (Pressure Groups in Postwar Japan), Tokyo: Tokyo Keizai.

Murofushi Tetsuro (1987) *Kokyū kanryō* (National Bureaucracy), Tokyo: Kodansha.

Mutō Ichiyō (1986) "Class Struggle in Postwar Japan," in Gavan McCormack and Yoshi Sugimoto (eds) *Democracy in Contemporary Japan*, Sydney, Australia: Hale and Iremonger, pp. 114–37.

Nader, Laura (1972) "Up the Anthropologist – Perspectives Gained from Studying Up," in Dell Hymes (ed.) *Reinventing Anthropology*, New York: Pantheon Books, pp. 284– 311.

Naitō Takashi (1990) "Moral Education in Japanese Public Schools," *Moral Education Forum* 27–36.

Najita, Tetsuo (1974) *Japan: The Intellectual Foundations of Modern Japanese Politics*, Chicago: University of Chicago Press.

Nakajima Makoto (1978) *Shōwashi o irodoru kakushin kanryō no jidai* (The Era of Bureaucratic Reform that Colors the History of Shōwa), Tokyo: Gendai no me.

Namiki Nobuyoshi (1989) *Tsūsanshō no shūen: shakai kōzō no henkaku wa kanō ka* (The End of MITI: Is the Structural Change of Society still Possible?), Tokyo: Daiyamondo-sha.

Nisbet, Robert (1980) *History of the Idea of Progress*, New York: Basic Books.

Ohnuki-Tierney, Emiko (1993) *Rice as Self: Japanese Identities through Time*, Princeton: Princeton University Press.

Ojimi Yoshihisa (1975) "A Government Ministry: The Case of the Ministry of International Trade and Industry," in Ezra Vogel (ed.) *Modern Japanese*

Organization and Decision-making, Berkeley: University of California Press, pp. 101–12.

Okada Akira (1994) *Gendai nihon kanryōsei no seiritsu* (The Formation of Contemporary Japan's Bureaucracy), Tokyo: Hōsei University Press.

Okano, Kaori (1993) *School to Work Transition in Japan*, Clevedon, Philadelphia, Adelaide: Multilingual Matters Ltd.

Okimoto, Daniel (1989) *Between MITI and the Market: Japanese Industrial Policy for High Technology*, Stanford: Stanford University Press.

Okin, Susan Moller (1979) *Women in Western Political Thought*, Princeton: Princeton University Press.

—— (1991) "Gender, the Public and the Private," in David Held (ed.) *Political Theory Today*,Cambridge: Polity.

Ōkita Saburō (1984) *Nihon kanryō jijō* (Conditions of Japanese Bureaucrats), Tokyo: TBS Buritanikia.

Ōkura kanryō no shōtai (The True Character of the Ministry of Finance) (1994) Takarajima (ed.), *Bessatsu* 214 (Supplement 214), Tokyo: Takarajimasha.

Ōmae Kenichi (1994) *Heisei kanryō-ron* (Essays about Heisei Bureaucracy), Tokyo: Shōgakkan.

Ōmiya Tomonobu (1991) *Sekimatsu nippon no kanryōtachi* (Japan's Bureaucrats at the End of the Century), Tokyo: Sanichishobō.

Önis, Ziya (1991) "The Logic of the Developmental State," *Comparative Politics* 24 (1): 109– 26.

Ortner, Sherry (1974) "Is Female to Male as Nature is to Culture?" in Michelle Zimbalist Rosaldo and Louise Lamphere (eds) *Woman, Culture, and Society*, Stanford: Stanford University Press, pp. 67–87.

Ōtsuka Yoshikazu (ed.) (1994) *Oyakusho to no toraburu kaiketsuhō* (How to Solve the Government's Troubles), Tokyo: Jiyū Kokuminsha.

Park, Yung H. (1986) *Bureaucrats and Ministers in Contemporary Japanese Government.* Berkeley: Institute of East Asian Studies of the University of California.

Parsons, Talcott (1951) *The Social System*, Chicago: Free Press.

—— (1960) *Structure and Process in Modern Societies*, Glencoe, Illinois: Free Press.

Pateman, Carole (1983) "Feminist Critiques of the Public/Private Dichotomy," in S. I. Benn and G. F. Gaus (eds) *Public and Private in Social Life*, London: Croom Helm, pp. 281–303.

—— (1988) *The Sexual Contract*, Cambridge: Polity.

Peak, L. (1989) "Learning to Become Part of the Group: The Japanese Child's Transition to Preschool Life," *The Journal of Japanese Studies* 15 (1): 93–123.

—— (1991) *Learning to Go to School in Japan: The Transition from Home to Preschool Life*, Berkeley: University of California Press.

Pempel, T. J. (1974) "The Bureaucratization of Policymaking in Contemporary Japan," *American Journal of Political Science* 18: 647–74.

—— (1978) *Patterns of Japanese Policymaking: Experiences from Higher Education*, Boulder, Colo.: Westview Press.

Pempel, T. J. (1984) "Organizing for Efficiency: The Higher Civil Service in Japan," in Ezra Suleiman (ed.) *Bureaucrats and Policymaking*, New York: Holmes and Meier, pp. 72–106.

—— (1987a) "The Unbundling of 'Japan, Inc.': The Changing Dynamics of Japanese Policy Formation," *Journal of Japanese Studies* 13: 271–306.

—— (1987b) "The Tar Baby Target: 'Reform' of the Japanese Bureaucracy," in Robert E. Ward and Sakamoto Yoshikazu (eds) *Democratizing Japan: The Allied Occupation*, Honolulu: University of Hawaii Press. pp. 157–87.

Pharr, Susan J. and Ellis S. Krauss (eds) (1996) *Media and Politics in Japan*, Honolulu: University of Hawaii Press.

Polanyi, Karl (1957) "The Economy as Instituted Process," in Karl Polanyi, Conrad Arensberg, and Harry Pearson (eds) *Trade and Market in the Early Empires*, New York: Free Press, pp. 243–70.

Prestowitz, Clyde V., Jr (1988) *Trading Places*, Tokyo: Charles E. Tuttle.

—— (1993) "Introduction," in Eisuke Sakakibara (ed.) *Beyond Capitalism: The Japanese Model of Market Economics*, New York: University Press of America and the Economic Strategy Institute, pp. vii–xxi.

Quinn, Charles J., Jr (1994) "The Terms *Uchi* and *Soto* as Windows on a World," in Jane M. Bachnik and Charles J. Quinn Jr (eds) *Situated Meanings: Inside and Outside in Japanese Self, Society, and Language*, Princeton: Princeton University Press, pp. 38–72.

Ramseyer, J. Mark and Frances McCall Rosenbluth (1993) *Japan's Political Marketplace*, Cambridge, Mass.: Harvard University Press.

Raz, Jacob (1992) "Self-presentation and Performance in the Yakuza Way of Life: Fieldwork with a Japanese Underworld Group," in Roger Goodman and Kirsten Refsing (eds) *Ideology and Practice in Modern Japan*, London: Routledge, pp. 210–34.

Reed, Steven R. (1982) "Is Japanese Government Really Centralized?" *Journal of Japanese Studies* 8 (1): 133–64.

—— (1986) *Japanese Prefectures and Policymaking*, Pittsburgh: University of Pittsburgh Press.

—— (1993) *Making Common Sense of Japan*, Pittsburgh: University of Pittsburgh Press.

Rix, Alan (1988) "Bureaucracy and Political Change in Japan," in J. A. A. Stockwin (ed.) *Dynamics and Immobilist Politics in Japan*, London: Macmillan Press, pp. 54–76.

Rogers, Susan Carol (1978) "Woman's Place: A Critical Review of Anthropological Theory," *Comparative Studies in Society and History* 20 (1): 123–62.

Rohlen, Thomas P. (1974) *For Harmony and Strength: Japanese White Collar Organization in Anthropological Perspective*, Berkeley: University of California Press.

—— (1983) *Japan's High Schools*, Berkeley: University of California Press.

—— (1989) "Order in Japanese Society: Attachmnent, Authority, and Routine," *The Journal of Japanese Studies* 15 (1): 5–40.

Rosaldo, Michelle Zimbalist (1974) "Woman, Culture, and Society: A Theoretical Overview," in Michelle Zimbalist Rosaldo and Louise Lamphere (eds) *Woman, Culture, and Society*, Stanford: Stanford University Press, pp. 17–42.

Rosaldo, Michelle Zimbalist and Louise Lamphere (eds) (1974) *Woman, Culture, and Society*, Stanford: Stanford University Press.

Rosenberger, Nancy R. (1989) "Dialectic Balance in the Polar Model of Self: The Japan Case," *Ethos* 17: 88–113.

Sahlins, Marshall (1976) *Culture and Practical Reason*, Chicago: University of Chicago Press.

Said, Edward W. (1985) *Orientalism*, Harmondsworth, Penguin.

Sakakibara Eisuke (1977) *Nihon o enshutsu suru shin kanryō-zō* (A Portrait of New Bureaucrats Who Direct Japan), Tokyo: Yamade Shobō.

—— (1993) *Beyond Capitalism: The Japanese Model of Market Economics*, New York: University Press of America and the Economic Strategy Institute.

Sakakibara Eisuke and Noguchi Yakio (1977) *Ōkurashō, nichigin no bunseki* (Analysis of the Ministry of Finance and the Bank of Japan), Chūō Kōron (August).

Sakamoto Hideo (1992) "*Monbushō wa hitsuyō ka*" ("Is the Ministry of Education Necessary?"), in *Monbushō no kenkyū: kyōiku no jiyū to kenri o kangaeru* (Research on the Ministry of Education: Thinking about the Freedom of Education and Rights), Sakamoto H. and Yamamoto H. (eds) Tokyo: Sanmitsu Shobō, pp. 288–311.

Samuels, Richard (1983) *The Politics of Regional Policy: Localities Incorporated?* Princeton: Princeton University Press.

—— (1994) "*Rich Nation, Strong Army*": *National Security and the Technological Transformation of Japan*, Ithaca, NY: Cornell University Press.

—— (1987) *The Business of the Japanese State: Energy Markets in Comparative and Historical Perspective*, Ithaca, NY: Cornell University Press.

Sano Toshiyuki (1989) "Methods of Social Control and Socialization in Japanese Day-Care Centers," *Journal of Japanese Studies* 15 (1): 125–38.

Sataka Makoto (1989) *Nihon kanryō hakusho* (White Paper on the Japanese Bureaucracy), Tokyo: Kōdansha.

Sato Ikuya (1991) *Kamikaze Biker: Parody and Anomy in Affluent Japan*, Chicago: University of Chicago Press.

Satō Tomohiro (1994) *Shakai shinrigaku* (Social Psychology), Tokyo: Chūō Daigaku Seikatsu Kyōdō Kumiai.

Schaar, John H. (1969) "Legitimacy in the Modern State," in P. Green and S. Levinson (eds) *Power and Community: Dissenting Essays in Political Science*, New York: Random House, pp. 277–327.

Schoppa, Leonard James (1991) *Education Reform in Japan: A Case of Immobilist Politics*, London: Routledge.

Schwartz, Frank (1993) "Of Fairy Cloaks and Familiar Talks: The Politics of Consultaion," in Gary D. Allinson and Yasunori Sone (eds) *Political Dynamics in Contemporary Japan*, Ithaca, New York: Cornell University Press, pp. 215–41.

Scott, W. Richard, John W. Meyer *et al.* (1994) *Institutional Environments and Organizations: Structural Complexity and Individualism,* London: Sage.

Seito Makoto (editor-in-chief) (1989) *Dōtoku shidō no tame no wazai senshū* (Selection of Discussion Materials for Moral Guidance), Tokyo: Bunkyō Shoin.

Sennett, Richard (1976) *The Fall of Public Man,* New York: Vintage Books.

Seward, Jack (1968) *Hara-kiri: Japanese Ritual Suicide,* Rutland, Vermont: Charles E. Tuttle.

Shakai kyōiku chōsa hōkokusho (Survey of Social Education) (1994) Ministry of Education (ed.), Tokyo: Ministry of Education.

Sharistanian, Janet (ed.) (1986a) *Beyond the Public/Domestic Dichotomy: Contemporary Perspectives on Women's Public Lives,* Westport, Conn.: Greenwood Press.

—— (ed.) (1986b) "Introduction: Women's Lives in the Public and Domestic Spheres," in Janet Sharistanian (ed.) *Beyond the Public/Domestic Dichotomy: Contemporary Perspectives on Women's Public Lives,* Westport, Conn.: Greenwood Press, pp. 1–9.

—— (1986c) "Conclusion: The Public/Domestic Model and the Study of Contemporary Women's Lives," in Janet Sharistanian (ed.), *Beyond the Public/Domestic Dichotomy: Contemporary Perspectives on Women's Public Lives,* Westport, Conn.: Greenwood Press, pp. 170–84.

—— (ed.) (1986d) *Gender, Ideology, and Action: Historical Perspectives on Women's Public Lives,* Westport, Conn.: Greenwood Press.

Shindo Muneyuki (1984) "Relations between National and Local Government," in Tsuji Kiyoaki (ed.) *Public Administration in Japan,* Tokyo: University of Tokyo Press, pp. 109–20.

—— (1992) *Gyōsei shidō* (Administrative Guidance), Tokyo: Iwanami Shoten.

Shingikai sōran (An Overview of Advisory Councils) (1994) Management and Coordination Agency (ed.), Tokyo: Ministry of Finance.

Shiono Hiroshi (1984) "Administrative Guidance," in Tsuji Kiyoaki (ed.), *Public Administration in Japan,* Tokyo: University of Tokyo Press, pp. 203–15.

Shō gakkō: dōtoku kyōiku jūjitsu no tame no kōnai kenshū no tebiki (A Primer on School Training for Realizing Moral Education in Primary School) (1984) Ministry of Education (ed.), Tokyo: Ministry of Finance.

Shō gakkō: dōtoku kyōiku shidō jō no shomondai (Various Problems Concerning Guidance for Moral Education in Primary School) (1990) Ministry of Education (ed.), Tokyo: Ministry of Finance.

Shō gakkō: omoiyari no kokoro o sodateru shidō (Guidance for Cultivating a Heart of Empathy in Primary School) (1986) Ministry of Education (ed.), Tokyo: Ministry of Finance.

Shō gakkō shidō sho: shakai hen (Primary School Guidance Manual: Social Studies) (1994) Ministry of Education (ed.), Tokyo: Ministry of Education.

Shō gakkō shidō sho: tokubetsu katsudō hen (Primary School Guidance Manual: A Compilation of Special Activities) (1994) Ministry of Education (ed.), Tokyo: Ministry of Education.

248   *Bibliography*

Silberman, Bernard S. (1964) *Ministers of Modernization: Elite Mobility in the Meiji Restoration 1868–1873*, Tuscon: University of Arizona Press.
—— (1967) "Bureaucratic Development and the Structure of Decision-Making in the Meiji Period: The Case of the Genrō," *Journal of Asian Studies* 27: 81–94.
—— (1970) "Bureaucratic Development and the Structure of Decision-Making in Japan: 1868–1925," *Journal of Asian Studies* 29: 347–62.
—— (1973) "Ringi-sei – Traditional Values or Organizational Imperatives in the Japanese Upper Civil Service," *Journal of Asian Studies* 32: 251–64.
—— (1976) "Bureaucratization of the Meiji State: The Problem of Succession in the Meiji Restoration, 1868–1900," *Journal of Asian Studies* 35: 421–30.
—— (1978) "Bureaucrtric Development and Bureaucratization: The Case of Japan," *Social Science History* 2: 385–98.
—— (1982) "The Bureaucratic State in Japan: The Problem of Authority and Legitimacy," in Tetsuo Najita and J. Victor Koschmann (eds) *Conflict in Japanese History*, Princeton: Princeton University Press, pp. 226–37.
Simmel, George (1988) "The Stranger," in Donald N. Levine (ed.) *On Individuality and Social Forms*, Chicago: University of Chicago Press, pp. 143–9.
Singleton, John (1993) "*Gambaru*: A Japanese Cultural Theory of Learning," in James J. Shields Jr (ed.) *Japanese Schooling*, University Park: Pennsylvania State University Press, pp. 8–15.
Smith, Robert J. (1992) "The Cultural Context of the Japanese Political Economy," in Shumpei Kumon and Henry Rosovsky (eds) *The Political Economy of Japan: Cultural and Social Dynamics* (vol 3), Stanford: Stanford University Press, pp. 13–31.
Social Education and Its Administration in Japan (1972) Ministry of Education, Social Education Bureau (ed.), Tokyo: Ministry of Education.
Sone Yasunori *et al.* (1985) *Shingikai no kiso kenkyū: kinō taiyō ni tsuite bunseki* (Basic Research on Advisory Commissions: An Analysis of Their Functions and Conditions), Tokyo: Keio University.
Spaulding, Robert M., Jr (1967) *Imperial Japan's Higher Civil Service Examinations*, Princeton: Princeton University Press.
Steiner, Kurt (1965) *Local Government in Japan*, Stanford: Stanford University Press.
Stephens, Michael D. (1991) *Japan and Education*, Hong Kong: Macmillan.
Sugano Tadashi (1971) *Gendai no kanryōsei* (Contemporary Bureaucracy), Tokyo: Seishin Press.
Suzuki, Takahiro (1993) "Policy Development and Think Tanks in Japan," in Raymond J. Struyk, Makiko Ueno, and Takahiro Suzuki (eds) *A Japanese Think Tank*, Washington, DC: The Urban Institute, pp. 1–15.
Tada Michitarō (1978) "The Glory and Misery of 'My Home,'" in J. Victor Koschmann (ed.) *Authority and the Individual in Japan*, Tokyo: University of Tokyo Press, pp. 206–17.
Tahara Sōichirō (1979) *Nihon no kanryō* (Japan's Bureaucrats), Tokyo: Bungei Shunjū.

Tahara Sōichirō (1990) *Heisei-nihon no kanryō* (Bureaucracy in Heisei Japan), Tokyo: Bungei Haruaki.

Tambiah, Stanley J. (1979) "A Performative Approach to Ritual," *Proceedings of the British Academy* 65: 113–69.

Tanaka, Stefan (1993) *Japan's Orient: Rendering Pasts into History*, Berkeley: University of California Press.

Taussig, Michael (1980) *The Devil and Commodity Fetishism in South America*, Chapel Hill, NC: University of North Carolina Press.

—— (1992) "Maleficium: State Fetishism," in *The Nervous System*, New York: Routledge, pp. 111–40.

Teraoka Hideaki (ed.) (1993) *Japan's Public School Program: A Public Junior High School Program in a Prefecture of Japan*, Nagoya: Maruzen Self-Publishing Service.

Tester, Keith (1992) *Civil Society*, London: Routledge.

Tiffany, Sharon W. (1979) "Woman, Power and the Anthropology of Politics: A Review," *International Journal of Women's Studies* 2 (5): 430–42.

Titus, David Anson (1974) *Palace and Politics in Prewar Japan*, New York: Columbia University Press.

Tobin, Joseph J. (1991) "Japanese Preschools and the Pedagogy of Selfhood," in Nancy R. Rosenberger (ed.) *The Japanese Sense of Self*, Cambridge: Cambridge University Press, pp. 299–323.

Tokushu hōjin o kiru (Kill the Special Legal Entities) (1980) Tōkyō Shinbun Tokushu Hōjin Shuzaihan (Tokyo Newspaper Special Legal Entities Coverage Team), Tokyo: Sanshūsha.

Tokushu hōjin sōran (An Overview of Special Juridical Persons) (1995) Tokyo: Gyōsei Kanri Kenkyū Sentā.

Tönnies, Ferdinand (1957) *Community and Society* (trans. Charles P. Loomis), East Lansing: Michigan State University Press.

Tsuji Kiyoaki (1964) "Kanryō kikō no onzon to kyōka (The Preservation and Strengthening of the Bureaucratic Structure)," in *Gendai nihon no seiji katei* (Political Process in Contemporary Japan), Tokyo: Iwanami Shoten. Excerpted in *Journal of Social and Political Ideas in Japan* 2 (3): 88–92.

—— (1968) "Decision-Making in the Japanese Government: A Study of Ringi-sei," in Robert Ward (ed.) *Political Development in Modern Japan*, Princeton: Princeton University Press.

—— (1969) *Shinpan nihon kanryōsei no kenkyū* (A Study of Japanese Bureaucracy, new edition), Tokyo: Tōkyō Daigaku Shuppankai.

—— (1976) *Nihon no chīhō jichi* (Local Autonomy in Japan), Tokyo: Iwanami Shoten.

—— (1984) *Public Administration in Japan*, Tokyo: University of Tokyo Press.

Tsukada, Mamoru (1991) *Yobiko Life: A Study of the Legitimation Process of Social Stratification in Japan*, Berkeley: Institute of East Asian Studies, University of California.

Tuchman, Gaye (1980) "Some Thoughts on Public and Private Spheres," in

Women: The Dialectic of Public and Private Spaces – Centerpoint: A Journal of Interdisciplinary Studies (special issue) 3 (3/4), pp. 111–13.

Tucker, Robert (ed.) (1978) *The Marx–Engels Reader*, New York: W. W. Norton and Co.

Twine, Nanette (1991) *Language and the Modern State: The Reform of Written Japanese*, London: Routledge.

Uchida Yoshihiko (1981) *Sakuhin to shite no shakai kagaku* (Social Science as a Piece of Work), Tokyo: Iwanami Shinsho.

—— (1985) *Dokusho to shakai kagaku* (Reading and the Social Sciences), Tokyo: Iwanami Shinsho.

Ueda, Atsushi (1994) "How Bureaucrats Manage Society," in Atsushi Ueda (ed.) *The Electric Geisha: Exploring Japan's Popular Culture*, Tokyo: Kodansha, pp. 127–38.

Ueno, Makiko (1992) "Think Tanks – A Key Institution for Promoting National Civil Virtues," *Asahi Shimbun* (October 23) (author's reprint).

—— (1993) "Weak Nonprofit Sector Handicaps Japan," *The Asian Wall Street Journal* (June 21) (author's reprint).

—— (1994) "Moving Toward a Nonprofit Sector for Japan," in *Sekai* (February) (author's reprint).

Upham, Frank K. (1987) *Law and Social Change in Postwar Japan*, Cambridge, Mass.: Harvard University Press.

Van Bremen, Jan and D. P. Martinez (eds) (1995) *Ceremony and Ritual in Japan: Religious Practices in an Industrialized Society*, New York: Routledge.

Van Wolferen, Karel (1989) *The Enigma of Japanese Power*, London: Macmillan.

Wade, Robert (1990) *Governing the Market: Economic Theory and the Role of Government in East Asian Industrialization*, Princeton: Princeton University Press.

Waga kuni no bunka to bunka gyōsei (Our Country's Culture and Culture Administration) (1987) Agency for Cultural Affairs (ed.), Tokyo: Agency for Cultural Affairs.

Waga kuni no bunkyō shisaku (Our Country's Education Policy) (1994) Ministry of Education (ed.), Tokyo: Ministry of Education.

Waga kuni no tokushu kyōiku (Special Education in Our Country) (1994) Special Education Division, Elementary and Secondary Education Bureau, Ministry of Education (ed.), Tokyo: Ministry of Education.

Weber, Max (1978) [1922] *Economy and Society: An Outline of Interpretative Sociology*, 2 vols, Berkeley: University of California Press.

Westney, D. Eleanor (1996) "Mass Media as Business Organizations: A US–Japanese Comparison," in Susan J. Pharr and Ellis S. Krauss (eds) *Media and Politics in Japan*, Honolulu: University Of Hawaii Press, pp. 47–88.

White, Merry (1987) *The Japanese Educational Challenge*, Tokyo: Kodansha.

—— (1992) *The Japanese Overseas: Can They Go Home Again?* Princeton: Princeton University Press.

Whyte, William H., Jr (1957) *The Organization Man*, New York: Doubleday.

Wilks, Stephen and Maurice Wright (eds) (1991) *The Promotion and Regulation of Industry in Japan*, London: Macmillan.

Williams, David (1994) *Japan: Beyond the End of History*, London: Routledge.

—— (1996) *Japan and the Enemies of Open Political Science*, London: Routledge.

Woodall, Brian (1996) *Japan under Construction: Corruption, Politics and Public Works*, Berkeley: University of California Press.

Woronoff, Jon (1986) *Politics the Japanese Way*, London: Macmillan Press.

Wrong, Dennis (ed.) (1970) *Max Weber*, Englewood Cliffs, NJ: Prentice-Hall.

Yakushiji Taizō (1989) *Seijika, kanryō* (Politicians and Bureaucrats), Tokyo: Tōyō Keizai Shihō-sha.

Yamada Yuichi (1993) *Ringi to Nemawashi*, Tokyo: Kōdansha Gendai Shinsho.

Yamaguchi Jirō (1987) *Ōkura kanryō no shihai no shūen* (The End of Domination by Finance Ministry Bureaucrats), Tokyo: Iwanami Shoten.

Yamamoto H. (1992) *"Monbushō to kyōiku i-inkai"* (The Ministry of Education and Boards of Education), in *Monbushō no kenkyū: kyōiku no jiyū to kenri o kangaeru* (Research on the Ministry of Education: Thinking about the Freedom of Education and Rights), Sakamoto H. and Yamamoto H. (eds) Tokyo: Sanmitsu Shobō, pp. 50–73.

Yamanaka Einosuke (1974) *Nihon kindai kokka no keisei to kanryōsei* (The Formation of Japan's Modern State and Bureaucracy), Tokyo: Kōbundō.

Yasuhara Kazuo (1974) *Ōkurashō* (The Mininstry of Finance), Tokyo: Kyōikusha.

Yeatman, Anna (1984) "Gender and the Differentiation of Social Life into Public and Domestic Domains," *Social Analysis – Gender and Social Life* (special issue series), 15: 32–50.

Yoda Kaoru (1994) *Oyakusho no shikumi* (Organization of the Governmental Bureaucracy), Tokyo: Nihon Jitsugyō Shuppansha.

Yoshino Kosaku (1992) *Cultural Nationalism in Contemporary Japan: A Sociological Inquiry*, New York: Routledge.

Yoshino, M. Y. (1968) *Japan's Managerial System*, Cambridge, Mass: MIT Press.

Yoshino, Shōji (1994) "The Japanese Home: A Grab Bag of Tradition, Trends, and High-Tech," in Atsushi Ueda (ed.) *The Electric Geisha: Exploring Japan's Popular Culture*, Tokyo: Kodansha, pp. 116–23.

Index

Affairs, cultural essentialism, cultural homogeneity, culturalism, culturalist mythologies, "tradition," traditionalism
culture centers 135
culture industry 134

De Certeau, M. 195
de-orientalizing 14; of knowledge about Japan 194
democracy 4, 44, 48, 101, 104, 119, 179, 183, 193
Department of Education 131; *see also* Ministry of Education
Diet 64, 72, 73, 77, 80, 81, 83, 89, 101, 125, 134; and educational policy 129–30
diligence 162, 163, 169
Ding, X. L. 191
diploma-oriented society 134
Doi, T. 52, 56
Dore, R. 138, 139, 158
"double schoolers" 139
Douglas, M. 23, 106
dual economy 121
Duke, B. 168
Durkheim, E. 18, 24, 107

economic nationalism 125, 126, 152, 180; and "common sense," legitimacy, rationality 118, 121; *see also* capitalist developmental state, Japaneseness, neomercantilism, nationalism
economics: American regulatory orientation 124; beliefs about religious in nature 195; as defense 72; and education 126, 127; as moralistic endeavor 118; Japan's developmental orientation 124; symbolic production of 31; *see also* economic nationalism *passim*
education xiv 103, 113, 180, 189, 194; bureaucratic control of 137; bureaucratized 156; ideology of 137; "total" 13; of cultivation 124; rationalized 140; state's activist role in 124; state-centered philosophy 128–9; strategic 156,

157; *see also* moral education, school(ing), strategic schooling
educational clique 129, 130
educational credentials 77
educational system 12, 97, 109
elections xiv 63, 104
Elementary and Secondary Education Bureau 133, 137–41
Elias, N. 18
elites 3, 6, 8, 9, 21, 69, 70, 72, 75, 81, 89, 104, 117, 119, 121, 122, 124, 125, 127, 159, 179, 190, 194, 196; and journalism 64; and media 65; and revolution from above 71
emotion 13, 18, 170, 174; *see also* emotionalizing experience
emotionalizing experience 173, 174–5; *see also* emotion
empathy (*omoiyari*) 43, 59, 163, 164, 165–6, 191; as social facilitator 60
emperor 11, 20, 94, 104, 114–17, 162, 168, 186, 193; "bodies" of 116; and Japaneseness 115; legitimizing belief in state 80; Meiji 115; and *omote* 116; and Pacific War 116; and rituals 116–17; and Shinto 116; Shōwa 115, 116, 117; and *soto* 116; and state 116; as symbol of state 114; as "tool" 115; and *uchi* 115; and *ura* 116
equality: Japanese version of 111–13; and welfare 112
ethnomorality: advocated by state 51, 67, 161
etiquette 1, 25, 67, 72, 164, 172, 192; and empathy 60; manuals 43; and moral education 160; *see also* *aisatsu*, manners, sociolinguistic codes, speech (proper)
Euro-American (societies) xvi, xviii 10, 44, 46, 47, 50, 52, 56, 57, 58, 68, 69, 81, 83, 104, 192, 193, 194, 196, 19; political thinking of 48, 49, 61
European nations 4, 20, 109, 146
everyday practices 102, 106; and ideology xv
exam hell 158; *see also* examinations
examinations 109, 111; and rationalizing 138; pyramid of 138, 139; *see also* exam hell

Herzfeld, M. 7, 17, 23, 32, 101, 102, 104, 105, 106, 107, 109, 110
hierarchies 7, 21, 43, 44, 58, 59, 74, 81, 100, 101, 106, 111, 112, 124, 148, 154, 192; and education 158; and media 65; *see also* hierarchization, verticality, vertical society
hierarchization xiv 3, 10, 12, 67, 178, 180, 184; and education 127; and moral education 159; *see also* hierarchies, verticality, vertical society
Higashi, S. 134, 136
Higher Education Bureau 141–2, 153
Hirata, K. 48
Hiroshima 113; and annual rituals of "peaceful Japan" 113
historical essentialism 19; *see also* historicism, "tradition," traditionalism
historicism 19; *see also* historical essentialism, "tradition," traditionalism
hitomae (publicness) 53
hitome (publicness) 53, 56
Hobsbawm, E. 17
Hollerman, L. 77
"homogeneity" (Japan's) 21, 112, 193; *see also* culturalist mythologies, Japaneseness, race
honne (real intention) 10, 51, 55, 56, 60, 65, 80, 83, 177
Huber, T. M. 12, 117, 119, 121, 122, 124, 125

ideologies: and culture 16; imperialistic 162; nationalizing 6; and nonconscious constructs 7; two aspects of 7; *see also* "common sense," cosmology, invisible institutions, legitimacy
Imperial Household 186
Imperial Palace 116; *see also* space
imperial officials 71
in-group 61, 68; *see also* out-group
in-group/out-group boundaries 67, 81, 192; mentality of 65
industrial policy 91, 124; *see also* Bureau of Industrial Policy

interest groups 65, 68, 91, 99, 100, 122
international(ism) 20, 21; and state organs 108–9, 167, 168; *see also* Japaneseness, nationalism
"invisible institutions" 7, 8, 16, 101, 189, 195; *see also* invisible political processes
"invisible" political processes 80; *see also* "invisible institutions"
Isomura, E. 50, 82
Ivy, M. 190

Japan Airlines 87
Japan bashing 5, 19
Japan Chamber of Commerce and Industry (*Nisshō*) 130
Japan Foundation 87
Japan Teachers Union 131, 155, 160
"Japan, Inc." 1, 3
Japanese Committee for Economic Development (*Keizai Dōyūkai*) 130
Japanese Federation of Employers' Associations (*Nikkeiren*) 130
Japanese Language Council 130; *see also* Japanese language
Japanese language 2, 11, 17, 21, 27, 52, 56, 102, 111, 139, 141, 168, 172, 176; and Agency for Cultural Affairs 147; and moral education 111; and nationalism, national identity 110–11, 114; and nation-state building 111; and rationalized schooling 130; problems with 187; *see also* national language (*kokugo*)
"Japanese miracle" 3; myths of 110–11
Japanese state: ideology of xv; as paradoxically strong and weak 49; *see also* government, state
Japaneseness 11, 12, 13, 18, 20, 27, 99, 102, 128, 130, 133, 134, 165, 167, 180, 187, 190, 191–4; and Agency for Cultural Affairs 145, 146; and civil society 113; construction by state 108; and emperor 115, 117; and equality 111–13; essentialist, naturalist view of 113; and gender definitions 108;